RESEARCH AND REGIONAL WELFARE

Papers Presented at a Conference on Research at
the University of North Carolina at Chapel Hill
May 9-10-11, 1945

Edited by

ROBERT E. COKER

KENAN PROFESSOR OF ZOOLOGY

With a Foreword by

LOUIS R. WILSON

DIRECTOR OF THE SESQUICENTENNIAL

CHAPEL HILL
THE UNIVERSITY OF NORTH CAROLINA PRESS
1946

Copyright, 1946, by

THE UNIVERSITY OF NORTH CAROLINA PRESS

Printed in the United States of America

The William Byrd Press, Inc.
Richmond, Virginia

FOREWORD

IN PROVIDING FOR a Conference on Research and Regional Welfare as a part of its Sesquicentennial Celebration, the University of North Carolina was moved by several major considerations.

In the first place, the University has long recognized that while it is the function of all educational institutions to disseminate knowledge, it is the particular function of a *university* to discover and extend knowledge. As a state university, by virtue of its public support, the obligation unmistakably rests upon the University of North Carolina to employ its libraries, its laboratories, and its personnel in the prosecution of research not only for the discovery of new knowledge, but also for the advancement of the material, intellectual, and spiritual welfare of the public which it serves through the application of knowledge thus discovered. In evidence of its understanding of this responsibility, the University can point to the long record of sustained investigation and publication which appears in *The Graduate School: Research and Publications*, and *The Graduate School: Dissertations and Theses*, issued by the University in its Sesquicentennial Publications.

The second consideration has grown out of the recognition of distinct limitations which the University has experienced in the development and support of its research program. These limitations have been made evident in many ways. They have been most notable, however, in lack of funds, of laboratory and library facilities, and of personnel to carry on an extensive program at a high level. World War II clearly revealed this situation in that the assistance, though extensive and highly important, which the University could render the armed services, was largely limited to the provision of physical facilities, of instruction, and of research facilities in a few fields rather than at higher levels and in many subjects. The more highly specialized types of investigation had to be left largely to the major universities of the Northeast and the Middle West, to governmental research agencies, to private research foundations, and to industry.

The third consideration stemmed from the obvious lag, which the papers in this volume make all too clear, in the development of industrial research in North Carolina and the South generally. Industry, in this region of abundance of raw materials, has depended to a far greater extent than it should on research carried on elsewhere. Consequently, the region has not enjoyed the advantages which flow from the application of the findings of laboratories to the processes of manufacturing. Obviously, this lag must be eliminated, and the best in science and technology must be put to work on a large scale for the advancement of the public good.

The final reason for holding the Conference was the very compelling one that this is the hour of the South's greatest opportunity. The tremendous advances made during the war through research and the applications of research must be released and extended to the people in the postwar period. Pure and applied research, made possible through universities, governmental agencies, foundations, and industrial organizations, must be put to work on a scale commensurate with the needs and resources of North Carolina and the region. By greatly extending its own program of research, and by joining other institutions and organizations in the South in promoting fundamental and applied research—and by these means only—can the University of North Carolina, in all of its branches, play the part of a modern state university and make its full contribution to the civilization of tomorrow.

The papers reproduced in the following pages were presented in a series of meetings at Chapel Hill on May 9-11, 1945. Unfortunately, the remarks of those who participated in the discussions and of the following presiding officers were not available for publication: Robert B. House, Chancellor and Vice President, University of North Carolina, Chapel Hill; Howard W. Odum, Head, Sociology Department, University of North Carolina; Milton J. Rosenau, Dean, School of Public Health, University of North Carolina; Newman I. White, Professor of English, Duke University; J. E. Mills, Chief Chemist, Sonoco Products Company, Hartsville, S. C.; L. D. Baver, Director, Agricultural Experiment Station, North Carolina State College of Agriculture and Engineering of the University of North Carolina; J. M.

Broughton, ex-Governor of North Carolina, Raleigh, N. C. Representing Under-Secretary of War Robert P. Patterson, who was unavoidably absent, Brigadier General Georges F. Doriot, Director, Military Planning, Office of the Quartermaster General, U. S. Army, delivered an address, "Wartime Science Builds for Peace." The paper was accompanied by an exhibit concerning the application of research in the solution of problems met with by the Office of the Quartermaster General in providing food and equipment for the Army.

The conference was made possible through the generous contribution of funds by a number of alumni and friends of the University and through the planning of the Sesquicentennial Committee, of a special committee representing the Divisions of the Humanities, the Social Sciences, and the Physical Sciences, and of individual departments and members of the Faculty of the University. The cordial thanks of the University are extended to all who assisted in these ways and to all the speakers, presiding officers, discussion leaders, and others who participated in the Conference. Special acknowledgment is made of the services of Dr. R. E. Coker, who assumed the principal responsibility for planning and directing the Conference and editing the papers in this volume: to Dr. Claiborne S. Jones, who assisted Dr. Coker in carrying out the details of the program; and to W. D. Carmichael, Jr., Controller of the University, who aided in planning the Conference and secured the funds for carrying it out successfully.

L. R. W.

Chapel Hill, N. C.
May, 1945

THE NEED FOR RESEARCH

Robert E. Coker

KENAN PROFESSOR OF ZOOLOGY
UNIVERSITY OF NORTH CAROLINA

I would have all our people believe in their power to accomplish as much as can be done anywhere on earth by any people.
—Charles B. Aycock, Governor of North Carolina, 1901-1905.

WHATEVER THE TITLE of this Conference may seem to suggest, it is not meant to place undue emphasis on the Southeast as a region apart from a greater whole. Particularly in these times our thoughts and aspirations go beyond any small region; they reach even beyond the nation to the peoples of the world as they may be served in a thousand ways by research. Nevertheless, it is an actual and indisputable fact that our own nation, to say nothing of the world as a whole, is now out of balance industrially and economically. Some of the authoritative papers to come will show this conclusively. To remedy a deplorable state of imbalance, it is a practical necessity for us to begin at home in the hope that we here may carry our share of the burden of greater productiveness and better living.

The time is now. The cessation of battles in Europe and the cessation certain to come in the Far East compel us to think of adjustments to a new situation. If new soil is to be turned, we can begin nowhere better than in the cultivation of our own backyard garden. So, with the stimulus and friendly counsel of distinguished leaders in a dozen fields of action and learning, we gather at Chapel Hill to consider needs and opportunities for research and creative effort in advancement of general human welfare in the southeastern region.

Our competent speakers will set the signposts and mark the special paths of potential progress. Yet at the outset we may ask for answers to two basic questions. (1) What is the occasion for such a conference? In a way, the occasion is the observance of the Sesquicentennial of the oldest operating State University, and one which, like other State Universities, is particularly dedicated to broad public service; but, if the Sesquicentennial were not with us, there would still be a compelling call for this gathering. (2) Why is there special and immediate need for consideration of research in relation to welfare? A few general answers to that question may be timely and suggestive of the constructive educational service contemplated for this Conference.

1. Research is needed because new times call for new ideas and new practices. This is a period of *change*. According to all indications, those privileged to live through the next score of years will see more drastic reorganizations of society, of industry, and of human life in many of its aspects than have been witnessed in any previous period of corresponding duration. Perhaps this is an overstatement. Assume, if you will, that we shall return to normalcy. Even so, to be normal is to change. Actually we need not single out the present time as a particularly critical one. All periods in the history of the world are periods of change. No one would deny that in times of change those fare best who are prepared; those are most fortunate who can anticipate the directions of change; they lose least and they gain more. The game of life is not a mere gamble; foresight, judgment and skill always draw a large share of the winnings. Yet all those favoring qualities are founded on superiority in knowledge, which is just what is to be gained by research.

2. Research is particularly needed because the changes, whatever they may be, and whether for good or for bad, will be made by *people*, including ourselves. One does not anticipate a changed physical world. Whatever is done that was not done before will come out of the action of human beings. It is for the movements of a dynamic human system that we want preparation. We want, also, some share in their control. The changes in agriculture, in industry, in education, and in social organization will be made by wise people or by foolish people. Might we not better say: They will be made by folks, ourselves included, who combine some knowledge with some ignorance? If we want predominance of the right sorts of change we must try, and try

hard, to shift the balance from ignorance toward knowledge. Education will go a long way, but first we must have the stuff with which to educate. We need the answers to the crucial questions that will regularly confront us: but the answers are not always in the books; for many of the questions will be new. How shall we get the answers except by persistent inquiry, by rooting out all the stubborn facts and by applying a measure of logic—or, let us say, a little common sense. But that is just the method of reasearch, whether it is done in the laboratory or on the farm, in the study or the studio, in the administrative office or the accounting house. Intelligent, controlled inquiry is research: certainly nothing to be feared.

3. Research is required for *self-defense*. We do not want to trail our neighbors and always take their dust. Research will be done somewhere, let us make no mistake about that: the peoples of this world as a whole will not stagnate. There will be improvements in agriculture, in the use of products of forests and fisheries, in manufacture, in transportation and communications, in social organization, and in the arts. Not only will there be new types of material products and new industries based upon them; there will also be better art and literature and law. Somewhere these things will be worked out and the results will be profitable to the communities that lead the van. It is not merely that they will enjoy pecuniary profit; along with material gain they will have intellectual, esthetic, and spiritual advantages. We do not ask to do all of the leading in every field: let the prizes be distributed; but we want to do our share of the running and to enjoy our proportionate part of the material and spiritual rewards.

4. Research is needed if we are to make the most of our raw materials. We have the soils, actually or potentially productive of annual crops. We have the minerals that are being extracted or are extractable from the earth. We have the waters and their living resources. To no little extent we harvest these materials, such as cotton, tobacco, corn, fish, wood, coal, and iron. Sometimes, through processes of technology and manufacture, we add values to them; to the extent that we do, we pass beyond a *raw materials economy*. Everyone knows, however, that, except in respect to a few materials, such as tobacco, we do not generally

take our products far beyond the stage of raw material. We in the South import many more kinds of finished products than we export. And what of the techniques of adding values to the raw stuff? Where were these originated? Who profited first from them? Who now make the tools and machinery? We have done something in this line—there is no attempt to disparage what, here and there, has been done—yet the origination of techniques by which values are added and their first applications are not being done in the Southeast to anything like the extent to which they are done elsewhere or might be done here. Let us look a little farther. In the practices of conservation of our natural resources, do we employ procedures originated by us or do we more commonly adopt such as have been worked out by scientific inquiry and controlled experiment in adaptation to needs and conditions that do not necessarily coincide precisely with our own? In the protection of our crops against plant diseases and pests, did we originate the techniques through the research of our own plant pathologists, entomologists and chemists? Do we usually invent and manufacture the chemicals employed in crop protection?

5. Let us not think only of physical raw materials. We ought to be deeply concerned about our boys and girls who look ahead to careers of usefulness and a genuinely good life. Many of these *raw materials of social life* are certain to become, somewhere, more finely finished human products and to form socially valuable parts of some community. We might well be concerned, also, about the extent to which we now "export" the young folks or make it virtually necessary for so many of them to leave this region for the training that will make them expert chemists, physicists, plant pathologists, historians, physicians, government administrators, artists, or musicians. This is not disparaging our regional educational institutions; it is implying, simply, that we are not yet keeping pace in diversity of specialities. Furthermore, to what extent do the finished human products, refined here or elsewhere, have to find profitable careers and rear families in other regions? Socially and economically, it does not pay to send away for their training or for their careers too many of our ablest young men and women. It does not pay socially to foster conditions under which the most attractive careers must be

sought in other regions than our own. We produce young folks who want the high training required to reach the top rung of the ladder and who will find, somewhere, the chance to follow careers appropriate to their natural talents and their acquired skills. We like such young men and young women; it would be nice to keep them about. Regional interchange of talent is proper and desirable; but let us not sell too cheaply our inheritance in *human resources*—the boys and girls with the good minds and with high aspirations for achievement and service.

6. We want research because we cannot escape paying for it. Whether we foster research at home or not, we will do our share, and more, in footing the bill. If we leave creative work to other regions and use here only what our neighbors will pass on, then, most certainly, those distant and keener neighbors will, in one way or another, charge us for what we get from them. The profits from research will not be donated to us. If new products are devised and manufactured elsewhere from our cotton, our wood, our minerals, or our fish and shellfish, we may get a little better return from raw materials; but we more than pay it back when we purchase the final products for our own enjoyment. It does not pay to export raw materials to too great an extent and then buy the finished products at higher prices. Even if the "foreign" concern establishes a branch plant in our midst, and we thus gain in employment of regional labor, the greater share of the profit will be banked and checked out elsewhere. *We pay for research*, whether or not we let it be done by our own young folks in our own region. We feed the cow, whether or not we get the cream and butter or let others take the rich fat and drain the skimmed milk down our way. Of course, if we do our own research, we pay in advance for the return that may be expected eventually. Actually, however, the advance payment need not be relatively great. Let us take the State of North Carolina as an example: if we were to spend for research only one-fourth of one per cent of the aggregate personal income, we should have now an annual research budget of more than five million dollars. Quite conceivably, wisely conducted research costing a fourth of a per cent might ultimately result in increasing total personal and corporate income by one hundred per cent.

7. There must be *basic research*. If it be asked where research

is to be done, the answer is "almost everywhere." There is need for industrial research laboratories, in which the South lags far behind. There is need for research by various state agencies. In respect to government and public administration, research may be highly productive of public good, as the Institute of Government in Chapel Hill has so effectively demonstrated. There is need for more research in experiment stations. There is need for an institute of fishery research. There is need for more creative work in private and public studies and studios. Underlying the whole situation is the need for more research and graduate instruction in educational institutions. Beyond any possible question, the fountainhead of both theoretical and applied research is in universities. It is only there that one finds the diversities of skills and the broad freedom of analysis that must be brought to bear on special problems of all sorts. It is only there that the essential personnel for research can be primarily selected and given the basic training to produce competence in practical research. It is chiefly in universities that the solid foundation of fundamental or so-called "pure" research can be laid. After all, it is the facts and the ideas of fundamental research that keep filling the reservoir into which the industrial researcher inevitably must dip.

Research is needed because we want our place in the sun, where there is a richer and better life. The wise old preacher, author of Ecclesiastes, said: "Wisdom is good with an inheritance and by it there is profit to them that see the sun." We of the South have the inheritance in resources and in persons. We could apply more wisdom in the use of that great estate, and we might then see a little more of the sun. The same preacher said that "wisdom is a defense"—which is something else we may need. Finally on this point, he added: "the excellence of knowledge is that wisdom giveth life to them that have it." Life and more of it is a good thing to have. It might well be a guiding theme for the Conference, that we want more life. By life we mean not mere subsistence, not just financial wealth, but, rather, more life in the widest and best sense, the life that comes from wisdom. How is wisdom arrived at but by inquiry and creative effort? And this is the essence of research.

CONTENTS

THE KEY TO THE FUTURE

RESEARCH FOR THE COMMONWEALTH

The Honorable R. Gregg Cherry
GOVERNOR OF NORTH CAROLINA

I CAN THINK of nothing more fitting, as part of the Sesquicentennial celebration of the University of North Carolina, than this Conference on Research and Regional Welfare. I am happy to be with you tonight and officially to welcome you here in Chapel Hill to this original part of a now enlarged State University, which is today doing a magnificent job of finding and disseminating knowledge at its three units, here, at Greensboro, and at Raleigh.

You are gathered here as a part of our Sesquicentennial celebration in the name of the most interesting, the most dramatic, and the most useful thing that I know in the entire universe: Research.

I find that Webster describes research as "careful inquiry" or "diligent investigation." I find that this "careful inquiry" has conquered many of the diseases that have plagued man, given him both wings and fins, given him invisible energy and fire over wires leading into his home, sent his voice and his likeness through endless space, and laid the groundwork for even more wonderful accomplishments to come.

As a layman who can boast only of an A.B. degree from Duke University, and of no discovered scientific talent, I found that I could not even attend a research meeting to discuss research without first doing a little research. And because I have just been faced with that proposition I commend to some of you, as a project, a program of research on research. It might be very helpful to people in my dilemma.

My own very brief research brought to my attention such highly dramatic accomplishments in the field of research as the conquering of smallpox, diphtheria, and typhoid. I found that, because of research, what was a worthless fungus one day became penicillin the next. I also found that research divides itself

3

into the two main classifications of immediate pressing work on current problems, looking toward a quick and practical solution, and the storing up and classifying of assorted knowledge against the day when another researcher may take this information in a new combination or a new application and make of it a new solution to a problem of mankind.

In this second classification we find that all knowledge in all fields is valuable. In fact, all knowledge that is wrung from nature seems to be useful—today and hereafter. I find, too, that research, as such, develops character and ability in those who stick to it.

It is the function of a college to transmit knowledge from generation to generation. You men do not stop there; you dig deeper; you carry on research; you find new knowledge to add to the stream. If all past knowledge were wiped out, we would revert to savagery. If we found no new knowledge, we would stagnate. Practical research needs no advocate, but those of you who work at the business of delving for further knowledge know that the real force behind all practical work in research is the fundamental, or "pure," research that makes the practical solution of current problems possible.

Not every project under way in every laboratory will ultimately turn to some practical use. On the other hand, many useful discoveries and inventions have grown out of what appeared at the time to be useless. Take, for example, the story, familiar to you I am sure, of Michael Faraday and his dynamo. This was exhibited at a meeting of the Royal Society. Gladstone, who was then the Prime Minister, looked at the plaything, said it was interesting, and then asked of what value it could ever be. Whereupon, Faraday is said to have replied: "What good is a new-born baby? Some day you will be taxing it."

Many fine developments in the life of mankind have at first appeared as useless academic research, only later to revolutionize whole fields of human operation. It was so with Pasteur when he was developing the germ theory of disease. Mendel played with peas, and laid the modern foundation for scientific plant and animal breeding. Luther Burbank hybridized his plants at random, and from the sports developed new and better varieties of grains, fruits, and vegetables.

And now has come war, fast drawing to a close. It has spurred twentieth-century Pasteurs and Mendels to provide us with synthetic rubber, 100-octane gasoline, nylon, plastics, sulfa drugs, penicillin, quinine substitute, radar, B 29's, bazookas, jelly bombs, Garand rifles, bomb sights, tanks, and thousands of different mechanisms and formulas for both destroying and saving life and for annihilating space.

After that quick glance around the world, let us come back here to the South, to North Carolina, to Chapel Hill. We should be interested in what all this surge of doing and accomplishing means to us here.

In the past the South has been referred to as the nation's economic problem No. 1. In the face of recent developments, and with such leadership as that assembled here tonight, I think it is generally agreed that the South is now, today, the nation's economic opportunity No. 1.

Research programs must recognize that the South is not an isolated part of the country, nor of the world. What happens to cotton production in Brazil, India, and China is of immediate concern to North Carolina. Planning for the most effective utilization of our human and natural resources can result in a prosperous and happy people. Research pointing in this direction is badly needed.

Progress comes through research and the results of research as applied to something for somebody. Scientists and scholars ferret out the basic facts—the "pure" knowledge—and industrialists build the plants, operate the mines, and convert the raw materials.

North Carolina and the South for many years lagged in scientific research and in the application of the results of research to industry and agriculture and daily life and living. A survey shows that only 4 per cent of the pages of *The Journal of the American Chemical Society* are filled with material from the South, and that one fourth of this material came from two institutions in North Carolina. This small proportion does not mean that southern men and women have less of brain power. It means that too many of our most able workers in the fields of research have moved on to the northern states to make reputations in this field. Today, I am delighted to say, we are bringing many of these leading scientists back to North Carolina and the South and are keeping other young men and women here to do their work and to gain the first fruits of their labors at home. This is necessary if we are to reap the greatest benefits from our natural resources. Not only must we locate the industries in the South, but we must also have the research laboratories that improve these industries, and by that means improve also our people and their way of life. The resources of North Carolina can best be developed by those who know North Carolina and who know her resources through close contact with them.

Not all research is with test tubes. A great poet once said, "The proper study of mankind is man," and so researchers also look into the dim and almost forgotten past of man. An ever-continuing study goes on, far back in the library stacks, of the practices, customs, ideas, beliefs, and superstitions of man. Back to the very childhood of the race we go with our probing, and by that study penetrate deeper into the mystery of man today and come to a fuller understanding of him. In old caves and grottoes, archaeologists continue finding out things about man of today by finding out about man of yesterday.

Looking at the usefulness of research in this field we find that military men still study the campaigns of Alexander, Hannibal, and Caesar. The German general staff based much of its strategy in recent years on Hannibal's battle of Cannae.

Nor is this research on mankind entirely a matter of sifting the dust heaps of Egypt or other ancient centers of civilization. It moves on up to a more modern day. Here at Chapel Hill is being built a Southern Historical Collection of bound diaries, account books, loose manuscripts, letters, speeches, pamphlets, and printed matter. It has become in just a few years the most important body of source material for the history of North Carolina and other southern states anywhere in existence. In it is to be found information on every phase of southern life from politics to religion and including agriculture, industry, education, and health conditions. It covers all periods of southern history and is especially strong in pre-Civil War times and the days of the Confederacy. The collection is of inestimable value for research into the history of North Carolina and the South, for appreciating the part the South has played in the history of the United States, and for understanding present-day conditions in the South.

There is great need for continued basic research in animal life. How else would we know today that ticks carry Texas fever in cattle, that mosquitoes can give us malaria, that Rocky Mountain spotted fever and typhus fever come to us by way of animal parasites? Fleas scattered bubonic plague until research found them hidden in the drab hair that covers the loathsome rat. The guardians of our health have some, but not yet adequate, knowledge of how to deal with the animal carriers of diseases of man and those of domestic and economic animals.

And let us look in another direction in this matter of research in the field of animal life. Those who have long studied the oyster and oyster culture in North Carolina and elsewhere, and who know whereof they speak, assure us that we have in this state possibilities for oyster farms that should bring millions of dollars annually into the state. These millions of dollars would pay wages, support merchants, employ physicians, and—as some grim listener might suggest—the same millions would also be taxed for schools, libraries, highways, health, and—more and more research. But if we are to make this progress, we need studies and experiments in the field of biological science, as well as in other fields.

I am told that in many places along our coast there is a shell-fish, unfit for human food, that was long looked upon as waste— a mere weed in the marine garden, so to speak. Just since the beginning of this war, it has been discovered by research, done elsewhere, that this "horse mussel" is one of the very best sources of a commercially valuable vitamin, previously derived in this country from raw material imported from Europe. Now there is demand for its cultivation, and no one has yet the basic knowledge necessary for that purpose. We ought not to have to wait for a war to prompt discoveries in our own backyard. Research on this shellfish is now actively in progress in a neighboring state.

Many aspects of our marine fisheries are calling for research. We have never made a full survey for possible offshore fishing grounds. We ought to know more of the changing currents off the southeast coasts, the conditions of food supply for fish, and the relations of these to the fluctuations in abundance, from year to year, of the commercial fish. It is wasteful to prepare for a big run of fish in a year when the run is poor. It is not most profitable to be unprepared when the run is exceptionally large.

Research in the social sciences presents complex and challenging problems. Unlike the natural sciences, the method of controlled experiment cannot be widely employed. The Bretton Woods agreement needed a great backlog of work in the field of social-science research before it could be accomplished. Researchers in this field can arrive at business forecasts that will be workable predictions—not perfect, perhaps, but establishing a high degree of probability.

For instance, social scientists in North Carolina know that during the past five years the marriage rate has increased sharply. The birth rate has also risen. It is also known that, during the decade of the thirties and the first four years of the present decade, the rate of construction of residential units in the United States has been less than 60 per cent of the rate in the 1920's. It is also true that an enormous volume of liquid savings has accumulated in the hands of individuals. Some 53 billion dollars of United States obligations are owned by individuals. (Incidentally, from July, 1941, through January, 1945, over 533 million dollars of United States Savings bonds were sold in North Carolina.)

With these determinate facts, it is possible to project a postwar decade of active residential construction in the United States which should assume a magnitude of one million residential units a year as a conservative estimate. These illustrations of the possibilities of social, economic, and business research briefly suggest the objectives.

In this field of social science, a comprehensive study was once made by the Institute for Research in Social Science in more than sixty of the hundred counties of the state, and these detailed findings were reduced to a confidential report that was placed at the disposal of a legislative committee appointed by the late Governor McLean to study existing systems of government in North Carolina and to bring in recommendations for the revision and improvement of county government. In 1930 the Institute made a study of the penal system of the state at the request of

Governor Gardner. The report provided the basic data for a subcommittee report of the state Prison Advisory Commission appointed by Governor Gardner. Youth, balanced industry, resources, and deficiencies—all these have provided fields for research. The matter of housing, rural and urban, should be the subject of an early study.

Chemists, dressed in long aprons, have stood before their benches for many back-breaking hours to rediscover cellulose, one of nature's most abundant raw materials. Cellulose was formerly used chiefly in the making of paper and cotton textiles. In its new and ever expanding fields of usefulness, cellulose has now become cellophane, rayon, cellulose acetate, plastics, explosives, and, under the magic wand of research, all manner of household commodities. From these discoveries have come entirely new industries. From these new industries have come wholesome influences on the economy and the life of this particular section. There is not a North Carolinian, or an American, today who does not enjoy the uses to which cellulose has been put in recent years.

In 1859 the first oil well was sunk in the state of Pennsylvania. Here was just another product of nature. Its chief use at first was for illumination, in the form of kerosene. Then came gasoline for internal combustion engines. Then came ether, fuel oil, Diesel oil, lubricating oils, paraffin, and so on. With each new product came a ready market. Cracked refinery gases gave us the best aviation fuel in the world.

When this nation entered World War II and our source of rubber fell into enemy hands, chemical research again played a dramatic role. Synthetic rubber was developed from petroleum, enabling our war machine to move forward with increasing fury on wheels cushioned with a new kind of rubber that scored a new victory for research. These things, you will remember, were developed from the black and almost useless oil that came from the first well opened in Pennsylvania just eighty-six years ago.

The wonders which chemical research has wrought with petroleum and cellulose are no greater than those which might be brought about if co-ordinated research were applied to others of nature's products. Here in the South we are blessed by nature with an abundance of raw material. Already the growing and processing of whole cotton as a source of alpha cellulose has been subjected to an extensive laboratory study here in the chemical laboratory in Chapel Hill. Other raw materials of the South which are worthy of study are farm waste products, mineral resources, marine resources, southern forests, and the volatile oils. These raw materials need to be studied just as the chemist studied petroleum and cellulose.

I have touched briefly on these many and varied aspects of research to remind you of its vast accomplishments and its infinite future. The things I have mentioned might indicate that the job has been pretty well accomplished. It looks as if we have gone far and done much. Indeed we have. But as we meet here tonight, we are within two miles of eroded and impoverished fields, containing tumble-down cabins that house fly-besieged and spindly youngsters suffering with rickets. These places and these people are in need—desperately in need—of some of this research we are talking about. Within two miles of this conference on "research and regional welfare" are wasted lands and wasted people. I am afraid that the deliberations and the findings of this body will not reach these people or these acres. Crumbs from this learned table will not roll even that far. To these and many like them we have been too late with too little.

But the gullies will wash deeper on these red Orange County hillsides, and other children with knotty legs will sit on those rotting and sagging porches. They do not deserve to have the first bright, peering inquisitiveness in their eyes snuffed out. If this thing called research is all that you and I say it is, we can lift up our people, put new radiance in their faces, make their feet light, and give them dreams—even as you and I have dreams. There are people in North Carolina and in the South who need spirit. Can your combined delvings find that spirit and give it to those who need it so badly? I believe so. Your work is necessarily slow and painstaking. But it is so badly needed that I feel urged to hurry you. What you will accomplish tomorrow will halt death that is too early and too wasteful, death of people and death of the things that people love.

Both practical and spiritual values are at stake. They lean on each other. The results of your work will be found in dollars and cents, in corn and potatoes, in balance sheets and cash registers, in tax premiums and life insurance policies.

Research will also help man to follow his primal impulse and impetus towards the making of a truly beautiful and vital world. Utility and physical benefits do not entirely satisfy the hunger of his soul. Man will eternally struggle and continue to strive towards the making of such a world. However obscured, hindered, and detoured by false doctrines and prophets, he will somehow stumble on toward that goal. But he needs help, we all need help, and it is the business of our leaders, our spokesmen, our men of study and of research, to help us toward this creative living.

Research for the creative life is research for the really abundant life.

THE OPPORTUNITY AND RESPONSIBILITY
OF RESEARCH

Frank Porter Graham

PRESIDENT, UNIVERSITY OF NORTH CAROLINA

IN THESE DAYS when Americans have joined with British, Russians, and French in dictating terms of unconditional surrender in Germany, and with Australians, Dutch, Indians, Chinese, and British in pushing back the Japs in Asia and in the Pacific, and with the representatives of forty-four nations organizing, in San Francisco, the future peace of the world, it is clear to the wayfaring man that America is not only a part of the world, but is in the very middle of our one world, yet to be organized for freedom and justice, peace and plenty, for all people.

In this hour of our rejoicing over victories won in Europe and our hopes for combined and decisive victories in Asia, as we close ranks behind our new able and devoted Commander-in-Chief, we would, in grateful memory, acknowledge the prophetic insights of that major prophet of international organization, Woodrow Wilson, and the present foundations for the structure of world security already laid out by Franklin D. Roosevelt. In mankind's most fateful hour we find the over-all strategy in building the world's most powerful Navy, the largest Merchant Marine, the most modernly equipped Army, the largest Air Force, and the gigantic production of food and munitions, which have been decisive on all the battlefronts of the world. We see, too, the over-all strategy for peace and the unity of the world in the early recognition of Russia by the Old World and in the good-neighbor policy of the New World; in the Atlantic Charter, the Four Freedoms, Bretton Woods, Dumbarton Oaks, Yalta, and the promise of San Francisco. In the center of it, between the two great oceans, and fronting on both the wide responsibilities of the Atlantic Charter and the high opportunities of the San Francisco Conference, we see the United States of America in this hour of her destiny.

As one of the four basic regional parts of this America, we see, and are a part of, the southern section of the United States. We gather here tonight in commemoration of the 150th anniversary of the founding of a southern State University, the first existing State University to open its doors in America. In this Conference on the relation between research and southern regional welfare, we would rededicate this old but young University to a more creative part in rebuilding old commonwealths for a nobler part in the remaking of the world.

Too long has the South been the dependent colonial province of a financial industrial empire reaching from Boston to Chicago. Rising now to something like independence and power is a new industrial region reaching across the Old South from the Chesapeake to the Gulf. What the South does agriculturally and industrially depends, in intelligent part, on what the South does educationally. What the South does for educational leadership depends, in vital part, on what our universities do in basic researches in all fields, in co-operative leadership in agriculture, industry, business, and labor relations, and in the general fulfillment of the economic, scientific, cultural, and spiritual aspiration of all the people.

The states of the South have come to grips with all the mighty possibilities of the industrial revolution. The people of this section have the opportunity to make a joint and wise utilization of their geographic, economic, educational, and human resources in co-operation with its marvelous mechanical energies. Through the very value of intelligent social regulations and high human standards the South could give attractive economic and social welcome to highly skilled, highly waged, and highly productive new and diversified industries. The lists of crops and industries still missing from our economic structure are appalling. Clear-headed, scientific, humanly-disposed men and women in the South from within the industries and from within the commonwealths are pounding away at such fundamental things as pedigreed seeds, engineering skill, balanced production, scientific marketing, economic diversification, balanced nutrition, home-making, more dedicated professions, more creative schools, and more spiritual churches. Diversified agriculture, supplementing staple crops; diversified industries, supplementing basic manufactures; and nine months' schools and county-wide libraries, supplementing both agriculture and industry, with the liberal arts and sciences undergirding them all, make up the groundwork upon which to build nobler commonwealths in the risen South.

In this region of the Old South, where human slavery made its last stand in the modern world, industrialism makes fresh beginnings on virgin soil. We have the lessons, in the tragedies of the one, and the opportunities, in the power of the other, to make a contribution to the cause of mankind and the history of civilization, distinctive and rich in a deeper sense of human personality and in social relations to be worked out, on the basis of freedom and justice, by a friendly folk who live under the southern sun in a pleasant land between the mountains and the sea. We have the opportunity not only to install the new machinery seen on all sides and to utilize the new techniques of our agricultural, textile, and engineering schools, and our liberal arts colleges and universities, but also to develop with intellectual freedom nobler human attitudes than have yet characterized the history of any people.

We stand at the gateways of industry, through which increasing thousands of our people and mounting millions of our wealth will pass for the potential production of a fairer life. Out into the waste places and up the hillsides move the mills and factories with creative power. Down from the mountains, the rivers come rushing with the power for the electrification of our civilization, cleanly charged with something more of the good life for all our people. As we do our day's work and dream our dream that the farms and factories, printing presses and dynamos, schools and churches will all join in the building of a more economically productive and spiritually beautiful civilization, we will find, near the center of it all, colleges and universities calling to youth, who stand with inquiring minds and stout hearts along the research frontiers of the vast wilderness of our yet unmastered civilization.

It is the responsibility of the state and the nation to make appropriations for research as an investment for the welfare and progress of the people. This responsibility has been accepted both by the Congress and by the State Legislature for agricultural development. State, regional, and national welfare and development require public appropriations for research no less in the fields of engineering, industry, business, the fundamental sciences, the social sciences, and the humanities. Research in the pure sciences is fundamental to research in the applied sciences and to agricultural and industrial progress. Research in the social sciences is necessary for the social mastery of our great modern civilization for the public welfare. Research in the humanities provides the background for understanding the humane, ethical, and spiritual foundations and directions of our modern world. No people concerned with their present welfare and future advancement can afford not to make intelligently adequate appropriations for both fundamental and applied research. In North Carolina and all the other southern states we have lagged too long, to the damage of the state, the region, and the nation.

Great teachers, libraries, and laboratories, patient and profound research, generous and free publication in a community of scholars devoted to truth, goodness, and beauty, and dedicated to make them increasingly prevail, through youth, in a world desperately in need of the best which youth has to give—these are the stuff of conviction, purpose, and spirit which we need and for which we pray for all our colleges and universities.

In this hour we stand committed, with all our resources, to winning the war for human freedom; to the improvement of the productive resources of our free economic society so that every human being, regardless of race, color, or creed, has a fair chance to earn a decent living; and to the organization of a society of nations for the international guarantee of liberty, justice, and peace in the world. North Carolina is becoming an example of co-operation and sharing on a state-wide basis of more equal opportunity in schools, roads, libraries, suffrage, health, medical care, and the welfare of all our great family of people called North Carolina. Let us challenge our region and generation with plans for research in all fields, which the people, free and unafraid, will rejoice to fulfill in the service of all the needs of all the people more wisely and nobly from generation to generation.

THE USEFULNESS OF USEFUL
KNOWLEDGE

Wilson Compton

PRESIDENT, WASHINGTON STATE COLLEGE

D URING THE LAST half century in the United States more
than one half of our new national wealth has come
from new ideas which were not known fifty years
ago, or at least were not applied to the production of things.
But for the South as a whole, like the Pacific Northwest,
that proportion has been less than one tenth. This contrast is
something for the South to think about. Rich in diversified
natural resources, the South has not been proportionately rich
in ideas or in opportunities. The ratio of ideas to resources
in the South, to be sure, is greater now than ever heretofore. But that fact is due primarily to the great war industries
brought in by force of arms and Federal fiat; and, over a longer
period of time, to the pulp and paper and petroleum industries.

During this half-century period new ideas and novel applications of old ones have on the whole had the best chance in the
East and the Central West, not in the South and not on the
Pacific Coast. The records of the Patent Office and of the development of new industries show this clearly. In the South the
inventor, the "queer" man with quaint ideas, still has a hard
time graduating from the street to the office and to the factory
and the shop. He is still regarded as a bit troublesome—maybe a
nuisance, as sometimes he is—and generally as more of a threat
than a promise. The South, like the Pacific Northwest, has been
engaged busily, and for the most part profitably, in the exploitation of its soils, forests, and mines. Largely, the South, like the
Northwest, is still living off its resources, not off its ideas. We
must learn to depend less on resources, which have been made
for us, and more on ideas, which we must make and apply for
ourselves. This is the heart of the "scientific spirit." The South,

I think, stands to gain from it as much as any part of our country with the possible exception of the Pacific Northwest, from which I come. We have been exploiting our resources. We must learn instead to develop them. To do that we must join boldly in the March of Science, which is fashioning the arts of triumphant war, and is capable equally, with our help, of fashioning the arts of triumphant peace.

One of the foremost American scientists, speaking in New Orleans on "The Industrial Resources and Opportunities of the South," said this to a great group of industrialists and chemists:

Foremost among the industrial problems of the South would seem to be the suppression of wastes, the vastly greater development of labor values in its products and the keeping at home of money now needlessly spent elsewhere. The South has been too generally content with shipping crude materials and primary products and too ready to accept from other sections the things which it might better produce at home. The South has been selling raw materials. It should sell brain values and labor values.

This is the statement of Arthur D. Little, founder of perhaps the most eminent industrial research organization in this country, a man intimately familiar with the strength and the weakness of the South's economy. This statement was made not in 1945, but in 1915. It may have been merely prophetic then.

A quarter-century later another public commentator, Thurman Arnold, valiant gladiator before the law, he of orthodox economics and picturesque speech, speaking in 1939 on "Monopoly and the South," expressed the same basic idea from a different angle and, of course, in a different way. Said he:

The industrial East has been the Mother Country. The South and West have been the Colonies. The Colonies have furnished the Mother Country with raw materials. The Mother Country has been exploiting the Colonies by selling them manufactured necessities. The industrial East has been the principal source of both capital and organization to develop the South and West. Under such conditions it has been natural enough that the South and West have been developed in the way which would contribute the most to the domination of the industrial East. This is the age-old principle of Colonial empires.

That is a mild impeachment, which the South, I dare say, relishes as little as does the West. But even more than its germ of truth is its challenge—a challenge to both the South and the West which, if they are as wise and alert as I think they are, they will accept. In fact, I think they have no real choice. Of Britain it has been said: Export or die! Of the South and the West it may equally be said: Utilize, conserve, and diversify; or decline! For this purpose, great natural resources are not enough. Only ideas, inspired by the scientific mind and implemented by the tools of research, will pave the way.

THE POSITION OF THE SOUTH

Here we stand at the close of a century and a half of distinguished service to the South by this great institution. We are interested in the record of the past only as it throws light on the promise of the future. We are looking ahead from behind; and if we are to be guided by the light of reason we must let our minds be bold. I like the way in which the Under Secretary of War, Robert P. Patterson, whose magnificent contribution to our war production cannot yet be fully measured, recently introduced a forum on Industrial Research and National Security, in these words:

There is a great voice in the world today, the voice of science and technology. It is a voice heard since ancient times. But never until today has it spoken with such authority, have its words been so filled with promise, has it been listened to with such hope. And in no country in the world does the voice speak as eloquently as in our own.

You have invited me to speak on Research and Southern Welfare. Perhaps you might as well have asked me to speak on Research and the National Welfare, for, as I sense the future, there will be no enduring progress in the nation except there be, in both the South and the West, a great adventure in what I may call the "scientific spirit," as an access to the promise of American life.

Now I do not want to smother you beneath a barrage of figures. Statistics, it has been said, explain everything without giving you any information. But if it is true that the South as a whole has had an unbalanced economy—unbalanced, that is, between richness of old resources and poverty of new ideas—that fact should be evident in the record. So, for a moment, let us look at the record, not of the ambitious hopes of an imaginative publicist, nor of the bashful claims of a chamber of commerce, but of the unsmiling census analyst and his expressionless adding machine.

The South includes a third of our national population, 40 per cent of our land in farms, 52 per cent of our mines production, 61 per cent of our petroleum, 46 per cent of our lumber and timber products. But the South has only 17 per cent of our national banking resources, 10 per cent of our savings deposits, 24 per cent of our property value, 21 per cent of our electric power, 15 per cent of our manufactures, and 13 per cent of our exports.

As compared to the United States as a whole based on comparative population, the South in 1940 had individual income 60 per cent of the national average; and bank deposits 50 per cent; and provided funds for its public schools only 63 per cent of the national average, and for public health still less.

These, you may say, are only statistics, and they are. But they are also much more than that. They are a mirror of the economic weal and woe of millions of the American people, and they show, at least, that the abundant natural resources of the South have not yet been reflected in any comparable income for its people, or in comparable increase in purchasing power, or in comparable progress in public education or in public health. To achieve that, I suggest, is no more a challenge of the present than a promise of the future, if we do our part.

THE PACIFIC NORTHWEST

We have today in the Pacific Northwest an analagous problem. We stand, as you in the South do also, on top of some of the largest ore resources in the world in light metals of aluminum and magnesium. Beneath our feet are billions of tons of dolomite and magnesite and alumina-bearing clays. Gradually we are learning, as you are learning, how to extract these ores; and, in the meantime, from high places we are told of the "infinite possibilities" of these metals beneath our feet.

This war has indeed dramatized the great promise of the light metals. But what are we doing with them? We are doing what, as a nation, we never would think of doing except in wartime, where *speed* of production is primary and *cost* of production is secondary. Familiar bauxite ore, some of it from the South but more of it from South America, is now shipped to processing plants in the East and the South. The extracted alumina are shipped by rail to the Pacific Northwest. Aluminum "ingot" produced by familiar electro-metallurgical processes is then shipped back to rolling mills in the East. Finally aluminum sheets are shipped again by rail to our West Coast aircraft factories, whence they now fly the Seven Seas.

This promiscuous and expensive "joy ride" of wartime aluminum back and forth across the continent is possible only because the electric power costs of ore conversion in the Pacific Northwest are only a third or perhaps only a fourth of the average power costs elsewhere in the United States. But that is no reason that the permanent place of the Pacific Northwest, any more than of the South, in these light metals should be merely to provide cheap ingot to be processed and fabricated in Illinois, or Pennsylvania, or Connecticut. The South likewise has low-cost hydro-electric power. In fact, the lowest power rates of record today are at local points in the South, although the power costs in the Pacific Northwest as a whole are, I believe, substantially lower than the power costs in the South generally.

Today in the Northwest we have six great plants producing ingot aluminum and magnesium and employing at full time about forty-five hundred persons. We have one aluminum sheet rolling mill employing about an equal number. There are in the Northwest today no producers of aluminum castings, forgings, shapes and tubing, and only a few small aluminum and magnesium foundries. The processing, refinement, and fabrication of light metals is done almost entirely in the East.

The production of a ton of ingot aluminum provides three days of employment for one man. The same ton of aluminum in its diversified fabricated forms may provide one hundred days' work for one man. If the Northwest produced not only ingot metal but also the rolled sheet, castings, forgings, and shapes which are now being made from it elsewhere, the industrial employments in the Northwest, based on the light metals alone, would be multiplied more than fifteen times.

This is not a fantasy. It is simple arithmetic. It cannot be done all at once. But it can be done. I am sure it can be done in the Northwest. Equally I believe it can be done in the South. But it will take bold ideas, courageous capital, and the initiative of enterprising men who understand what Edison meant when he said that "invention is one per cent inspiration and ninety-nine per cent perspiration."

FORESTRY

The South, again, has 36 per cent of the commercial forest area of the United States. Almost all of this is in private ownership. It will be well if most of it may so remain. These lands today hold a fourth of the nation's saw timber supply. Forty years ago the South was producing over 40 per cent of the national production of lumber and timber products. It is still producing that proportion; temporarily in wartime a little more. The ratio of timber growth to timber drain in the South in 1936 was 0.83; and, including cord-wood sizes, a ratio of 0.97, a close approach to balance between drain and growth. The pressing wartime demands for timber products have substantially increased the inroads on timber supply and undoubtedly have reduced, temporarily at least, the ratio of growth to drain. But Dean Korstian, of the School of Forestry at Duke University, in his recent excellent book on *Forestry on Private Lands in the United States*, has said, "It is doubtful that the increased wartime drain would exceed the annual growth if the South had adequate forest fire protection.

Only half of the forest lands of the South even now have organized continuous fire protection. What a tragedy! What a reflection on southern stewardship of its greatest resource! What a challenge to both public and industry leadership! These forest lands are today only half as productive as they may readily be made with continuous South-wide fire protection and with the better forest management which is being gradually encouraged by improved forest protection, better education of forest owners, and the developing public regulation of timber-cutting practices.

WOOD UTILIZATION OPPORTUNITIES

In addition to the thousands of its sawmills, the South now sustains forty-eight great pulp mills. Most of these have been built since 1920. Now that practical methods have been developed for pulping hardwoods as well as pine, the wood supply in the South is sufficient to sustain a pulp capacity twice its present volume. The pulp industry in the last quarter century in the South has advanced from a basis of four hundred thousand cords of pulpwood annually in 1920 to six million cords annually, a fifteen-fold increase which again may be doubled.

But there is an even greater opportunity in the South in wood conversion. Eventually it should not only provide employment opportunities to replace the waning cotton, but also, over a period of years, it should contribute to the restoration and improvement of the forests of the South, its one greatest renewable resource. Many of you in the South have grown up within sight of sawdust piles, slab pits, and wood-refuse burners. Perhaps you take them for granted as an essential part of a great industry which after all has provided much of the backbone of the development of the South.

THE SAWDUST PILE

What do you see when you look at a pile of sawdust? I have asked that question of hundreds of people in the West and the South. Most people answer, "I see a pile of sawdust." Some say, "I see a lot of good stoker fuel." But that is not what I mean. When you look at a ton of sawdust you are looking at over eleven hundred pounds of wood sugar, the same kind of sugar, by the way, which you put in your coffee this morning. You are looking, too, at about six hundred pounds of a brownish, blackish substance called lignin, which experts, who know much better than I, say may have many of the mysteries of the "benzene ring," which is at the foundation of our modern great chemical industries.

Or if you are not interested in the wood sugar itself, it may be converted readily and at low cost into fifty-five gallons—maybe more—of ethyl alcohol, not the wood alcohol which you shun, but the same kind of alcohol which many of you crave but cannot get, the same alcohol which familiarly comes from Caribbean molasses, or now more expensively from the distillation of wheat. Or you may have the alcohol in the form of synthetic rubber for your tires or your overshoes. I myself have a pair of good overshoes which once was a pine tree or a fir tree, I don't know which.

Or, if you are interested not only in alcohol or synthetic rubber but also in improving the feeding of livestock, you may see also in this ton of sawdust three hundred pounds of a feeding yeast of a protein content higher than oil meal or oil cake and apparently at a lower cost. Taking wheat at a dollar a bushel and sawdust at four dollars a ton, it would take eight dollars' worth of wheat to furnish as much carbohydrate as one dollar's worth of wood. There are many other factors involved, of course, as the organic chemist will promptly point out. But this margin of eight to one is big enough for somebody with constructive imagination to work on. Some day somebody will, and that will be a day of thanksgiving for the South.

In woods operations throughout the United States, large and small, for lumber and timber products, there is annually a volume of between fifty and sixty million tons of wood which is not now utilized for any important purpose. Much of it is not used at all. This, of course, is an adventure in astronomical statistics. But this amount of so-called "wood waste," if it were converted by present known and proven processes, would produce thirty-three million tons of wood sugar, which is as much as the present world total production of sugar of all kinds from all sources. Or it would yield over three billion gallons of alcohol, thrice our present national alcohol production for all purposes. Or it would provide nearly ten million tons of feeding yeast sufficient for the livestock of this country and Europe combined. And it would provide twenty million tons of lignin, which, if it cannot be used in the production of perfumes, extracts, water purifiers, and the like, can at least be used, as on a large scale in Europe it has been used, as a road binder or a soil fertilizer, or perhaps a glue.

I mention these staggering figures not because any such approach to complete timber utilization may in fact be expected, now or later, but because there is so vast a difference between our present 30 per cent utilization of our timber and the 60 or 70 per cent utilization to which science has already opened the door; and because that extent of improved utilization, if established in the forest industries alone, in the South alone, would provide permanently more employment for more people and at higher wages than have ever gained their livelihood from the production of cotton in its most confident days.

SOUTHERN FORESTS

The name of Charles H. Herty is one of the most respected names in the annals of science and industry in the South. Dr. Herty's faith in the chemical future of southern pine has been vindicated by the achievement in recent years of a successful newsprint industry in the South, a development which over the years undoubtedly will be multiplied throughout the South. I knew Dr. Herty. I have sat on the same end of a log with him. I have been in his modest laboratory. Latterly I worked with him in the National Recovery Administration. He had hope. He had patience. Above all he had faith. In 1938, testifying before a U. S. Senate Committee, he said:

I am an optimist on forestry in the South. There is a simple foundation for my optimism. Here in the South we have 200 million acres of land not needed for agriculture or for town expansion. Every acre of this will grow timber and *if properly protected from fire and properly managed*, can yield a cord an acre per year. Two hundred million cords is a goal that we can look forward to *if our people are educated*.

At that time the Senate had before it a forecast for 1950 of a total national consumption of twenty-five million cords of wood for pulp and paper in the United States, a quantity which in Dr. Herty's vision, and under conditions of forest protection and management no more favorable than can readily be brought to pass through intelligent public and private co-operation, may eventually be supplied many times over in southern pine alone.

A few days ago in the Congress of the United States the Honorable Harris Ellsworth, Congressman from Oregon, speaking on the subject "New Jobs Grow on Trees," threw this challenge not only to the Pacific Northwest, which he so capably represents, but to the South as well:

Present employment in the manufacture of forest products is estimated by the Forest Service at 3,500,000. If, by turning to account what has heretofore been regarded as waste wood, the total forest production figure is increased even 10 per cent—a modest goal—some 350,000 more jobs will be provided in the post-war era. This I consider a minimum figure; other estimates place the potential increase in employment as high as 2,000,000.

During recent years, particularly the war years, important strides have been taken toward utmost usefulness from the produce of our greatest, renewable natural resource—the forests. Yet an uncharted continent lies ripe for exploration by research, and the reward will be new products, new industries, and *new jobs*. The challenge is so compelling and the prize so rich that we should think of the forest products research program on a national scale.

Our forest industries, I am proud to say, are gradually learning that their future is to be written in the chemist's test tube as well as with a sharp saw; that an industry which eventually must grow its own raw materials had better find out how, practically and profitably, to use more than a third of the timber which it grows and cuts and sells; and that, with the aid of ingenious science and patient research, the future of forest enterprise in this country may be far greater than its past.

MINERAL RESOURCES

How prophetic, too, of our present problem is the warning given a quarter-century ago to the industries and scientists of the South by a far-seeing industrial leader of New England who, in commenting on the raw materials economy of the South, had this to say:

Bauxite is sold for $5. a ton to be subjected elsewhere to the purifying treatment which raises its value to $60. The South will one day benefit enormously by a cheap process for producing alumina direct from clay. It will give new values to Southern clay beds and to Southern water powers and transfer the aluminum industry to this section. It does not appear, however, that any effort is being made in the Southern States to develop such a process.

This was in 1915; and even today such a process has not been developed in the South, although it has been in the West. In the meantime the Northwest, with its abundant ore and low-cost power resources, right now is seeking to establish a dominant place in the light metals industries from raw material to fabricated product. Unless the South goes promptly on the march, its opportunity in light metals, so clearly envisaged a quarter-century ago will be realized—if realized at all—only under the sternest, stiffest, and strongest competition from the Pacific Northwest. In fact, one of the major objectives of the ambitious program of Industrial Research and Extension in the great institution which presently I head is the development in the Pacific Northwest of a diversified light metals industry in aluminum and magnesium, commensurate with the scope of its huge resources of ore and hydro-electric power and compatible with the vigor, ambition, and enthusiasm of its people. We in the Northwest look upon this field of development as one of the most promising means eventually of lifting the Northwest out of its traditional station as—so to speak—a "raw-materials colony" and toward an industrial economy and culture of its own.

AGRICULTURE

Again, in the processing of agricultural products the South, like the Northwest, is only on the fringes of great new opportunities. Recently I visited a new plant in the State of Washington converting ordinary wheat into starch and glucose and seeking additional recovery of multiple by-products. Its product cannot perhaps quite compete in taste with Vermont maple syrup. But it can at least make better corn syrup than corn. I also visited a plant for the production of starch from potatoes, a further precaution against the violences of over-production so characteristic of agriculture. These enterprises have been initiated by the Washington State Grange. They illustrate the new spirit of enterprise which is pervading agriculture in the Northwest. They are comparable to the developments in forest and vegetable processing in the South, such as the starch production in Mississippi and the alcohol production in Georgia, which are gradually lifting the lowly sweet potato to the status, not of a mere vegetable to be eaten or fed today or lost, but of a chemurgic treasure, a permanent source of permanent fuel, an endless resource, not like petroleum, which must live on its own capital.

Farmers in the Northwest, and I hope and believe in the

South, too, are no longer content to have all their eggs in one basket, or all their fruit, or their wheat, or corn, or potatoes, or their peas, or peanuts, or cotton, or their dairy products. Processing, by-products utilization, dehydration, refrigeration, and now even irradiation are opening up new opportunities, new resources, and new alternatives to agriculture.

MANUFACTURERS VS. MATERIALS

I have spoken of the companionable interest of the South and the West in light metals and in their long-range implications. These light metals are suitable, for example, for general use in machinery and tools and equipment. Eventually they will be so used on a large scale. But where will they be used? That, I think, is an appropriate and a crucial question for the South, as it is for the West.

Ordinarily in this country the production of "durable" goods, such as machinery, has provided one sixth of our national employment; production of "consumer" goods, such as food and clothing, has provided one third; and service industries including trades, transportation, professions, and public services have provided one half. The "key" to jobs has been the production of durable goods. During the great depression of the thirties, however, only one out of eight persons employed in consumer goods production lost his job. But four out of eight in durable goods, and even five out of eight in construction, lost their jobs. In the South as in the Northwest we should seek a better balance of production between raw materials on the one hand and processed goods and manufactures on the other; between durable goods and consumer goods; and between goods and services. We can then safely multiply our employment opportunities. We can make industrial operations more stable; and we can make jobs more secure.

We cannot do this by taking in each other's washing. We cannot do it by merely producing raw materials. We can do it through a balanced and diversified agricultural and industrial production. From the standpoint of abundant resources, ready accessibility, and inviting climate, no section of the United States has fundamentally a better chance to do just that than has the South. But great industries do not spring from great opportunities alone. They spring from the initiative of great people.

I have had occasion recently to analyze the types and sources of production of machinery used throughout the United States —agricultural, food processing, machine tools, metal working, electrical, engines, tractors, and the like. These are typical processed, fabricated, finished manufactures. They are not like the ton of ingot metal which provides three days' work for one man. Rather they are like the ton of processed and fabricated aluminum which provides from fifty to two hundred days work for one man.

The eleven western states use nearly 16 per cent of our national product of machinery. But altogether they produce only 1½ per cent. Of the combined national production of all machinery, the South produces barely 2½ per cent. But the South uses more than 25 per cent.

INCOME DISTRIBUTION

If an economy dominated by the production of raw materials is inferior to a diversified industrial economy, that fact should of course be reflected in the people's income. Let us look for a moment at *that* record, as of 1940, our latest prewar year. Our national income then was a little less than eighty billion dollars and our average individual income about six hundred dollars. Ten per cent of our total national population was engaged in the *production of raw materials*. Of the forty-eight states, thirteen had an average income *greater* than the six-hundred-dollar national average; and each of these expended *less* than the national average of its labor on the production of raw materials. Of these states, twelve were eastern and central states. The thirteenth was California.

On the other hand, thirty states had *less* than the national average of income and spent *more* than the average of labor time on producing raw materials. These states with a single exception were south of the Ohio or west of the Mississippi. The remaining five states were Maine, New Hampshire, Indiana, Wyoming, and Nevada, which had variable ratios of income and labor expenditure on production of raw materials.

With these minor exceptions the distribution of our national income in 1940 showed that those states had the *largest* individual incomes which spent the *lowest* proportion of their labor on the production of raw materials; and, conversely, those states had the *lowest* individual incomes which spent the *highest* proportion of their labor on the production of raw materials. Each of the southern states spent *more* than the national average of its labor on the production of raw materials; and out of the seventeen states in which the largest proportion of labor was used in the production of raw materials, fourteen were in the South. The other three were in the West, and those same seventeen states showed the lowest averages of individual income. Do we, in the South or the West, wish to debate with the adding machine? Or will we learn from it?

MORE EQUAL PURCHASING POWER

It is true, of course, that there are many manufacturing industries well established in other parts of the country to whose immediate interest it may be that the South, like the Northwest, should continue as a supplier of low-cost raw materials and not become a formidable competitor in processing, refining, and fabricating these raw materials. This interest of ownership and investment is understandable, logical, and fair. But it is not in their ultimate interest and certainly it is not in the interest of the people of the South and the West. Nor, in the long run, is it in the national interest. In the interest alike of progress at home and of peace abroad there is need in this country for a greater equalization of purchasing power, not by taking away opportunity from some but by adding opportunity for others; not by subtracting from the purchasing power of the more populous eastern and central states with the greater markets and the higher income, but by adding to the purchasing power of the less populous western and southern states with the lesser markets and the lesser income. So all may gain.

It is probably true that the West and the South will gain from a balanced and diversified economy proportionately more than the East and the central states. But it is equally true and, I think, much more important that, unless the purchasing power of the lower-income half of the South and the lower-income third of the West can be substantially increased, we shall all lose, for we shall have ahead of us in this country an endless sequence of alternating employment and unemployment, of boom and depression, and the continuing invitation to a type of social and political improvization which throughout history has been often tried, has always failed, and I think will fail again, if tried again—but in failure may nevertheless bring disaster.

The kind of economy and culture to which intelligent and ambitious people everywhere aspire cannot be built on a raw materials economy. It cannot be built on agriculture alone, or on industry alone, or on commerce alone. It can be built, and securely maintained, only on the kind of diversified economy of abundant raw materials, finished manufactures, and free commerce toward which the leadership alike of the South and the West for years has been reaching, and toward which science now gradually is paving the way.

INDUSTRIAL RESEARCH

There are today 2,300 industrial research laboratories in the United States. But of these there are in the entire South only 298, fewer than in the single State of New Jersey. In the four states of the Pacific Northwest there are only fifty-five, barely half of the number in the single small State of Connecticut, which, I may add, has the highest average individual income of all the states, expends the lowest proportion of its labor on the production of raw materials, and with one exception spends the highest proportion on the manufacture of finished goods.

But industrial research laboratories may not themselves be expected to find the answer to the basic problems of diversified industry and commerce on which the future of our society and of our American way of life so much depends. No single industry or group of industries may reasonably be expected to incur large continuing expenditures for work in pure science; and yet, without pure science, there will be little progress. Fundamental research today is applied research tomorrow; and day after tomorrow it may be blazing the way to important new opportunities.

Speaking a few years ago before the House Committee on Interstate and Foreign Commerce, Dr. Karl Taylor Compton, president of the greatest scientific institution in this country, the Massachusetts Institute of Technology, has offered in these simple words what seems to me to be a clear-cut and understandable basis for the evaluation of science as a collective responsibility of the community:

1. The scientific work of today is the basis for the industrial developments and for contributions to an improved standard of living for tomorrow.

2. The industrial developments which grow out of science have been the greatest factors in providing employment.

3. In general those industries are in a state of healthy growth which have maintained close contacts with the results of scientific work.

4. There are many other valuable results of science—such as contributions to medical science and public health, new means of education, recreation, and protection against natural and human hazards.

It is generally impossible to predict the direction in which so-called "practical" results will follow from any given line of industrial research. If a group of industrial engineers, one hundred years ago, had been asked to devise means of improving illumination, would they likely have explored the sparkling habits of electricity and magnetism or the nature of tungsten wire or the passage of electric current through gases? Probably not. More likely they would have made a sober study of the processes of oil lamps and tallow candles. No, we shall gain nothing by subordinating pure science to applied research. In the long run we shall then merely lose both. The support of pure science and the inspiration to industrial research are a legitimate and, I should think, for the present at least, a necessary "community investment."

THE UNIVERSITY OF NORTH CAROLINA

The University of North Carolina is one of the pillars of the growing scientific spirit in the South. Throughout its distinguished history it has contributed greatly to the arts and letters, and to the learned professions. It has before it, as have like institutions throughout the South, a unique opportunity now to contribute to the progress and welfare of the South and of the nation as a great fountain of inspiration to the March of Science, of which the South today stands in so great a need.

Research is a means of making people dissatisfied. To the

scientific spirit no way is right or final as long as there is a better way. The progress of mankind, it is said, has been marked by increasing satisfactions. Even more in recent times, I think, has it been stimulated by dissatisfactions—the kind of dissatisfactions which take nothing for granted, are content with present ways only until better ways may be found, and aspire always to a better life.

"Never be afraid to doubt," said Coleridge, "if you have the capacity to believe." We live indeed by faith—faith in the things which are eternal. We live also by doubt, through faith, paradoxically, in the ceaseless change of the things which are subject to improvement by the hand of man. As a great scientist said centuries ago, "That which man altereth not for the better Time, the Great Innovator, altereth for the worse." What momentous examples of that truth we have seen and are seeing today as we stand in the shadow of great events, of great tragedy, and of great anguish the world over.

Civilization is a race between education and catastrophe. So as educator, as promoter, or even, for the moment, as agitator, I invite you to encourage in this state and throughout the South a bold adventure in the scientific spirit. The South is rich in resources. You can help to make it rich also in ideas, in culture, and in opportunities.

James Branch Cabell, of Virginia, in that inimitable bit of prose which he entitled "The Rivet in Grandfather's Neck," had a vision, I think, of the Old South which was, and of the New South which is to be, when he wrote these words:

"To the Old South! She does not gaze unwillingly nor too complacently upon old years. For her all former glory is less a jewel than a touchstone; and with her portion of it daily she appraises her own doing, and without vain speech. And her high past she values now, in chief, as a fit foundation of that edifice whereon she labours day by day, and with augmenting strokes."

From the Great West I come to wish the Great South Godspeed as it climbs toward the Upper Road in its economy, its statesmanship, its culture, and its pursuit of happiness in a world which one day will be again at peace.

RESEARCH IN THE SOUTH

RESEARCH FOR PROSPERITY IN THE INDUSTRIAL SOUTH

Wilbur A. Lazier

DIRECTOR, SOUTHERN RESEARCH INSTITUTE

W E HAVE REACHED a decisive moment in history technologically as well as politically. Acceleration of research activities and advances in scientific thought and experiment have given man the power to stamp out forever the ravages of disease, starvation, exposure, and want. We are equally cognizant of having developed powers that if unleashed in some future war perhaps could wipe humanity from the face of the earth. While the power of science knows no geographical boundaries, the capacity to apply it has, happily for our welfare, reached its highest state of development under the conditions of freedom of thought and initiative unique to our own particular way of life.

I doubt if there ever has been a time when the importance of physical science was so generally appreciated, for with that science we have achieved a superiority in arms that has provided us with security at home and has undoubtedly spared the lives of thousands of our soldiers. I need mention only a few of the miracles of the laboratory at war: 100-octane gasoline flowing in a steady stream to our air armada in all parts of the world; light metals of fabulous strength extracted from the salts of the sea; a synthetic rubber industry founded on molasses, wheat, corn, and petroleum and built from scratch after hostilities began; startling new products of fire and forge; glass that will bounce, and glass that will float; penicillin now so plentiful that there is enough for everyone; sulfa drugs; rockets and radar; supersonic detection devices and microwave communications; range finders and stabilizers that make gunfire a matter of mathematical precision; ships to carry armies overseas; and trucks of a size and in sufficient numbers to transport whole navies over the land; that fabulous insecticide DDT; gas proof clothing and synthetic remedies for malaria and other tropical diseases. The fundamental science underlying these great nation-saving achievements was evolved not so often in the arsenals and government laboratories as in the private research departments of our great industrial concerns and the pure research laboratories of our colleges and universities.

Little wonder, then, that hope and promise should be inspired for an equally impressive application of science to postwar problems. If science can contribute so much to win the war, can it not do as much to win the peace? Recovery and reconversion from total war will be a new world experience on a scale that will strain to the utmost all measures of resourcefulness that can be marshalled to meet its problems. We have good reason to look hopefully to physical science for help with our problems. Under the pressure of war, decades of progress most certainly have been compressed into a few short years. It remains for us wisely to turn the instruments of war to the pursuits of peace.

Dr. Charles F. Kettering of the General Motors Corporation has said that "research is an effort to find out what we are going to do when we can no longer keep on doing what we are doing now." In the field of applied research activities, this definition expresses quite adequately the objectives of research for the postwar period. There can be no victory in this war if its end brings widespread unemployment and want in our land. Many jobs must be created by industry after the war in order to employ our returning soldiers and to provide new jobs for those of our war-plant workers who wish to remain in industry.

As a research chemist, I invite your attention to the fact that in twenty-five years since World War I, new industries resulting from research have created millions of new jobs that had never been dreamed of before. We can be confident that in view of the peacetime possibilities of the wartime advances in science and technology this performance can be repeated. It is a maxim of research that every new product produces wealth greater than it destroys, for the human need or desire which makes it possible for the new to displace the old gives to the new a greater market than the old ever enjoyed.

It is quite possible, however, for us to be caught napping. Already, we of the South are far behind other regions in our technological resources. The South can no longer permit its vast resources of raw materials to remain unused, but must instead do what is necessary to bring these materials into profitable use for the comfort and enrichment of the region. If we in the southern area grow only the things in agriculture that we have been growing, and no more cheaply, and use them in the same manner; if we manufacture only the things we have always made, and in the same traditional way; if we use our forests and minerals only as they have been used in the past decades, we shall remain, as we have been, contributors mainly to the prosperity of others.

Other speakers of this conference will, no doubt, emphasize the economic heritage of the South and certain deficiencies in the most fruitful exploitation of that heritage. I shall note only one of these deficiencies. In matters of scientific research especially, the South lags far behind the more highly industrialized regions of our country. Committed for many decades to an agrarian economy, manufacturing facilities have arrived late in the South. The machinery and tools and know-how have, in the main, been brought in from elsewhere. In view of the fact that so great a part of the industry established in the South has consisted of subsidiary plants of northern and eastern concerns, it is not surprising that the research laboratories and development departments have so frequently been left behind. The important extent to which industrial research has been lacking in the South is revealed by a roll call of industrial research workers made by the National Research Council just before the war. It was found, for example, that in 1938 the industrial research personnel claimed by the nine states constituting the region usually referred to as the South totalled only 983 or 2.2 per cent of all such research personnel in the entire country. By way of contrast, 39,431 industrial research workers or 89.2 per cent of the total, during the same year, were residents of the sixteen states located in the region north of the Ohio and east of the Mississippi Rivers. As we all know, in this region to the north and east also is concentrated the bulk of the nation's manufacturing facilities.

Lest these statistics, unfavorable as they are, be found too depressing, I am glad to add that the trends are now entirely in the South's favor. Taking, for example, a comparison of the number of industrial establishments reporting the maintenance of research facilities and personnel, the percentage increase during the five years immediately preceding the war has been greater for the South than for any other comparable region in the country. The research trend has definitely turned South. It is our duty as citizens interested in the well-being of our Southland to aid and encourage it and provide whatever is necessary to maintain and accelerate it.

Opportunities for research in the South as elsewhere are legion. As elsewhere, the emphasis will and should be on securing a better co-ordination between business and agriculture. The late President Roosevelt once characterized the South as the "number one economic problem of the nation." By the same token I think we should look upon the South as the number one opportunity for research and development, for here the least has been done. Containing as it does some twenty-eight millions of people, the incomes of many of whom have seldom risen above a bare subsistence level, the South has a unique future market unto itself. It need not look far afield for outlets for its products. It needs only to provide more adequately for its own people through agricultural diversification and industrial balance. A well balanced animal industry and increased facilities for the making of finished manufacturing goods are urgent and essential needs if the South is to achieve a proper economy and a decent living for all. Medicine, nutrition, and sanitation must receive further research attention in the interest of public health and the general welfare. Scientific research on a previously uneqalled scale is needed if we are to achieve these objectives in good time.

In planning a regional program, let us look first to our agricultural set-up. Industry must work more closely with the farmer. He needs help in improving the fertility of the soil, in the control of insect pests, in the development of power tools and labor saving devices. The public school system, the telephone, the radio, the automobile, and rural electrification have brought enlightenment and comfort to millions, but other millions are yet to be reached. Labor-saving devices must be further developed and cheapened in price in order that man's toil may be made more productive. The tractor is replacing the mule, and the mechanical cotton picker has become an established reality after long years of experimentation, though only a beginning has been made. Revolutionary developments are in the making that will greatly affect the southern economy. A planter in Mississippi, who believes that wages on mechanized farms should be as high as factory wages, is looking for a new use for his forest lands that will provide all-year-round employment to utilize the spare time of his cotton workers. In Georgia, the Callaway farming enterprises are putting theory to practice for the benefit of the skeptics. Marginal land is being put to more profitable uses, and the standard of rural living is being raised. These and similar agricultural developments are of the greatest scientific and social significance.

Laboratory science must be brought to bear on the greater utilization of our farm products, to extend their applications and to avoid waste. A great corporation, primarily interested in the production of cane sugar in the Everglades of Florida, is carving out of undeveloped land an empire based on the unification of industry and agriculture. At Clewiston, Florida, the focal point of this huge undertaking, scientific research is piloting developments of factory and field. Investigations are under way ranging from the evolution of new varieties of sugar cane through the whole gamut of special tillage practices, soil biology, and livestock nutrition. Announcement was made a short time ago of plans for the construction there of a plant to produce 50,000,000 pounds of starch annually from the sweet potato, the culture of which can be dovetailed into that of cane. Here is a full-scale demonstration of what can be accomplished by the joint efforts of science, industry, and agriculture boldly and adequately backed by venture capital.

In many parts of the South the satisfactory development of the beef cattle and dairy industry is impeded by a shortage of starchy feeds. The relatively low yield of corn and the poor keeping qualities of the sweet potato challenge the research laboratory to solve these problems, or alternatively to develop a new feed crop for the region. Wood wastes suggest to the scientist a possible source of feeds for the livestock industry. Notwithstanding its regional production difficulties, corn is still the second most important cash crop of the South. Researchwise, corn and its component parts are already recognized as important industrial chemicals and are the subject of intensive investigation and exploitation in the Midwest. More typically southern crops are cotton, citrus products, tobacco, and peanuts, which constitute the four other most important cash crops. The limitations of this hour will not permit an adequate discussion of the manifold problems presented by these four items alone. The future of domestic cotton is so involved in national and international policies that it is most difficult to treat of it on a truly economic basis. Moreover, wood is embattled with cotton as a competitive source of pure chemical cellulose, the raw material for rayon textiles, tire cord, acetate yarns, and the artificial sausage casing.

Nevertheless, the cotton fiber and the cotton textile industries present two of the greatest opportunities confronting the southern scientist. Not only must the performance of the fiber be improved to meet competition with other textile fibers, but entirely new uses must be found for cotton. If, through mechanized production the cost of cotton can be substantially reduced, there is considerable basis to hope that cotton can retain its well established outlets in textiles, tire cord, and mattress filling; that it can enter new fields such as plastics, paper-making, insulation, and blended textiles, and perhaps even become a more important raw material for synthetic fibers of several types.

In Florida the citrus farmers have organized themselves into co-operatives and trade associations to solve their common problems. The ravages of the Mediterranean fruit fly, which once threatened the whole industry with extinction, have conditioned them to the needs and values of co-operative research effort. This spring there was organized in Tampa the Citrus Products Research Council for the purpose of co-ordinating all research activities of interest to the industry. Through the active co-operation of the State Experiment Station, much progress has been made in fruit culture. Some, though not yet enough, attention has been given to the by-products of the orange and grapefruit; to the constituents of the pulp and peel; to new feeds, food products, confections, and extracts containing the citrus ingredients; to the manufacture of pure organic chemicals from the oil and juice.

In the tobacco field, research information is scanty and fairly localized. Only a few companies have undertaken to investigate the fundamental reactions taking place in the curing, compounding, and combustion of tobacco. Much improvement is undoubtedly possible. At Duke University experiments have been under way for a number of years in an effort to duplicate the aroma of Turkish tobacco in domestically grown varieties. The medical profession is undoubtedly interested in research that will eliminate those components of the smoke responsible for harshness and irritation, and will reduce the nicotine content of the smoke.

War has transformed the peanut industry. Domestic production, which incidentally is all concentrated in the South and Southwest, has soared to an all-time high under the sponsorship of the War Food Administration. In 1944, 4.4 million acres were planted in peanuts, and in that year peanuts picked and threshed had a total farm value of 188 million dollars, more than a fivefold increase over the 31 million dollar value of the 1939 crop. What peanut growers want to know is how this vast expansion in production can be sustained in the years to follow the war. New food products from peanuts appear to be a large part of the answer. Although the production of oil and meal has increased substantially, both of these products will be in sharp competition with very similar products available from the soy bean. Peanut butter, peanut confections, and salted nuts are now the principal outlets in the food industry. The interesting chemical composition and high nutritional value of the peanut stir the imagination to further effort in the improvement of existing peanut foods and the development of new ones. The National Peanut Council is alert to its responsibilities and is seeking additional funds and laboratory space for research.

Another of our unique and relatively undeveloped resources is our fast-growing timber. Before the war there were, in eleven southern states, about 58 million acres in farm woodlots. This acreage constituted 30 per cent of all the forest land in this area and about 40 per cent of the total volume of timber in the South. Under favorable conditions of rainfall and temperature the southern pine reaches pulpwood size in from ten to fifteen years. Through systematic planting and selective cutting a new crop of pulpwood can be made available each year without depletion and with a cumulative asset in the trees that are allowed to stand for saw timber. Millions have been invested in kraft mills throughout the South in the past decade, and continual progress has been made on the utilization of southern woods for newsprint and as a source of alpha cellulose. Appalling wastes are evident in all phases of wood utilization, which invite the attention and demand the ingenuity of the researcher. Better labor-saving devices are needed for cutting operations. Top and limb waste is substantial, especially in the hardwoods industry. Sawmill refuse is largely unused, notwithstanding the brilliant developments in some quarters in the steaming and vulcanization of chips into wall boards and the recovery and utilization of lignin in plastics. The kraft mills exude a characteristic objectionable odor that has sometimes made their entry into a community unwelcome. Removal of this odor is one way in which negative research can be put to positive benefit.

Cellulose from wood, which is the product sought in papermaking, constitutes only a fraction of the whole wood substance. Disposing of the by-products creates problems in stream pollution. In time the chemist will find a way to separate and recover many of the other chemical substances in the wood just as the Marathon Company of Wisconsin has discovered through research the secret of recovering vanilla flavor (vanillin) from the lignin of the northern woods.

Turning now to saw timber, more research is needed in the lumber industry to prevent end-checking and fungi-staining, to preserve wood against the ravages of insects, to upgrade wood quality in such characteristics as hardness and grain weakness. Adhesives for plywood constitute another legitimate field for study in wood chemistry. Brilliant advances in the laboratory have taken place in many of these lines of wood chemistry during the war, and even as the glass industry has risen to spectacular performance under the skillful guidance of the research chemist, may it not be possible that wood chemistry, too, will burst forth to hold its own in the competitive race with light metals and plastics for structural applications? Picture if you can the impact on the lumber industry of a completely successful rapid and continuous process for the seasoning of green lumber.

Although the need for research on agricultural products cannot be overemphasized, our problem does not end here. Prominent in our regional economy are the extraction, fabrication, and fishing industries. In and around Birmingham, coal and iron dominate the scene; and, farther to the South and West, petroleum, natural gas, sulfur, and salt form a unique aggregation of chemical raw materials for future exploitation by industry. Louisiana, Mississippi, and Texas in particular are richly endowed with oil and other chemical raw materials, which, when properly combined with the elements of the air, can form an industrial empire all by themselves. Natural gas reserves can, according to a newly announced development, be turned into liquid fuels to piece out our dwindling supply of petroleum. Cheap electric power has brought to our Southland specialized metallurgical practices relying on an abundant supply of electric current. In the coastal regions the shipbuilding industry is greatly expanded and will have one of the most difficult postwar labor re-employment problems to be found anywhere. Announcement has just been made of the retooling of one of these yards for the manufacture of diesel locomotives, a new departure for the South.

Throughout the South the metals industries are not well diversified. There is a need generally for research in the manufacture of goods for the consumer trade, such as building hardware, household appliances, farm implements, heavy and fine chemicals, drugs, ink, pigments, paint, glass, ceramics, shoes, clothing, and the finer lines of textile products. The flow of northern and eastern capital to new plants in the South promises to continue unabated, but there are also many small locally-owned businesses which, if given a chance, could through properly managed research activities find new opportunities for expansion and development.

The research problems of some industries are being handled on a national scale as, for example, the coal industry, which is pouring millions into the research activities of Bituminous Research, Inc., a trade organization representing chiefly the mine operators and railroads. A research fund of $600,000 has been established by the American Gas Association representing the needs of both the natural and manufactured gas interests. It would be a healthy condition for the South if facilities could be made available so that a portion of these huge outlays for research, which are normally distributed elsewhere, could be spent in the South to provide employment for southern scientists and add prestige to southern institutions.

Air conditioning is a field for research in which the South should take a special and proprietary interest. In no other region is the potential market so great or the comforts to be derived more necessary. I have no doubt that extensive adoption of the practice of cooling residences and places of business during the hot summer months would pay for itself everywhere many times over in the added comfort and well-being of the people. Because of the mild winters, the South is particularly well situated for the economical application of the single-unit summer-winter air conditioner. Electric utilities in the Southeast are showing increasing interest in their research responsibilities in connection with developments in conditioned weather comforts. As a load builder for power-generating equipment and transmission lines the possibilities are tremendous.

Assuming that we have established a case for scientific research in the South, how can the South meet the challenge of its post-war destiny and provide a research set-up that will be adequate to its needs? First of all, much benefit will be derived in the form of an overflow from the activities of others. Companies like the American Telephone and Telegraph Company, Westinghouse and General Electric Company and DuPont maintain large and efficient establishments for the production of improvements that ultimately benefit everyone. Some companies with research laboratories dispense a brand of research information to their customers and potential customers which, although sometimes biased, is often of great benefit in helping to improve products and processes. Then there are the centralized laboratories of the Federal Government, such as the National Bureau of Standards and the U. S. Public Health Service, which are organized to carry on fundamental investigations in the interest of the public generally. With a closer kinship to specific industries we have the U. S. Bureau of Mines, the Forest Products Laboratory, and many others. More recently, with regional differences in mind, the Congress has established for agriculture the four new Regional Research Laboratories of the Bureau of Agricultural and Industrial Chemistry.

But these agencies of the government are not enough. They are interested in the more general problems of agriculture and industry. Their findings require local application and adaptation, which must in the final analysis be carried out by those who are to profit by the advances made.

It has long been the practice of private industry, especially when in some kind of temporary technical difficulty, to go to the nearest state or city university seeking the services of a specialist. Out of this practice has grown the Engineering Experiment Station or University Research Foundation, providing more formalized service for industry and giving practical research experience to advanced students in scientific or engineering courses. Many schools in the South and elsewhere are for the first time organizing new university research foundations. Commenting on this trend, Dr. Harold Vagtborg, President and Director of Midwest Research Institute, has this to say: "It must be kept in mind that the greatest contribution of the university is in training research men. Some kinds of research are most beneficially pursued in the university laboratory with its thorough and leisurely attack on problems of a fundamental nature, but the industrial research laboratory is generally regarded as geared to the tempo of industry."

It is to the privately sponsored industrial research laboratory, be it large or small, but multiplied over and over again, that we must look for a real broadside on our regional research objectives. The small business need not feel unduly handicapped. There are advantages in smallness as well as in largeness. Decisions can be more quickly reached and projects more closely scrutinized. Dr. Clyde Williams, Director of Battelle Memorial Institute, asserts: "The major difference between small business and big business is one of history. The one has grown either because it is older or has had more business acumen or was more progressive. Small business is really young, potential, big business. The reason that many small businesses became large is that their managements undertook research and were successful not only in the origination and commercial application of the new development, but also in protecting it under the U. S. patent system." Dr. Edward Herbert Land, the head of Polaroid Corporation, a small company, puts it even more strongly when he says, "No

company can afford not to have some scientists on its staff. . . .
This bright new world depends on two things: The company
must stay small, the company must be scientific."

Research management is a matter of education and experience,
and the uninitiated manager may quite naturally feel confused
and unequal to his research responsibilities. A good place to
begin a company research program is, therefore, in a research
institute. Such an organization can provide valuable counsel in
defining suitable research objectives, sound judgment in the
selection of research personnel, and facilities for initial work
that would be entirely too costly for the company just entering
upon an excursion into research. As the first few years pass by,
management has an opportunity, from first-hand contacts with
the institute, to observe research methods and to develop a point
of view helpful to the later establishment of a research department of its own. Meanwhile, in the institute the sponsor enjoys
the same privileges of proprietorship that would prevail if the
work were done under his own roof in the beginning. Under
the usual contractural arrangements, any inventions or discoveries made in the institute within the field of the sponsor's interest become the sole property of the sponsor. There are a
number of outstandingly successful non-profit research institutes
prepared to render this service provided a prior commitment in
the field of the sponsor's interest has not already been made.
The three largest are Mellon Institute in Pittsburgh, Battelle
Memorial Institute in Columbus, and Armour Research Foundation in Chicago. All are endowed, splendidly equipped, and well
managed. More recently, groups of enterprising business men in
the South and Midwest have seen fit to take the initiative in
organizing the Southern Research Institute at Birmingham,
Alabama, and the Midwest Research Institute at Kansas City.
Both organizations are non-profit and both are dedicated to the
services of their respective regions. Great promise is held for
institutions of this kind which can work close to the regional
interests of their sponsors. Some trade associations have established special laboratories such as the Institute of Paper Chemistry at Appleton, Wis., and the Institute of Textile Technology
at Charlottesville, Va.

In industrial research the all-important factor in success is the competence of the research personnel employed. After this there is required, on the part of sponsors, something of an appreciation of the difficulties and expense involved in conducting research for profit. It is not only unfair but unenlightened to expect a research chemist or physicist to solve all your problems the first day or even the first year. Companies experienced in research know that much patience, time, and money are needed to bring satisfactory results.

Those who have given thought to planning our postwar recovery program are concerned about the prevailing apathy towards the deferment of technological and research personnel, and the training of youth for a career in science. It takes at least seven years of academic training or four years of intensive schooling with added years of practical experience to make a research man. The fountain-head of research is the undergraduate enrollment in technical studies, and this has been cut to a trickle. Here in the South there is a special problem, because too little attention has been given to the science branches of our colleges and universities, relatively few of which are qualified to grant the doctor's degree in the physical sciences.

The American Association for the Advancement of Science makes a practice of honoring scientists who in the opinion of their fellows have achieved most in their chosen fields of endeavor. Few are the awards which go to the South. In the 1944 edition of *American Men of Science* there were 255 scientists who were awarded the star of distinction. Out of this number only eight went to the South. It is interesting to note that among these eight, three were distinguished members of the faculty of the University of North Carolina. In the whole 1944 class of awards, there were only eight chemists and four physicists connected with industrial concerns. All of these were in the North and East. Dr. Wilson Gee has pointed out most ably that if we are to succeed in scientific research for industry the technical prestige of our southern schools must be built up. There are those in industry who would gladly lend aid by providing fellowships to support worthy students who have the inclination and the qualifications to continue their scientific studies at the post-graduate level. In the distribution of these fellowships on merit, there necessarily has been a selection which tends to exclude the less well qualified schools of the South. Some means should be found to increase the incentive on the part of our schools to warrant these awards on a deserving basis.

There is just one more job that must be done by all if privately sponsored research in the South is to accomplish what it has done elsewhere. This is to create research-mindedness in those to whom we must look for the sponsorship of research projects. It is natural and easy for the initiated to be research-minded. To the uninitiated there are doubts that lead to indecision and an over-cautious attitude towards the continuation of projects. It is those who stay in research who succeed best. Research is like life insurance; it increases in value with time; it stands ready to meet an emergency only if it is in force. We must be prepared to deal with the lack of research-mindedness wherever we find it. We must be optimistic. We must use all the devices known to public-relations work to remove research from the realm of temporary expediency and to establish it as a fixed policy of business.

One hundred and twenty years ago Daniel Webster said, "And there is open to us, also, a noble pursuit, to which the spirit of the times strongly invites us. Our proper business is improvement. Let us develop the resources of our land, build up its institutions, promote all its great interests, and see whether we also, in our day and generation, may not perform something to be remembered."

THE DEVELOPMENT OF SOUTHERN RESEARCH

Raymond R. Paty

PRESIDENT, UNIVERSITY OF ALABAMA

TODAY THE SOUTH is more research-minded than at any time in its history. This is inevitably true of a region which has had the attention of the entire country focused upon it as an economic and social problem of the nation. When we look at the history of research in the South we find that (as elsewhere) progress has been made in both the pure and applied phases. At times in the development of research in the South, the emphasis has been laid predominantly upon pure research. This was particularly true until comparatively recent times. A review of the history of research at any southern university will bear out this observation. One of the reasons is, perhaps, the influence of the training of faculty members at European centers of learning at a time when abstract studies were emphasized to the almost complete exclusion of the applied field of research. During recent years the pendulum has, perhaps, swung too far the other way and the emphasis on applied research has made investigators forget the importance of fundamental studies.

It is interesting to note that in some of the southern states even in the days before the Civil War—when research of any type was meager—the need for applied research was recognized and bureaus were established to investigate the natural resources of the region for their increased utilization. This work was subsidized by the state governments, either through the universities or by the formation of a bureau of survey, and indicated a recognition of their obligation to further investigations into new or unexplored fields of knowledge as well as to disseminate it through education.

Most of the scientific research in the South, however, came from the almost isolated laboratories of the universities—the product of the minds of educators who considered finding new knowledge as important as teaching old knowledge. In a recent

49

article on the "Future of Science," Dr. F. R. Moulton makes these comments: "On looking over the great names in science one is struck by the fact that most of them are of scientists who worked in relative isolation. It is true of Archimedes and Aristotle, of Galileo and Newton, of Lyell and of Darwin, of Dalton and Mendeléeff, and of many other men whose names are bright on the pages of science." He adds: "These scientists were not simply, or even primarily, observers; their active and penetrating minds grasped the observational and experimental evidence relative to the subjects in which they were interested and organized it into coherent scientific theories." In essence this was the way that research in the sciences advanced in the South in the past. Would it not be wise to see that this method is still encouraged in the future along with those methods which involve the concerted action of many men upon a common front of investigation? Would not this mean attracting to our campuses more outstanding personnel and furnishing them the time and facilities to follow their natural bent?

More recently in the South research has been encouraged by government-supported research bureaus. Some of these are branch laboratories or offices of the federal government and others have been created by state agencies. In most cases they have the advantages accruing to a group of specialists working upon related problems and with the necessary facilities for research work. Those bureaus supported by the Federal government usually work upon problems of a regional nature, while the state-supported bureaus generally confine their activities to investigational studies within state boundaries. Through careful and recorded experimentation and observation, these agencies have produced much new knowledge of our resources. Some of it has been unreliable, but much of it has contributed to the betterment of the South.

The value of this method of promoting research is unquestioned, but it represents only one front of attack. These governmental bureaus in many cases have been established on or near the campuses of universities and colleges and have stimulated related research at these institutions through co-operative efforts. They have sometimes provided opportunities for the part-time use of faculty members and graduate students in a research environment. This is particularly important if we are to have a steady flow of talent into the research field. Our institution has trained many young men in this way and has thereby contributed not only to the region but to the country at large in producing young research workers in a highly specialized but important field.

The tangible results of this means of developing research are hard to evaluate. There is at times a decided lag between the completion of the investigation and its utilization. Much of it is probably never used, and some of it is rendered obsolete by later developments in other sections. One criticism frequently voiced is that this method produces bureaus which tend to become staffed with non-productive workers who rest on their past laurels. Another criticism is that careful preliminary studies to evaluate the worth of a proposed program are disregarded in the rush to secure additional appropriations. Sometimes political pressure is brought to bear on a particular bureau to investigate problems of doubtful merit. And there is frequently loss of a vast amount of valuable research time in unwinding the red tape which seemingly is indigenous to government bureaus. Should there not also be better means of co-ordination and co-operation between these government bureaus and, indeed, between all research agencies working in related fields? This method of developing research in the South has, however, been the means of producing well-equipped laboratories, upon which the progress of science is so much more dependent now than in years past.

A more recent movement for promoting research in the South has been the establishment of research foundations predominantly but not exclusively in the field of industrial research. Some of these follow the patterns set up in other parts of the country. A number of the institutions of higher learning have formed industrial research foundations, somewhat independent of their educational divisions, although utilizing in some cases both personnel and facilities of the institutions. The movement is so young in the South that it is impossible to judge its effectiveness, but at some of the universities in the North it has been successful to a marked degree. Certainly, research foundations will have the interest and support of those industries which are forward-looking and which realize the value of research as a tool for their own betterment and the betterment of the region. That industry at large recognizes this need in the South is evidenced by its substantial support, which resulted in the establishment of research foundations such as the Southern Research Institute and others independent of the educational institutions. This does not mean that they will not be dependent upon the educational institutions, for most of their staffs will have received their education and, indeed, their scientific training at some university. There will continue to be close co-operation between the research organizations and the educational institutions. In some cases the laboratories and personnel of the institutions may actually perform the research work under contract with the foundation.

One interesting development of the trend of large industries to support scientific research has been the increasing tendency on the part of industries to subsidize pure or fundamental scientific investigations which seemingly have little present commercial application. Of course, this is recognition of man's difficulty in forecasting future technical development. The research which is highly abstract today may become eminently practical tomorrow. Perhaps the willingness of large industries in Germany to finance pure research may account for the tremendous technical and scientific developments within the past few years in that country.

In an article on "British Industry and Research," Sir Harold Hartley stresses the increased dependence of industries upon both pure and applied research in order to refashion existing industries effectively and to create new ones. He says:

Great industrial developments usually depend on fundamental discoveries; thus the electrical industry grew from Faraday's researches in electro-magnetic induction, and the radio industry sprang from work on electro-magnetic waves carried out by Hertz in a university. In more recent times the technique of radio location was first devised and used for a purely scientific purpose without any thought of its practical application.

It is in the university laboratories, the outposts on the frontiers of knowledge, that fundamental research is mainly done. At any time a new industry may be born there which will meet some new human need. It is in the atmosphere of the university laboratory, too, that the men on whom we shall have to rely as leaders of industrial research are bred and trained.

It is no wonder, therefore, that in the South industry is becoming more and more interested in research and in co-operating in the establishment of industrial research laboratories at the universities.

The increased demand for industrial research, which at most educational institutions in the region had been handled in the past within the general framework of the university with little co-ordination, has led in recent years to the founding of special bureaus or institutes, where the necessary ingredients of research —time, space, personnel, and equipment—can be organized and utilized more efficiently than in the haphazard fashion formerly existing at many institutions. Industry prefers to deal with an organized bureau through businesslike contracts, where applied research problems can be initiated, pursued, and completed with dispatch. Most of these organized bureaus of research in the southern states utilize the services of the faculty of the university with which the bureau is associated, although they frequently have full-time research personnel as well. The research fields covered by this type of organization include not only the natural and applied sciences but the social sciences as well. Even in the humanities some start has been made in the South with this type of research organization. In a recent preliminary statement by the Institute for Research in Social Science of the University of North Carolina, following an inquiry into college and university research in the southern states, the following statement was made:

The research agencies have been established as units within the general administrative organization of the institution but with their own advisory or administrative boards. This type of organization has made possible concentration and co-ordination of research activities with efficient provision of direction and various aids to research, and general supervision by a group of faculty members and administrators selected for their interest in the particular field or fields represented by the agency. The overall supervision by university officials has insured responsibility in financial matters and in general policies. The agencies are usually independent of the other parts of the university except for this quite general supervision, usually exercised by the chief governing official.

The question naturally arises as to the success of the research bureau for prosecuting research in the South. Where bureaus are ably directed and adequately financed and equipped, much progress seems to have been made, even in the South, where the movement is relatively young.

In recent years there has been a trend in this region for universities to co-ordinate and control research activities in a central body in addition to the established bureaus or stations. This has developed in some cases because of special appropriations or subventions for research in special fields and the desire to secure the most effective results from them. In the establishment of these centralized agencies, such as committees, councils, or foundations, the functions of the organized bureaus have not been appreciably disturbed.

A more recent development in the South has been the establishment of institutes at various universities for regional studies in specialized fields. Many problems of the South require this regional approach for the securing of sufficient source material and the subsequent broad utilization of their findings. They have been particularly effective in enlisting the collective aid of several institutions, which by themselves could not adequately finance a program of sufficient scope, and in securing assistance from some of the national research foundations and governmental agencies which look with favor on the regional approach to difficult economic and industrial problems.

It is indeed gratifying to see within the last few decades the growth of great foundations in America for the betterment of civilization. As Dr. F. R. Moulton has so aptly stated in a bulletin of the American Association for the Advancement of Science:

Within a few decades a considerable number of great foundations have been created in this country for the purpose of advancing science, improving education, or otherwise benefiting mankind. The wisdom with which they have been set up and administered matches the princely sums that have been made available for their purposes. The founders have clearly regarded themselves as trustees of the vast resources they have commanded, and several of them have provided that both principal and income shall be completely expended within a specified period of time in order that one generation, after it is dead, shall not directly interfere with the destinies of another. In spite of the dissipation of wealth by war, it is not likely that the patterns set by these foundations will be forgotten in the years to come.

A number of the large foundations whose interests include the natural, technological, and social sciences have made notable contributions to the furtherance of research in the South and, as the universities place more and more emphasis on research themselves, it is to be hoped that they will receive even more support from the outside agencies.

The need for research here in the South is so great that we must push forward with every means at our command through individual research, through organized bureaus and foundations, and through regional institutes. This would be true under normal circumstances, but is not such a program many times as imperative under the approaching impact of postwar adjustments?

At the close of the first World War, the need in southern social sciences and humanities was for research. There was pitifully little, of any sort or intent, being conducted. Now, after twenty-five years of slow but appreciable progress, the needs are more refined. The studies made of some phases of southern culture need to be extended to other phases. Studies made in some areas need to be made uniformly throughout the region. For example, the rural social economics of parts of the South is well documented, but the problems of the small urban business men have received little study. The farmer has available tremendous research facilities for investigating the production and marketing of his products, but many a public official is carrying on his duties by rule of thumb, navigating his department "by the seat of his pants."

At a time when the federal government is planning to finance battalions and regiments of returned veterans in small businesses, our knowledge of the local factors of success and of the business needs of the South is woefully, even cruelly, meager. Business research bureaus and business research direction we have in plenty, but the bureaus are small, unco-ordinated, starved for funds, and starved for personnel. The South, perhaps more than other regions, should welcome the suggestions being made for a federally assisted system of business research comparable to the federal agricultural research organization.

In promoting research the need for trained personnel, adequate financial support, and facilities must be stressed over and over again. Of these, perhaps, the most important is trained personnel, and here we in America have been most negligent. Many outstanding scientists have warned us of our reckless expenditure of young scientists. To quote Dr. Raymond B. Fosdick, President of the Rockefeller Foundation, in his review of their activities in 1944:

The policy of the American government in regard to the training of scientific men during wartime has been characterized in many responsible quarters as fundamentally short-sighted. Unfortunately the accuracy of the characterization can scarcely be challenged. Where England and Russia have sought to protect their future by guarding the flow of new scientific personnel, our policy seems to have been largely dictated by expediency and the apparent necessities of the moment.

With few exceptions our young teachers and research workers have largely left the universities as have our science and engineering students. The question arises in the minds of the leading scientists as to whether we will be able to meet the needs of the next generation with so much of our technical strength lost. This sobering thought of the lack of young men to carry on research is even more pregnant here in the South, where we have had difficulty in normal times in holding our most promising young graduates in competition with other sections of the country where greater recognition of the value of their services exists. Must we not bend every effort to halt this flow of research talent away from our shores?

Clyde E. Williams, Director of Battelle Memorial Institute, recently said:

In the intensified research program to follow the war, our most precious and critical resource will be well-trained research men. Our universities will do well to intensify and broaden their programs to include the training of men for research. Industry will do well to assist by the financial support of these programs. In this most essential activity, however, it is important that we do not lose sight of the product being sought—namely trained research men.

Battelle has recently moved in this direction by expanding the educational activities of the Institute. Should not university and college administrators in the South meet this challenging need for the postwar period? Mr. M. H. Trytten, Director, Office of Scientific Personnel of the National Research Council, has aptly presented the oncoming situation in his paper on "The Impending Scarcity of Scientific Personnel." In the concluding paragraphs of this most interesting paper he states:

If this constant technological expansion is necessary for continued prosperity and if a steady flow of new technically trained persons is needed to carry on the technological expansion, the full danger of our policy of curtailed training becomes apparent. The present supply of technically trained persons will apparently be so busy keeping up with the status quo that the necessary tempo of new development may not be possible.

These considerations should mean to science teachers a special awareness of the need for the highest devotion in the teaching of sound, solid work in the sciences at the beginning levels. We need an enhanced flow of capable men into the advanced levels of scientific and engineering instruction. It is in the interests of the nation as a whole that a flow of capable, sincere students in the sciences return as soon as possible to the regular training courses in the universities and the graduate schools.

At the universities in the South, in order to meet the postwar needs for regional adjustment, we should encourage the promotion of research through every possible avenue—through stimulating individual research, through establishing organized bureau research, through research foundations, through regional studies by groups of educational institutions working co-operatively with government agencies and national foundations. The need is great and the time is short.

Research in the humanities demands trained workers, time, and extensive libraries. Our ubiquitous poverty has limited the humanists no less than the physical and social scientists, and until recent years humanistic research in southern institutions was rare and fitful. During the past two decades the quantity and the quality of southern research in language and literature, religion and philosophy, art and history, have improved, but we are still backward.

In the humanities there is a conflict of philosophies that does not seriously trouble the scientists. It is between those who believe that southern research should be merely *in* the South and those who believe that southern research should be *about* the South. One school of thought scorns local and native art, literature, and traditions, holding that the humanist studies man in general, not man in Mississippi or Georgia. Adherents of this view have followed the leads of their non-southern university training, studying remote and ancient cultures despite inadequate libraries, and, with notable exceptions, achieving only moderate success. On the other hand, the documentation of southern culture has proceeded slowly and is still far from adequate.

No one would seriously propose that all southern humanistic research be focused on southern subjects; the contention of the humanist that he is above political and geographic boundaries is unquestionably valid. Yet it is pertinent to ask whether the cultural heritage of a region cannot be best studied and interpreted by the scholars who are actually in that region, close to the surviving relics and documents of the heritage. It is not a rejection of humanism to believe that man should know the shape and story of the ground from which his roots draw his very nature.

This is not a suggestion that our Shakespeare scholars should become experts on Confederate poetry and neglect the Bard; it is a suggestion that, along with Shakespeare scholars, we might well encourage the student of native culture and provide him with the facilities and respect that no other region can or should give him.

A few southerners have returned from eastern or foreign universities to build international reputations in fields far removed from the life of the South. A few have returned to apply their training to study of southern literature, theater, folklore, or music, and have attained eminence in so doing. But far too many have lacked the facilities to continue their early interests and have lacked the inclination or stimulation to take up new and more accessible subjects; they constitute a large part of the great majority of holders of the doctorate whose research and publication stopped with the printing of a dissertation abstract.

The necessary dependence of the humanist on books may make it advisable for southern universities to plan deliberately and farsightedly to foster research in particular disciplines, spending up to the hilt for documents in those fields and, while not stultifying their scholars in other fields, avoiding the dissipation of library funds on inadequate collections in too many fields.

A quarter of a century ago the development of research in the South was a subject with little past and only sketchy plans for a future. Now we can look back to enough of a past to make evaluations, to decide that some avenues are dead ends, some are too costly, and some are fruitful and deserve vigorous pursuit. Many of the problems which a generation ago were theoretical are now real and immediate. At the opening of an era in which research seems destined to flourish, we are much better prepared to make plans and develop philosophies, and much of our improved preparation is attributable to the magnificent groundwork laid here at the University of North Carolina.

NUTRITION AND PUBLIC HEALTH

RESEARCH IN NUTRITION: IMPORTANCE TO THE PUBLIC HEALTH

Russell M. Wilder

DIVISION OF MEDICINE, MAYO CLINIC; HEAD, DEPART-
MENT OF MEDICINE, MAYO FOUNDATION FOR
MEDICAL EDUCATION AND RESEARCH

THE PROSPECTUS, written by North Carolinians, to explain this Conference on Research and Southern Welfare is severely critical of the part played by North Carolina and other southern states in developing research. The criticism must have been intended to apply to fields in which I am not well acquainted; because in the field of public health, and especially as regards nutrition and its effects on public health, I cannot agree. For if the criticism were valid in all respects, I should not now be suffering from feelings of humility for attempting this address, on the home lot, so to speak, of many colleagues whose contributions to the knowledge of nutrition have been of great importance.

General Simmons will speak later on problems which I suppose relate to transmissible diseases. The triumphant march of modern medicine, with its impending conquest of plagues such as typhoid fever, hookworm, malaria, and amebic dysentery, has been nowhere more dramatic than in these southern states. Nor have state and county health departments anywhere been better organized, or manned by more faithful public servants. Millions of persons today owe their lives to the vision and devotion of those who made possible these triumphs.

Indeed, the victory over diseases caused by micro-organisms has been so conspicuous that possibly one ill effect of it can be observed, a tendency, namely, to retard advance in another field of public health, that of the nutritional deficiencies. Sir Edward Mellanby of the British Medical Research Council recently made mention of the fate of the French scientist, Chatin.[1]

1. Edward Mellanby, *Nutritional Science in Medicine* (*Brit. M. Bull.,* II [Nos. 10-11], 1944), pp. 202-4.

As long ago as 1850, Adolphe Chatin, then Professor of Pharmacy in Paris, thought that goiter developed from ingesting foods which contained insufficient iodine. However, the hypothesis of Chatin was actually suppressed in 1860 by the illustrious Académie des Sciences of France. At the time of Pasteur's epoch-making work with micro-organisms, it seemed impossible to imagine that lack of such small amounts of iodine as Chatin found in foods could in any way contribute to disease. So thoroughly was Chatin's contribution buried that no mention of his name appears in early editions of Garrison's classical history of medicine; yet Chatin's hypothesis now is well established, and application of it, in Switzerland especially, but also in our country, by adding iodine to table salt, has substantially decreased the incidence of simple goiter. In recent years it has become increasingly apparent that "factors of quality in food are as important for life as factors of quantity, that minute amounts of several inorganic elements and similarly minute amounts of several vitamins are essential to the maintenance of health." [2]

Deficiencies in diet are of several types. The total food may be inadequate in food energy units, so-called calories. Body building protein may be lacking or, if supplied, may be poor in quality and fail to contribute some of the amino acids known to be essential. Various salts may be missing or vitamins not be supplied in adequate amounts. The concept that ill health and disease may develop from deficiency of vitamins, although the term "vitamin" is of more recent coinage, began in 1897 in Java, where the Dutch physician, Eijkman, found that among prisoners who ate polished rice a form of neuritis known as "beriberi" developed. The major feature of this infirmity is paralysis, which is implicit in the name "beriberi"; the word is Singalese for "I cannot." Eijkman showed that this disease could be produced in fowls by feeding them a diet of polished rice; also, that it could be prevented or even cured by feeding the coverings that had been removed from the kernels of the rice in polishing or milling. The coverings contain the vitamin now long known as "vitamin

2. J. B. Orr and Isabella Leitch, *Iodine in Nutrition; a Review of Existing Information.* Medical Research Council, Special Report Series 1929, No. 123. 108 pages.

B$_2$" or "thiamine." Another landmark of this branch of medical science was the discovery, in 1907, that scurvy could be prevented and also cured by feeding of something that was present in fresh vegetables and fruits. This something was the vitamin later named "vitamin C" or "ascorbic acid." Another milestone was reached in 1917 when rickets was found to be preventable and curable by feeding certain animal fats, notably the fish oils. It later was shown that fish oils contain vitamin D.

THE CONQUEST OF PELLAGRA

The effect on medical thinking of these notable advances tended to be minimized by preoccupation with diseases caused by micro-organisms. Furthermore, beriberi in its full-blown form, as encountered in the Orient, occurs infrequently in America, and full-blown scurvy also is uncommon. The discovery of the cause of rickets was promptly put to work by giving cod-liver oil to babies, but even in this instance the general significance of the functions of vitamin D received but scant attention. However, in our South about this time pellagra appeared extensively, and the study devoted to pellagra by the scientists and physicians of southern states explains their pre-eminence today in nutritional research. For they showed in time that pellagra, much as was true of rickets, scurvy, and beriberi, resulted from defects in the nutritional quality of diets.

Isolated cases of pellagra had been described in several states, both North and South, but in 1905 in Alabama, in a hospital for insane Negroes, Dr. George Searcy immortalized himself by recognizing as pellagra what at first appeared to be an epidemic of a transmissible disease. Searcy stopped this "epidemic" by the use of better diets.

Don Gaspar Casal, physician to the King of Spain, first described pellagra, in the early eighteenth century, relating it to leprosy. Soon thereafter the disease appeared in southern France and later in northern Italy, in middle Europe, and in Egypt. The word "pellagra" means "rough skin." The major symptoms of pellagra stem from inflammation of the skin (dermatitis), inflammation of the tongue (glossitis), of the mucous membrane of the alimentary canal (enteritis) and of the brain (encephalitis). In its more baneful forms, pellagra, after nearly forty years, may have almost run its course in the United States, but at its height, in 1929, it claimed by death not less than 7,000 victims in this country. Pellagra is not limited to the southern states; yet the large majority of deaths have been reported from those states and seemingly in them it generally has been more virulent than elsewhere in the nation. In any case, physicians in the southern states early became more conscious of pellagra and more skillful in its recognition than their medical colleagues farther north.

Among the theories to explain pellagra, food deficiency was always popular, but it remained for Joseph Goldberger and his associates to prove the case. Deficiency of a specific vitamin, niacin, which is present in minute amounts in foods, is basically at fault. The search for this essential factor came to a dramatic climax in 1937, and parenthetically I should like to say that man's best friend, the dog, helped provide the answer to the riddle and thereby saved the lives of many thousand human beings. This fact and parallel facts in other fields are overlooked by those whose sympathy for dogs exceeds their sympathy for their fellow men. Such persons here and there oppose the proper use of dogs in medical research. Yet the mastery of disease which is now possessed, and which benefits other animals as well as man, would largely be impossible without our canine friends. Most notably the discovery of insulin and that of the significance of niacin in pellagra are owing to their helpfulness. Insulin makes life possible for persons who without it would have died of diabetes; niacin now saves the victims of pellagra.

"Black tongue," a spontaneous disease of dogs, came to be recognized as analogous to pellagra. Black tongue was induced in dogs by various investigators, but notably by Goldberger, with diets deficient in what Goldberger, for lack of more specific information, called the "pellagra preventive factor." He and his confreres in the United States Public Health Service, among them Dr. William H. Sebrell, his successor in that Service in research on pellagra, tested many foods and other substances and found that every substance of value for treatment of pellagra was equally valuable for treatment of black tongue; that every food or substance that was worthless for treatment of the one was also worthless for treatment of the other. Some foods were strikingly helpful, notably liver, but what the beneficial factor was remained a mystery. It at first seemed not to be a vitamin, at least not any vitamin then identified as such, that is, not vitamin A, which prevented night blindness, nor vitamin D, which helped in rickets, nor vitamin B_1, which cured beriberi, nor vitamin C, which relieved scurvy. The solution came from Elvehjem, a research worker in Wisconsin, who was led to prosecute his search by the many clues revealed by the workers on black tongue. In their brief original communication on this subject, Elvehjem and his colleagues wrote: "A single dose of 30 mg. of nicotinic acid gave a phenomenal response in a dog suffering from black tongue. The anorexia improved immediately. The animal showed a growth response similar to that obtained on . . . liver extract. The diarrhea disappeared." Nicotinic acid, recently rechristened "niacin," had long been known to chemists but not as a vitamin. Now its presence was detected in the very foods which were beneficial in pellagra. It furthermore was shown to be a vitamin; like certain other vitamins it functioned in the body as a part of enzymatic systems. The fact that it cured black tongue at once suggested that it was the missing link in the diet that provoked pellagra.

Let me here quote a dramatic passage from a book of Seale Harris, long a student of pellagra. The section is entitled: "The End of the Quest for the Essential Factor in the Etiology of Pellagra." It reads as follows:

"Stages were set in hospitals in Birmingham, Alabama; Durham, North Carolina; Augusta, Georgia; Cincinnati, Ohio; and Indianapolis, Indiana, to play the final act, following Elvehjem's 'Rin Tin Tin' scene laid in the experimental laboratories of the Department of Biochemistry of the University of Wisconsin. The actors in the last scene had been trained to perform their parts by years of clinical research in pellagra; and the curtain went down on the final act of the drama . . . leaving interested physicians impressed with the idea that they had witnessed another miracle of modern scientific research."[3]

The acute mental symptoms of pellagra responded almost overnight to niacin. The lesions of the skin rapidly improved. The sore tongue—fiery red—the diarrhea and dementia subsided

3. Seale Harris, *Clinical Pellagra* (St. Louis, The C. V. Mosby Company, 1941), p. 123.

promptly in large series of cases in which treatment was given by Spies in Alabama, by Ruffin and Smith in North Carolina, by Sydenstricker in Georgia, and by others.

Niacin also proved effective for prevention. Recurrence is a common feature of healed pellagra. Persons who have recovered from the worst symptoms of the disease usually break down again within a year or two. With niacin, however, recurrences were prevented. I made the comment earlier that pellagra in its florid form had largely disappeared from regions where it formerly was like an epidemic. In part responsible may be the recent addition of niacin to flour and bread. In this process of enrichment, standardized by regulation, niacin, as well as iron and two other vitamins, thiamine and riboflavin, are put in flour and bread. Seventeen states, and I am happy to say that North Carolina is one of them, have now adopted legislation requiring this improvement of nutritional quality of white flour and white bread. Several southern states also will require addition of niacin to corn grits and corn meal. Corn maize is naturally poor in niacin. Work by Elvehjem and his associates further shows that ingestion of much corn increases the requirement for this vitamin, which explains the prevalence of pellagra in regions of the world where the principal cereal food is corn.

THE LESS SEVERE NUTRITIONAL DEFICIENCIES

Physicians, especially physicians of the South, who have had experience with pellagra, are quick to recognize and to diagnose correctly full-blown cases of pellagra. They are less acute in recognizing the partial or milder forms of the disease, which undoubtedly are much more numerous and, although less threatening to life, provoke a greater total aggregate of disability in the population.

An immediate postwar goal of those who, in conference at Hot Springs, Virginia, drew blueprints for a United Nations Organization on Food and Agriculture was elimination of the obvious deficiency diseases, pellagra, beriberi, scurvy, and the like.[4] It was recognized, however, that the problem of combating

4. United Nations Conference on Food and Agriculture, Hot Springs, Virginia, May 18—June 3, 1943, *Final Act and Section Reports*, (Washington, D. C., U. S. Government Printing Office, 1943), p. 35.

the ill effects of malnutrition involved much more than this; for even many thousand deaths from actual deficiency disease is less of a burden for mankind than the *half* health from poor diets which appears even in regions of the earth where supplies of food are very liberal. The Mixed Committee on nutrition of the League of Nations had found, in 1936, that from a fifth to a third of the populations of Western Europe suffered from lack of foods necessary to satisfy nutritional requirements, that in Central and Eastern Europe there was lack of staple foods as well, and that in the Orient the deficiencies of food supply were great by any standard. Such conditions have been brought into even clearer focus recently. More information is available and opinion rapidly is forming that the next great battle to improve the public health must be waged against poor diets. In the conference at Hot Springs the problem was described in these words: "Malnutrition in varying degrees is found in all classes and countries, . . . the close and constant companion of poverty, both national and individual. . . . There is clear and convincing evidence of the association between faulty diets and ill-health. . . . The incidence of disease in general and mortality rates among infants, young children, women in the child-bearing period, and, indeed, among all age groups, are invariably higher in ill-fed than in well-fed populations."

It is in the field of less severe nutritional deficiency that research is called for now. Many questions require for their answering better information than we now possess. In particular, what influence does less than fully adequate nutrition have on the vigor of a population, on ability to learn, on capacity for work, on resistance to disease, and on longevity? Is it related to such chronic infirmities as ulcer of the stomach, deforming rheumatism, arteriosclerosis, and many of the other maladies which afflict mankind? With many diseases of this chronic type the physician gives a hand only when he sees the end results of processes which are damaging the tissues, the time for readjustment back to normal having long since passed. Greater training of physicians is required to recognize the commencement of disease.

I had the opportunity last August to be one of a party of physicians who carried out a medical survey of a cross section of the population of an island country near our eastern shore.[5] The people there were badly fed, not badly enough at the time we saw them to have pellagra or scurvy or beriberi, but badly enough so that a majority of the persons we examined showed marks or signs which are thought to be related to dietary insufficiencies. Examples of such signs are dry, staring hair; dry skin with roughening due to pouting of hair follicles and sweat glands, producing a goose flesh which is permanent in character; lack of luster of the eyes from thickening and coarsening of the conjunctivas; thinning, scaling, and fissuring of the lips; reddening of the tongue and atrophy of its coating; thick, bleeding gums; and other signs. The population of this island country has deteriorated badly. The children are backward in their school work; many of the men are incapable of a hard day's work. The proportion of infants who died within the first year of life was very high; four times as many deaths for every thousand live births as in better nourished populations. Also, the incidence of pulmonary tuberculosis was at least four times as great as is found in better nourished populations. Wherever large numbers of people get poor food, conditions similar to those described may be encountered, and that such conditions can be bettered by improvement in the diet is suggested by many observations. For example, a striking statement recently was made by Sir William Jameson of the British Ministry of Health: "The most sensitive index of a nation's general health is probably the proportion of infants dying in their first year." He continued: "In the last war this index rose steadily, but during the past three years it has declined steadily and last year was the lowest on record. . . . The death rates for children up to ten years of age were also the lowest on record last year, as was the puerperal death rate (deaths of women who are pregnant)."[6] Factors in this improvement, according to Sir William, were the national milk scheme, furnishing of vitamin supplements for mothers and young children, and the great extension of schemes for school meals and serving of milk in schools. Full employment

5. Colonel J. D. Adamson, et al., "Medical Survey of Nutrition in Newfoundland," Canadian Med. Assoc. Jour., LII (March, 1945), 227-50.
6. William Jameson, "Foreign Letters," excerpt from J.A.M.A. (January 20, 1945), p. 177.

and high purchasing power in many families doubtless played a part in securing needed food, as well as careful management of the restricted food supply. This experience is of great significance, for if the public health can be improved with fewer food resources and at a time when all other features of the environment are worse, as has been true in England, the potentialities for improvement in countries which have normal or increased supplies of food are indeed important.

Other effective demonstrations of the benefit of improved nutrition on infant mortality, the most sensitive index of national health, have been made by groups of children's doctors in Boston, Massachusetts, in Toronto, Canada, in London, England, and in other centers. Highly significant relations exist between the diet of mothers during pregnancy and the condition of their infants at birth. In one of these experiments[7] the 216 mothers on "good," that is, well-planned diets, had with only one exception infants rating "good" or "excellent" in physical condition, and none of their children died in infancy. The women on "poor" diets had poor infants with very few exceptions; a number of them were stillborn, and several others died within the first year of life.

An experiment by Harrell in a boarding school in Virginia, where the diets provided a relatively low level of thiamine, showed that adding thiamine resulted in a great improvement in the learning power of the children. The introduction of well-planned lunches in the schools of a Georgia county was followed by such improvement in scholarship that the saving effected by the fewer failures—children who otherwise would have been repeating courses—paid for the feeding programs.

EXISTING KNOWLEDGE OF REQUIREMENTS INSUFFICIENT

Although progress in the science of nutrition was rapid in the period between the two world wars, the specialists in the field were far from ready with answers to the questions that arose with the outbreak of this war. War calls for instant action and demands the best one has to give, no matter how inadequate that

7. Bertha S. Burke, Virginia A. Beale, S. B. Kirkwood, and H. C. Stuart, "Nutrition Studies during Pregnancy," *Am. Jour. Obst. & Gynec.*, XLVI (July, 1943), 38-52.

may be. The information put to work, although leaving much to be desired, proved to be of great importance. I have mentioned the contrast in England between the effect of this war and that of the last one on the health of the people. We also were made aware of the difference in the capacity of Germany to resist invasion. The collapse of Germany at the end of World War I was due primarily to lack of the right kind of food, whereas, by putting into practice what was known about nutrition, the German people in this war did not suffer from nutritional deficiencies. Indeed, in this war the Nazis used the science of nutrition as a weapon of offense. By purposely depriving prisoners and subject populations of the foods they needed they reduced their power of resistance.

The time now has arrived to scrutinize the data which currently are the basis of nutritional procedure. A natural law involved has long been recognized, but was first, I think, put in words by Professor Lafayette B. Mendel. It is that for every nutrient a minimum requirement exists and, lacking satisfaction of this minimum requirement, growth, development, health, and efficiency will suffer. The law applies both to factors of quantity and to those of quality; in other words, to calories and protein, as well as to the group of essential minerals and the somewhat larger group of vitamins. More complete information is needed concerning the requirement of each of these many nutrients. In such studies let me urge that we should not be satisfied with just enough to maintain life and freedom from the gross nutritional diseases. We want the best of health obtainable by dietary means, not merely what is passable. The basis for decisions as to requirements ought to be *how much is beneficial and not how little will suffice*. We can well afford the costs involved in improving national health. Such expenditure can be regarded as investment in the future of America.

BETTER FOODS REQUIRED

Planning for the future must include programs of research to improve the nutritive quality of foods. Nothing seems more certain than that eating refined staples in the amounts in which they contribute to most diets dilutes the vitamin content of the diet to a dangerous extent. I refer to white flour, white rice, white hominy, white sugar, all of them starchy or sugary foods deprived by refinement of varying large proportions of their vitamins and salts. We need more knowledge of how best to make these staple foods more nourishing. The answers reached so far are by no means wholly satisfactory. In England under-milled flour, retaining more of the vitamins and minerals of wheat than does white flour, further fortified with added cal-cium, was made mandatory early in the war, but large numbers of people do not like such flour, and it is very doubtful whether flour which is undermilled can ever compete in baking qualities with fine white flour. I have spoken of the efforts in our country to improve white bread and white flour by restoring to them the riboflavin, thiamine, niacin, and iron removed in milling.[8] The products thus obtained encounter no objection on the part of the consumer but fail to satisfy the critics who demand that little or nothing of nutritional value be removed from wheat by milling. Here is opportunity for research by biochemists, nutritionists, and food industrialists. Effort must continue until flour and other staples are obtained which are acceptable to the consumer and also possess the nutritionally important constitu-ents of the grains from which they are derived.

Another way to improve the diet is to enhance the nutritive qualities of foods which are produced by nature but with inter-ference by man. The idea that a diet which is limited to so-called natural foods is thereby assuredly adequate is fallacious. The major effort of the agriculturist has been directed to develop products which give maximum yields per acre or have ability to withstand shipment to market and appear attractive to the purchaser. These objectives are not to be decried, but in attain-ing them far too little attention has been given to the major pur-pose of all food; namely, to be nourishing to human bodies. In many cases commercial quality is in conflict with nutritional advantage. Take the tomato as an example. Nutritionists have urged production and consumption of tomatoes as a good source of ascorbic acid, vitamin C. However, in striving to produce tomatoes attractive in appearance, the small-fruited variety,

8. R. M. Wilder and R. R. Williams, *Enrichment of Flour and Bread; a History of the Movement. Bull. National Research Council*, November, 1944, No. 110.

which contained as much ascorbic acid as citrus fruits contain, has been replaced by commercial varieties with contents of this vitamin somewhat less than a fourth of those amounts. Professor Maynard of Cornell, from whom I obtained this information, showed that it is possible, through breeding, to improve not only yield but also content of ascorbic acid.[9] With cabbage, for example, four new varieties obtained by selection were higher in content of ascorbic acid than standard varieties, and with one exception higher in yield. Other examples of accomplishment by breeding could be cited, such as sweet potatoes high in carotene, the precursor of vitamin A, as well as high in yield, and apples nearly as rich in ascorbic acid as are oranges. Studies of this type are under way in many places. Important work with several crops has come from the United States Vegetable Breeding Laboratory at Charleston, South Carolina. Dr. Wade, the director of that laboratory, is quoted by Maynard as saying: "If some agency interested in the public welfare absorbs the cost of research in the production of new variety with improved nutrition values, then there is no reason for the public's paying increased prices [for these better products]. Our experience in breeding improved varieties would indicate that those with high nutritive value can be as productive as those with lower values."

In investigations of this type, seed plays a part of prime significance, but soil and climate also are important. When several varieties of tomato were grown in different soil, Dr. Karl Hammer of the United States Nutrition Laboratory found differences as great as 50 per cent in content of ascorbic acid. Among climatic variations to be studied were temperature, humidity, and light, the greatest effects being observed from variation in the intensity of light.

What I have had to say about vitamin C and vitamin A undoubtedly applies to other vitamins. Wheat, for instance, from different regions varies greatly in its content of vitamin B_1. Likewise products of animal origin can be improved nutritionally. Summer butter is rich in vitamin A, winter butter poor; yet, by appropriate feeding practices, winter butter and, more im-

9. L. A. Maynard, *Food Production for Better Health and Longer Life.* Proceedings of a Conference, November 3, 1944. Privately published by the Children's Fund of Michigan, Detroit, 1944.

portantly, the fluid milk supply could be substantially improved. Egg production has been increased today by feeding rations of high nutritive value, and with this increased production the nutritive value of the eggs has been increased without increase in cost to the consumer. It will take years to explore the many possibilities, and research in this domain promises to pay enormously in dividends of better public health.

In this connection may I address a special word to the women of this audience. Important as is the development of more nutritious foods, little progress can be made in improving diets unless pains are taken to avoid losses of nutritional values in the kitchen. Cooking is an art, but an art which can be greatly helped by a modicum of science. The appeal of the good cook is to the appetite, and flavor is important because of its effect on appetite and on assimilation. However, that is no excuse for wasting vitamins and minerals. In departments of home economics much research has been directed to development of methods to avoid this waste. More research is needed, with emphasis on finding methods which both conserve nutrients and improve palatability.

In this connection also to be emphasized is the need for research on food habits by psychologists. Habits are difficult to change, and yet without some change in the food desires of some segments of the population, improvement of nutritional status may be impossible. It is probable, however, that a systematic study of this subject will develop basic concepts which will be of help in suggesting educational and other means to effect desired changes.[10]

OTHER RESEARCH NEEDED

Turning now to medicine, we find controversy over the extent and significance of nutritional deficiency. The evidence of widespread prevalence of the milder degrees of nutritional deficiency was collected and reported recently in a bulletin of the National Research Council.[11] A concluding comment of

10. E. Guthe and Margaret Meade, The Problem of Changing Food Habits. Bull. National Research Council, October, 1943, No. 108.

11. H. D. Kruse, et al., Inadequate Diets and Nutritional Deficiencies in the United States: Their Prevalence and Significance. Bull. National Research Council, November, 1943, No. 109.

the report is that "data from numerous surveys with new methods among persons of all ages in many regions are entirely in accord in showing that deficiency states are rife throughout the nation." Some physicians refuse to accept this conclusion. The difficulty is in diagnosis of the milder states of malnutrition, a difficulty which is largely owing to lack of ease of application of existing diagnostic methods. Better methods must be found, methods like those employed to diagnose diseases resulting from infection. Before the latter were discovered, the less conspicuous forms of tuberculosis of the lungs were commonly overlooked and much syphilis remained obscure. Today in the diagnosis of deficiencies main reliance must be placed on clinical signs, which in milder forms frequently are overlooked by physicians who are inexperienced in their recognition. The practicing doctor has a threefold reason for taking an active interest in nutrition: first, many of the diseases which he has to treat have been occasioned by nutritional deficiency; second, virtually every illness may disturb nutrition; and third, convalescence from disease of any kind, or from operations, may be retarded by nutritional deficiency.

I mentioned the high incidence of tuberculosis in a population where the food supply was poor in quality. Nothing seems more certain than that poor nutrition plays a part in the etiology of many diseases of infectious origin. Malaria became so virulent in Greece, when the people were subjected to the starvation occasioned by the invasion of that country by the Germans, that mortality was terrifying. Furthermore, malaria spread farther north into Eastern Europe than it ever had before in recent years, as if the soil was fertilized by the misery of the people. Epidemics always have been bred by wars. The relative importance of the germ of an infectious disease and of the resistance of the body invaded by that germ varies greatly with different diseases. It nevertheless is true that the resistance of the body is one determinant in all infections, and much evidence indicates that nutrition plays a major part in such resistance. Here again, however, is a fertile field for much more study.

Encouraged by proper support, the sciences of biochemistry, physiology, pharmacology, and pathology will continue to contribute basic information of significance to nutrition. The chemical composition of many vitamins remains to be discovered; other vitamins are recognized by their effects on animals but are not as yet identified; the very existence of others is probably unsuspected. Inorganic minerals play enormous parts in life. With the role of some of them, such as calcium, iron, and iodine, we are reasonably well acquainted. The parts played by others are less well understood. We long have been aware of the significance of proteins—we have called them body builders—but recent work reveals that much remains to be discovered about them. The biochemical reactions in nutrition have just begun to be explored. The interplay of vitamins, minerals, and amino acids is a subject which as yet is largely speculative. The science of pathology, until lately, has been concerned with death, the end result of morbid changes, but new horizons open for this science. A number of chronic diseases, of unknown etiology, have been reproduced experimentally with diets restricted in respect to certain vitamins and amino acids. Light thus is thrown on their causation. Further study of this type and biochemical and biophysical research must in time reveal the nature of alterations in the enzymatic systems on which life itself depends, thus providing clues for an understanding of the processes of aging and degeneration. In these subjects your Dr. MacNider has been making contributions.

The practical importance of knowledge of nutrition ought to be apparent to everyone who is interested in the public welfare. However, more than welfare is involved—even national security. What part was played by malnutrition in the ill-health, which led to the rejection of so many of our boys, for military service, is difficult to estimate; informed opinion considers it important. At Hagerstown, Maryland, findings of selective service examinations were compared with findings in the same boys at physical examinations made in school fifteen years before.[12] Out of 323 boys, ninety-one, or more than one in every four, had been rated poor in nutritional status in school, and of them seven in every ten were rejected for military service when the Japanese at Pearl Harbor rang the bell which thrust this country into war.

12. A. Ciocco, H. Klein, and C. E. Palmer, "Child Health and Selective Service Physical Standards," *Pub. Health Rep.*, LVI (December 12, 1941), 2365-75.

Had such men formed our armies we probably should have failed to meet that challenge. I possess the greatest faith in the ultimate success of efforts to insure a peaceful world, and yet I must submit in the interest of security that this nation cannot now afford to fail to use existing scientific knowledge in efforts to maintain the health and vigor of its people. Nor can it possibly be safe to fail to keep abreast of other regions of the world in developing new knowledge through research. However, for research which reveals the major truths, dependence rests on fundamental work pursued, unhampered by considerations of expediency, in institutions of higher learning. The laboratories of the basic sciences in universities, therefore, form the vanguard in the never-ending struggle for better personal and better public health.

MEDICAL RESEARCH: THE FOUNDATION FOR FUTURE PROGRESS IN HEALTH AND PUBLIC WELFARE IN THE SOUTH

James Stevens Simmons, B. S., M. D., Ph. D., Sc. D. (Hon.)

BRIGADIER GENERAL, U. S. ARMY; CHIEF,
PREVENTIVE MEDICINE SERVICE, OFFICE
OF THE SURGEON GENERAL, U. S. ARMY

INTRODUCTION

MEDICAL RESEARCH is of fundamental importance to the welfare and security of our nation. The basic medical discoveries of the nineteenth century which established the causative relationship of micro-organisms to infectious diseases gave birth to the science of preventive medicine and made possible remarkable improvements in our national health. During the present war, the importance of medical investigation has been strikingly re-emphasized by the results produced through the gigantic research program which has been organized and operated so successfully to protect the health of our armed forces. Obviously these lessons of the past indicate clearly that medical research and its application to the health of all our people is essential to the further progress of this nation.

It is reassuring to know that specific plans are now being made to create a permanent and effective national organization to meet this obligation. At the request of the Secretary of War and the Secretary of the Navy, an interim body— the Research Board for National Security—has already been established under the auspices of the National Academy of Sciences, and leading scientists of the country are now working on plans for the permanent organization.

In view of these developments, it is appropriate that in this Sesquicentennial Conference, which the University of North Carolina has so wisely dedicated to research and regional welfare, we should give special consideration to the future need for research in medicine and public health in the South.

In this talk, I do not intend to enumerate the many health deficiencies of the nation or of the South, nor shall I attempt to furnish the detailed blueprint of a plan for their correction. Instead, I should like to tell you of the important role medical research has played in the development of military preventive medicine during this war, and of the mechanism by which the scientific resources of the entire country were brought to bear on this problem. It is hoped that this fine example of joint effort to meet the health needs peculiar to the Army at war may suggest lines of approach to the solution of some of the peace-time health problems of the South.

THE SCIENTIFIC MOBILIZATION TO MEET THE ARMY'S WARTIME HEALTH NEEDS

When the present war began in Europe, the United States had completed fifty years of remarkable progress in medicine, during which the federal government had shown an increasing interest in protecting the health of the public. This interest had been evidenced by the survey of the National Conservation Commission, of 1900; the reorganization and strengthening of the U. S. Public Health Service in 1912; President Hoover's White House Conference on Child Welfare in 1930; and, finally, by President Roosevelt's program of national security in 1935, which resulted in the Social Security Act and provided a responsible national health program under the leadership of the U. S. Public Health Service. The progress made was indicated by the facts that the incidence and death rates for certain of the acute communicable diseases in the registration area had declined remarkably, the average span of human life had been increased by at least 30 per cent, and living conditions were generally improved. There were still many unsolved problems, as there still are, in various sections of the country, but the peace-time health record for the United States as a whole, including both the civilian and military elements of the population, had reached an all-time high level. During 1940 it became increasingly apparent that this country might be forced into the war. Therefore, it was necessary to estimate America's emergency health needs and to make the special medical plans required to develop rapidly our military and naval forces, and to organize the industrial workers to support and assist them under the adverse conditions of war.

The Surgeon General of the Army immediately began the necessary revision and expansion of his plans in order to develop a Medical Department adequate to protect the health of a large wartime Army. This resulted in the development of the organization which now exists, to furnish medical and surgical care to the troops and to perform the even more important function of guarding the American soldier's health.

In making these plans, the Surgeon General was guided by three fundamental requirements, namely, to visualize the important health problems of the war, to apply the best medical information available to the solution of these problems, and, in instances where such information was deficient, to acquire new knowledge through an intensive program of medical research.

In estimating the important health hazards to which troops might be exposed, it was necessary to survey every region of the world, since at that time it was impossible to predict where the Army might be forced to fight. To accomplish this, there was established, as a part of the Preventive Medicine Service, a Division of Medical Intelligence, which has been actively engaged in the collection of exact up-to-date information about the disease and health problems of all countries. After analysis, this information, prepared in the form of comprehensive medical surveys, has been used as a basis for determining the special health precautions required for the protection of all American troops sent abroad. Thus, in planning for military operations in any given region, it has been possible to concentrate on those diseases most likely to interfere with our progress, and, when the available control methods were inadequate, to initiate investigations designed to correct these deficiencies. For example, all troops sent to regions where yellow fever is endemic have been protected with yellow fever vaccine. Likewise our soldiers sent to places where they might be exposed to such diseases as epidemic typhus or cholera have been previously immunized with the respective vaccines.

The second requirement was to develop an organization which would insure the most effective use of the medical knowledge already available for the preservation of the soldier's health. To accomplish this, the Surgeon General called on scientific leaders of American medicine, both military and civilian, for advice and assistance. At an early period he commissioned and brought into his office eminent specialists in the various branches of internal medicine, surgery, and preventive medicine, to help in the development of sound policies and plans, and to operate his entire medical program. For the control of disease, there was organized a special Preventive Medicine Service which includes ten divisions concerned with epidemiology, venereal disease control, tropical disease control, medical laboratories, nutrition, sanitation and hygiene, sanitary engineering, industrial medicine, and the health program for civilian populations of liberated and conquered territories.

Additional scientific advice was made available through the appointment as civilian consultants of a large corps of scientists in the leading educational and research organizations of the country, and through the civilian members of about sixty special advisory committees formed at the request of the Surgeon General by the National Research Council. These sources of medical advice have been further supplemented by close liaison and intimate co-operation with the Navy, the U. S. Public Health Service, the American Red Cross, the Pan-American Sanitary Bureau, the U. S. Department of Agriculture, the Institute of Inter-American Affairs, the International Health Division of the Rockefeller Foundation, and most of the scientific institutions and societies in the fields of biology and public health.

The third requirement was to develop new fundamental knowledge to be used for the solution of the many still unsolved problems of military medicine. To meet this situation, the Surgeon General initiated an enormous wartime program of medical research which has been carried on both by military and civilian scientists. This program has produced a wealth of new basic knowledge, and has furnished more effective methods for the care of the wounded and the prevention and treatment of many of the diseases which afflict troops.

The Medical Department of the Army has a long tradition of research. The studies of William Beaumont on gastric digestion, Sternberg's pioneer contributions in bacteriology, the work of Walter Reed on yellow fever, of Strong, Ashford, and Craig on tropical diseases, of Russell on typhoid fever, of Darnall on the chlorination of water, and the investigations of many other medical officers have contributed materially to the health and welfare not only of the armed forces but of the nation as a whole. The survival of this tradition of medical research through all the lean years between the two world wars when military appropriations were inadequate and trained investigative personnel was insufficient to meet the army's needs is a tribute to the strength and hardihood of the spirit of scientific service.

THE ARMY'S WARTIME PROGRAM OF MEDICAL RESEARCH

The Army research program during the present war may be considered under three main categories, namely, research projects developed within Army laboratories and field installations, others carried out in civilian institutions under Army contracts negotiated through the office of the Surgeon General, and still others developed for the Army by civilian scientists working under contract with the Office of Scientific Research and Development.

Research in Army Installations

The work carried on within the Army has covered a wide range of subjects; investigations dealing with the prevention and treatment of various diseases, including typhoid, dysentery, typhus, syphilis, and with certain veterinary and X-ray problems have been conducted at the Army Medical School in Washington. Studies have been made at the Armored Medical Research Laboratory, Fort Knox, Kentucky, to determine the effect on the soldier of gases, dust, temperature, noise, and the other occupational hazards of mechanized warfare. In the Army's Industrial Hygiene Laboratory at the Johns Hopkins School of Hygiene and Public Health in Baltimore, investigations have been made of the hazards encountered by workers in Army owned and operated industrial plants. At the Army Institute of Pathology in Washington, researches have been carried out on the pathology of many diseases, including infectious hepatitis and various tropical maladies. Veterinary problems have been studied at the Veterinary Research Laboratory, Quartermaster Remount Depot, Front Royal, Virginia.

Work on the development of field medical equipment has been carried out in the Medical Department Field Equipment Laboratory, Carlisle Barracks, Pennsylvania. Problems in nutrition and the medical aspects of clothing and equipment have been investigated in collaboration with the Office of the Quartermaster General, the medical phases of housing and ventilation with the Office of the Chief of Engineers, and problems related to gas warfare with the Chemical Warfare Service. The Army's Service Command Laboratories in this country, and our general and other medical laboratories abroad, have also engaged in research on a more limited scale, but with satisfactory results. In addition, important problems of aviation medicine have been studied under the supervision of the Air Surgeon at the School of Aviation Medicine at Randolph Field, Texas, the Aero-Medical Laboratory at Wright Field, Ohio, the Physiological Test Section, Army Air Forces Proving Grounds, Eglin Field, Florida, and the Army Air Forces School of Applied Tactics, at Orlando Army Air Base, Orlando, Florida.

Research under the Army Epidemiological Board

Another effective agency within the Army is the civilian Board for the Investigation and Control of Influenza and other Epidemic Diseases. At the request of the Surgeon General, this Board was established by the Secretary of War early in 1941, and was attached to the Preventive Medicine Service for administrative purposes. Its president is Dr. Francis G. Blake, Dean of the Yale University Medical School. It consists of a central board and about one hundred other members organized in ten commissions, each of which is concerned with a different aspect of disease control. The respective commissions are concerned with acute respiratory diseases, air-borne infections, epidemiological surveys, hemolytic streptococcal infections, influenza, pneumonia, measles and mumps, meningococcal meningitis, neurotropic virus diseases and tropical diseases. The consultants are on a part-time status and are stationed at their home institutions. The board functions in two ways: It affords a pool of highly competent specialists who may be sent into the field for various periods of time to assist the local medical officers in the investigation and control of specific disease problems. Its members also conduct long-term investigations in the laboratories of their respective civilian institutions. The Board and its Commissions do not own or operate any laboratories of their own, excepting the Respiratory Disease Commission which maintains a laboratory at Fort Bragg, N. C., under the jurisdiction of the Surgeon General. All of the work in civilian institutions is financed through War Department research contracts.

Since January, 1941, the Epidemiological Board has worked on more than one hundred research projects, the reports of which have been made immediately available to the Surgeon General and have been used to improve the welfare of troops. These projects have dealt with housing and living conditions in barracks; the control of respiratory diseases; the development of vaccines against influenza and Japanese B encephalitis; discovery of the virus of keratoconjunctivitis; improvements in the use of atabrine; the experimental production of atypical pneumonia, and the discovery of its etiologic virus; studies on infectious hepatitis and its causative agent; the collection of information on the distribution of leprosy throughout the world; the control of hemolytic streptococcal infections; and basic investigations of rheumatic fever, coccidioidomycosis, sandfly fever, schistosomiasis, and other important subjects. The Board has been in constant liaison with all of the other research activities of the Army. It has published about a hundred and fifty scientific papers and many more are in preparation. It represents a successful cooperative enterprise between the Army and the leading civilian institutions of the country and has been enormously helpful.

Research under the United States of
America Typhus Commission

The United States of America Typhus Commission is another agency which has been of great assistance to the Army through its extensive research activities. This Commission was initiated in the Preventive Medicine Service and is a joint Army, Navy, and U. S. Public Health Service organization, established by Executive Order of the President and administered through the Office of the Secretary of War. Its Director is Brig. General Stanhope Bayne-Jones, and its Field Director, Brig. General Leon A. Fox. It has the responsibility of protecting our armed forces wherever they may be against typhus fever and the related rickettsial diseases. It has conducted research in this country at the Army Medical School, the Army Institute of Pathology, the National Institute of Health of the U. S. Public Health Service, the Naval Medical Research Institute, and the Rockefeller Institute, and has collaborated with other investigators of typhus in this country and abroad. The Typhus Commission has done extensive laboratory studies and field control work on epidemic typhus in North Africa, Persia, Italy, the Balkans, and the European theater of war. It co-operated in the spectacular and successful attack on the incipient typhus epidemic at Naples, and it is now engaged in delousing the millions of displaced persons in Europe. It has sent groups to study tsutsugamushi disease or scrub typhus in the Western Pacific and in the Assam-Burma region, where its work has resulted in practical methods for the protection of troops against this disease.

The work of the Commission has advanced our fundamental knowledge of typhus fever, has improved the control of both epidemic and scrub typhus, and we have reason to believe that it may lead to the discovery of specific remedies for the several types of typhus fever.

The operation of this Commission again exemplifies the importance of combining the specialized scientific resources of the country in attacking a special health problem.

Research by Civilian Agencies

Realizing the urgent need for even more extensive investigative work than could be performed within the Army, the Surgeon General has taken full advantage of the splendid resources made available by other scientific agencies. The civilian response and the results obtained afford an inspiring example of what can be accomplished through a well organized and co-ordinated national research program. Since 1940, at the request of the Surgeon General, the National Research Council has maintained a large group of committees, under the direction of Dr. Lewis H. Weed, to advise the armed forces concerning its various medical problems; and since 1941, the Committee on Medical Research of the Office of Scientific Research and Development, under Dr. A. Newton Richards, has organized and supported numerous investigations which have been carried out by civilian workers in the scientific institutions of the country. Through this great organization, practically all the medical investigative resources and research workers of the country have been mobilized to assist the armed forces. The contracts made for CMR projects have totaled over seventeen million dollars. The new knowledge made available through this work has been applied immediately in the field.

There is not sufficient time even to list the subjects covered in this work, which includes studies to find more effective methods for the control of the dysenteries, cholera, plague, filariasis, malaria, and a host of other serious military diseases. Some of the better known contributions are the development of the blood substitutes, including plasma, the evolution of penicillin from the status of a laboratory curiosity to its present position as an important life-saving therapeutic agent, and, most important of all, the development of the Army's new repellents and insecticides, especially DDT. The latter has substantially removed the hazard of typhus fever and has afforded a most effective weapon against malaria and other insect-born diseases.

CONTRIBUTIONS OF WARTIME RESEARCH TO THE PROTECTION OF THE HEALTH OF SOLDIERS

The sum total of all this wartime research represents an enormous contribution not only to the control of military diseases, and thus to the successful termination of the war, but also to the entire science of medicine. Within the short space of four years, these joint researches within the laboratory and the field have afforded better methods for the prevention and treatment of a number of serious diseases. While these accomplishments cannot be considered in detail at this time, the results will be briefly summarized.

Excepting the dysenteries, the gastro-intestinal diseases, formerly the scourge of all armies, have been relatively unimportant in this war. All our troops are immunized with improved vaccines against typhoid and the paratyphoid fevers and cholera, and these diseases have been of no importance. An intensive search has been made for an effective dysentery vaccine with results which are encouraging, and experimental vaccines are now being tested in the field.

The respiratory tract diseases have been feared because of the unfortunate experience with influenza in World War I, and great emphasis has been placed on their investigation. Diphtheria, measles, mumps, scarlet fever, and acute rheumatic fever have been less common than in the last war, and the death rates have been negligible. Meningitis has occurred in the Army as in the civilian population, but its incidence has been lower than in World War I. Sulfadiazine has been used as a prophylactic, and the case fatality rate, which was 38 per cent in the previous war, has been reduced to less than 5 per cent. The pneumonias, including all types, have been less common, although the newly recognized primary atypical pneumonia has been fairly prevalent. The total fatality rate for all types of pneumonia during the last war was about 24 per cent as compared with less than 1 per cent in the present one. Two epidemic waves of mild, nonfatal, influenza have occurred, one in 1941 and the other in 1943-44. During the second outbreak, the Army's Influenza Commission carried out an extensive field experiment with a new vaccine containing viruses A and B. This vaccine is now being manufactured and stored for future military use, should it be required. Considered as a whole, the highest monthly mortality rate for respiratory disease in this war has been about one five-hundredth of the highest monthly rate during 1918.

Our researches have also improved the control of venereal diseases. The highest monthly rate reported during this war has been less than the lowest monthly rate for the last war. Chemotherapeutic researches have provided new prophylactic and therapeutic agents which have reduced the incidence of venereal diseases, practically eliminated complications, and have shortened the time lost during treatment. Until recently the soldier with syphilis required a minimum of six months for treatment, but today, using penicillin, the treatment lasts only two weeks and the results appear to be good.

Great progress has also been made in the control of the insect-borne diseases. Malaria has been completely controlled among troops in the United States. In certain tropical theaters the rates were undesirably high early in the war, but this situation has been corrected and there has been great improvement in the malaria control program throughout the army. This has been due to a number of factors, including better sanitary discipline on the part of unit commanders, the use of newly developed insect repellents and insecticides, and of suppressive drugs. The use of DDT residual sprays on the walls of buildings and tents, and the spraying of DDT from airplanes in certain theaters are important recent improvements. More than one million dollars is being spent in the search for new drugs for the control of malaria, and a number of promising ones are now being tested in the field.

The menace of epidemic typhus fever to our army has been substantially dispelled by the use of an improved vaccine and the development of the army's DDT louse powder. Scrub typhus, which has occurred in a few troops in New Guinea, the Philippines and Burma, with a mortality varying from 1 per cent to 30 per cent, is being controlled by the impregnation of clothing with dimethyl phthalate, supplemented by environmental mite control.

Effective methods have also been developed for the control of the insect vectors of yellow fever, dengue fever, sandfly fever, and plague, and vaccines are used for yellow fever and plague. The new weapons developed for the fight against these diseases have revolutionized the quarantine programs of the Army, Navy, and Public Health Service. They afford better methods for the protection of the country against the introduction of insect-borne diseases or their vectors.

Various other diseases have caused annoyance in many regions. Coccidioidomycosis has occurred on the West Coast. Infectious hepatitis is a vexing problem in certain areas, mycotic skin diseases have been common in all tropical locations, and schistosomiasis is a hazard in the Philippines. Although of little importance from the standpoint of mortality and disability, these diseases are still being investigated extensively.

Considered as a whole, the Army's health record has been excellent. During the last four years, it has mobilized more than ten million soldiers. It has examined and selected these men physically. It has provided them with healthful food, housing, clothing, recreation, personal and mental hygiene, environmental sanitation, and with individual protection against the innumerable diseases of every region of the earth. It has also provided excellent modern medical care and hospitalization for the sick and wounded. The Army has given these men training in temporary camps scattered throughout the United States, and has transported many of them in necessarily crowded conveyance across the seas. Our soldiers are now living and fighting in many foreign lands where the disease hazards are normally greater than in this country. In some of these areas, particularly in the Far East and the Pacific, the menace of disease is probably greater than anywhere else in the world. In spite of these environmental factors and the unhygienic conditions imposed by war, the death rate from disease among out troops in this country has remained far below that of the last war, and the rate abroad has been only slightly higher than at home. At no time has the loss of life from disease even approached epidemic proportions, and with a few exceptions similar statements can be made about the prevalence of disease. Moreover, 97 per cent of the wounded survive, and new medical discoveries are contributing to more rapid recovery and rehabilitation of these men.

These satisfactory results are a product not only of the investigations of the past and of the excellent training which our medical schools and hospitals have afforded to this generation of physicians, but also of research carried out during this war. It is obvious that we must keep up this work, and the Surgeon General has already made plans to continue the Army's program of medical research after the war. This nation affords unlimited natural resources and scientific talent which need only opportunity and facilities to bring them to bear upon the health problems of the nation in peace as well as in war.

APPLICATION OF THE ARMY'S WARTIME EXPERIENCE TO THE
POSTWAR HEALTH PROBLEMS OF THE SOUTH

The experience of the Army with research and its application to public health affords a pattern for the further development of the welfare of the entire nation and has created an intense interest in an effective national program of medical research.

At the request of the Secretaries of War and Navy, the President of the National Academy of Sciences has already established the Research Board for Security. This organization will continue the close co-operation between civilian scientists and the armed services provided during the war through the Office of Scientific Research and Development, pending the final establishment by Congress of a permanent postwar research agency. Naturally, the medical activities of such an agency must be closely integrated with the national health program, which is well under way.

The urgent need for further improvement in the health and welfare of this country is obvious. Remarkable progress has been made; but the United States still has many formidable health problems. The recent Selective Service examinations obviously do not afford a true index of national health, but they do serve to indicate that many of our young men are substandard physically and mentally. More than four million of the registrants examined during this war have been rejected as physically unfit for military service—a group as large as our total Army in World War I. The official health records show that each year millions of our citizens become sick, and many thousands die of preventable diseases. Recent national health surveys indicate that there is still a tragic waste of American manpower because of unnecessary accidents, industrial hazards, nutritional deficiencies, and the lack of adequate health facilities, including medical care and hospitalization.

Thus, we are again faced with the disagreeable fact that in the past we have neglected the opportunity to develop fully our national health and strength. Therefore, we must now prepare to meet the future demands of peace as we prepared to meet the demands of war four years ago. We must do more than talk about these health plans for the future. They must be made wisely and they must be carried out vigorously by an educated, informed citizenry in every section of the country.

While health deficiencies exist throughout the country, the problems of the various regions differ markedly depending on a wide variety of local factors. Because of climatic, social, and economic conditions, these problems are exaggerated in the South. In many of the southern states, the per capita income and the average level of adult education are relatively low. The birth rates are high, but so are the maternal and infant death rates. Certain states, including North Carolina, are making great progress in public health, but the health facilities of the South as a whole have not been adequately developed. This is indicated by the unusual prevalence of such preventable diseases as malaria, hookworm infestation, venereal diseases, tuberculosis, nutritional deficiencies, and dental defects. Nervous and mental afflictions are also common.

As already indicated, I shall not attempt to discuss these specific problems of the South or to suggest detailed methods for their solution. However, I wish to emphasize the fact that they can be, and should be, solved, and to propose that plans to improve the health of the South be developed along the lines followed by the Army in protecting the health of troops. As you will recall, these wartime plans were built with a view to fulfilling three basic requirements. The first was to collect specific information about the total health needs of the Army. This has been done for the South and many deficiencies are now recognized. The second requirement was to ensure the intelligent application of all the available knowledge to the correction of these deficiencies. In the South this is being done in part through the activities of the state and local health departments, medical schools, the great body of medical practitioners, and many voluntary health and welfare agencies. It is believed, however, that the effectiveness of these activities can be increased through a more aggressive, co-ordinated attack under broad leadership. The third requirement was to develop the research facilities necessary to discover new knowledge which might be applied for the prevention of the still unconquered diseases. This important requirement must be met in any program designed to improve the health of the South.

It is realized that the Army had certain advantages in the operation of its health program because of its more absolute control over the military population. Nevertheless, the lack of such centralized authority should not deter us from making similar broad plans to protect the civilian population. These plans should be the concern of all our leaders, including not only officials of the organized health departments, but our law makers, businessmen, and especially our educators.

It is suggested that the problem be approached by the formation in each state of non-political health and welfare councils headed by laymen but with representation from all the organizations and agencies concerned. Many state health departments now have lay health councils, but as a rule the scope of their activities needs broadening, and the role played by their members should be more dynamic. At frequent intervals periodic regional health conferences should be held at which the major problems of the South can be discussed from a broad viewpoint and practical programs developed. Such programs should be coordinated and integrated with the national programs of health and research.

Since so many of the important new ideas which have improved our national life have emanated from scientific researches conducted in southern institutions, it would seem appropriate that the great universities of the South should afford the leadership in the further development of her health and welfare.

It is reassuring to know that North Carolina has a good, progressive health department. It is stimulating to know that the citizens of North Carolina have resolved to provide adequate medical care for every person in the state. But it is inspiring to realize that those in charge of our State University have the vision to plan courageously to meet the health needs of the state, of the South and of the nation.

Medical research is the key to public health. Health is essential to the mental and physical strength of our people, and this strength is the real foundation of our national security.

THE HUMANITIES AND SOCIAL
SCIENCES

LITERARY RESEARCH IN MODERN LIFE

D. C. Allen

ASSOCIATE PROFESSOR OF ENGLISH, SCHOOL OF
HIGHER STUDIES, JOHNS HOPKINS UNIVERSITY

I HAVE SET MYSELF the task of explaining to you the place of literary research in modern life. In doing this, I shall, after a fashion, be telling you about my life; and yet, I hope that you will find in what I have to say none of the self-knowing, none of the ease and facility that is the index of the autobiographer. Time and again I have asked myself troublesome questions about the validity of my profession; I have examined my conscience to the very seams; and though I am not made dismal by too great doubt, I am by no means marked by the complacency of certainty. I must also tell you that it would have been far easier to have explained my point of view to you at the Centennial Celebration of the University of North Carolina than it is now; and, paradoxically enough, many of the difficulties that I must face were bred and nurtured within the corporate limits of this community.

It was here in 1929 that Professor Norman Foerster wrote and printed a little book that made vocal in this country a discussion that began in Europe before the end of the nineteenth century. Professor Foerster's manifesto against the literary historians of his time and his neo-humanistic program disturbed the academic world and put him at the head of a new school of literary thinking. But his views did not remain unchallenged, and interestingly enough the most telling opposition came from two of his colleagues, the late Professor Edwin Greenlaw and Professor Howard Mumford Jones. This was the first skirmish in a domestic quarrel that is not yet over. Traditional literary scholars have learned a great deal from Professor Foerster; those of us who were at that time beginning our careers modified many of our views and found it impossible to go on in the old tradition without making necessary discriminations. In that it stimulated a

97

counterreformation, the revolt of Norman Foerster and the subsequent proposals of his disciples did the study of letters a great service; but, by demonstrating the practical value of dissent, it may, like an armed madman, have given itself many wounds with one blow.

When Norman Foerster went scattering his corn over the academic ploughlands, he sowed some dragon's teeth too, and from his furrows has sprung an amazingly prolix, though sometimes unintelligible, brood of anti-traditionalists. Save in their opposition to the research techniques of the literary historians, this second generation of rebels agrees in little else. Having got the habit of schism, they have divided as tirelessly as one of the more agile *Saccharomyces cerevisiae*. They write endlessly—about literature, about themselves, about each other. The manner in which they write and the terminology that they invent carry us back to the decadent days of scholasticism and give us a good modern light by which to read the strictures of Rabelais on the doctors of the Sorbonne. These men have a great deal to say that is important, and the literary historian who has not learned from them is an unpliable fellow, indeed; but they are defective in humor, and some of them want grace, whereas others talk gibberish, and still others are undisciplined thinkers.

Some of the more enlightened members of this group must have perceived the logical conclusion of their program when the infection of their ideas spread to one of the great universities, which has departed from the tradition and gone lusting after a pseudo-philosophic vocabulary. At this institution, a visitor may hear an explicator, who is not perplexed by his ignorance of Greek, expound the *Poetics* and *Rhetoric* of Aristotle, whereas another malpractitioner, under the illusion that he is standing in a celestial pulpit a hundred light years from this world, dissects a specimen of literature and scatters the anatomical fragments in the void. While the clinical hacking and sawing is proceeding, the critics, as they call themselves, intone an incantation. I quote two sentences from a dithyramb of this sort with full malice because I cannot forget the remarks that these literary disintegrators have made about the historian, who, they say, has no artistic appreciation, no love of phrasing, no sense of style. The victim on the block, in this case, is Milton's *Lycidas*, and we have been informed that the method of the poem hinges on the double meaning of the word *shepherd* and its symbolical link with the poetic and religious experiences incorporated in the elegy.

The prospect of the resolution should be kept in mind as the opposition is explored; for it will be seen that Milton employs the complicating device of a partial expression of the basic problem of the opposition as the *internal* dialectic of one side or the other. Thus, we shall not erroneously suppose that he is tangling the lines of his oppositions, but will see that he is anticipating, by these wheels within wheels, the logical paradox of the resolution.

I think that I could say this in a simple sentence of a dozen words, but I am forced to ask why the "wheels within wheels" are laid at the door of Milton's study. This form of critical aberration is not likely to be too contagious; its jargon is an excellent antitoxin. Even John Crowe Ransom, who welcomed its conception by offering it a partnership in his critical brokerage association, is not so sure, now that it has been christened, that the child looks at all like a Fugitive Critic.

From the Humanists, the New Critics, and the Neo-Aristotelians has come the inner attack on literary research. The literary historian has been likened to a parrot picking up splinters in a dark wood; he has been accused of heaping up useless historical data; he has been called insincere; and he is said to have neither a sense of literary values nor a real understanding of literature and its problems. Mark Van Doren, a teacher of literature and a modern poet, says that the ambition of the literary research man is to explain literature away. In spite of the fact that it is the literary historian who has kept the interest in literature alive and provided most of the contemporary men of letters with their acquaintance with the tradition, there is truth in all of these charges. But these critics whose profession is literature should realize that they are revolting in a town already under siege, that, thanks to them, the state of literary studies is like a citadel beleaguered both without and within. If the citadel is taken from without, they will perish, too, and all their works with them.

It is the attack from without that is most to be feared because not only has it succeeded before, but, during the moments of its prevailing, there has been neither the study of literature nor literature itself. The historian of letters is more sensitive to this danger than many of the rebels in his midst, who are interested in "values," as they say, and not in history; for he has seen its face in other ages and knows the quarter whence it comes. Since the beginning of things, there has always been a section of mankind that has regarded the world as so many kilograms of leaves and rabbits and pebbles and robins. The trick, according to these people, is to discover the most efficient way of feeding the leaves to the rabbits and throwing the pebbles at the birds so that one can have robin pie today and rabbit stew tomorrow. This is the end of existence. This is the goal of all thinking. This is all ye know and all ye need to know. To pursue anything else—literature, art, music, pure science—is to make a beggar of time, to work at nothing with fool's hands. These are old opponents. We have known them when they wore the dress of Athens and when they spoke in the Latin tongue of Augustan Rome. Boccaccio, who did research on Dante, knew them at Florence, and Spenser, who wrote a book on the English poet, met them in Elizabethan England. If the current critic, who is sometimes a self-confessed "tortured modern poet," would emerge, to use his own phrase, from the jungle of "dialectic obscurity," he might learn something about them, too, and be not so ready to help them pull down his own house.

But the student of literature and the proponent of literary research are also responsible for the progress that the external attack has made, for they have invariably adopted a strategy of retreat and placation, of agreement and explanation in the language of the opponent and according to his terms. They have stressed the material value of the study of literature and illustrated it with charts and tabulations indicating how one's happiness or one's wealth or one's social prestige increased with each classic read. They have enumerated the favorite poems of successful wordlings as if the association gave luster to poetry; and, like the ancient sophists, they have even estimated the value of literary knowledge in terms of a weekly wage. Other defenders of literature and its understanding have talked in materialistic terms of a social bias. A knowledge of the best that has been thought and said in the world, by their admission, makes a colorful boutonniere for a dinner jacket. They tell us about the illiterate social failure who must sit tongue-tied because the conversation between bridge hands has drifted from rationing to Ruskin. The national high school study of *Ivanhoe*, according to their thinking, provides the boy from California and the girl from Georgia with a common topic of conversation. How little they know of *Ivanhoe!* How little of girls from Georgia! These withdrawing tactics lead only to defeat, and they are quite unnecessary. We have forgotten, I think, the true reasons for the study of literature, reasons that require no apology and that are different from those that dominate the pursuit of materialistic ends. These forgotten reasons are worth inspecting.

Great literature has never been concerned with the theory of causes, for there is something in the biology of the literary genius that makes it impossible for him to look at the world with the eyes of a scientist. Only on occasion, and then when he is least a man of letters, does he see even with the eyes of the philosopher. The poet and the mathematician begin to create, I think, in the same fashion; they share in the initial experience of intuitional perception. After this creative shock is over, they diverge at once. The mathematician pursues the impelling notion along logical courses; the poet performs conversely, following the idea through the realm of the supralogical or the transempirical. I should define a scientist by saying that he is a man realizing himself at the highest when he is tracing a given set of facts behaving according to a pattern of logic under conditions absolutely controlled. By using the antonym of each key word in this definition, I can establish a description of a poet, a description that I can epitomize by simply saying that a good poet is a bad scientist. The poet, then, does not write of the world as we are now inclined to see it because most of us have been brought up to look at our surroundings scientifically.

If the poet does not see as the scientist or as the average modern man sees, he is not unaware of the findings of science. They make for him an excellent basis of speculation. It is, however, poetical speculation, which adds to the data of the observer of causes the strangeness of an imagination that is aware that there is a half-world without causes. So the poetical mind gives to the facts of the scientist an unreality that makes them more real. This is a paradox only to him who insists on looking constantly at that half-nature which the poetical vision would make whole. There was a time when the scientific thinking of the world held that man was an earth-bound creature because his density was in unbalanced proportion to his area. Yet the poetic vision, which rebels at so-called tough facts, fashioned the dream of Daedalus, and in time the non-logical real begot the logical real. It is the purpose of poetry—and I distinguish between the poetic and the artistic—to make men see what they have not been taught to see and to understand those things that are not exactly in the realms of the knowable. In other words, the poetic now must perform for most men those functions that it once shared with the religious in providing man with experience that is unobtainable within the scientific limits of the understanding.

This service of literature to man blinded by three centuries of rationalism may, I think, be called illumination. Because of it, the reader of the poetic, like the creator, is enabled to stand outside the periphery of the logically knowable, savoring for brief moments the existence of a world that seems to be non-logical but is nonetheless real. But there is a second function of literature that is just as important. The best literature, and that is the only form of literature that should detain us, is the most effective transmitter of man's commentary on his personal experience. A photograph or a journalistic record of a moment in human history may tell us very clearly what was done, but it is literature that tells us what was thought and felt, that converts the concrete into the abstract, the particular into the universal. This ability of literature to reveal to us the experiences of the past on a universal plane that makes them frankly our own provides us with a sense of recognition that is no less vivid than the illumination that springs from it. Then, too, whereas the illuminative qualities of literature effect in us a new understanding of reality, the recognitory qualities lead us to a surer comprehension of the permanent. It is not improbable that the eternity of even a scientific fact may depend to a large extent on its poetic suggestibility. When modern man thinks of the cosmological system of Ptolemy with its intricate and revolving spheres of crystalline light, it is difficult for him to remember that it was once the central fact of our universe and that for more than a thousand years it was the basis of all accurate human thinking. To us this hypothesis seems not scientific but poetical; and, truly, this notion owes its permanence to Dante, who converted it at the time of its highest esteem into a poetical fact, and to our recognition, in the splendor of the Dantean elaboration, of man's eternal awe and wonder before the universe in which he finds himself and of his desire to comprehend it.

The main function of literature, I believe, is to provide modern man with this illumination and with this concept of the continuity of experience. This is a sublime and unique duty that is altogether wonderful; for though the second revelation may be had with less poignancy in the study of history or philosophy, the first, which provides the mind with infinite extension, is found nowhere else in this post-Cartesian world. Both of these fruits of the study of literature are undeniable gains in a non-materialistic sense and are the only reasons that can be advanced against the pragmatists, who would make literature work for its living, and the materialists, who would abolish it completely.

Now the sense of recognition and the force of illumination that come from the reading of literature are not enjoyed by each man in the same way. For the greatest of literature has the power not only to evoke different reactions in different men, but, what is much better, different reactions in the same man. Any work of art, as Professor Boas has pointed out, has a certain multivalence, which enables men to see in a painting like Whistler's *Mother* "a representation of a natural object, the expression of an introvert's libido, a moment in the history of the *Volksgeist*, and an exemplification of the laws of eternal beauty." The modern critic proposes to explain which one of these responses is the best, but he must ask himself such questions as, The best for whom? The best under what circumstances? His task is a distressing one, and I am not sure that it is a legitimate one. For it is the multifariousness of the experience, not the uniformity of the experience, that is important. For there is in a great work of literature not only the simple reaction of the ordinary reader but a multiplicity of experiences for the well-trained and sensitive reader; and the most valid reason for literary research is that it sharpens the sensitivity and prepares the mind for this manifold revelation. The approach to this place of suprarational experiences is by three bridges; yet each of them has its own intrinsic importance and, unlike worldly bridges, one may cross by all of them at the same time.

When the modern literary expert reads a work of a poetic nature, he is inclined to measure it by one or more of three sets of literary criteria. He may judge it according to its essence, viewing it *sub specie aeternitatis*. This is perhaps the noblest of approaches to a work of art, but it requires that its object be stripped of all its temporal impediments and estimated only in terms of its changelessness. Before this attitude, the scholar, whose duty is to tell how and why a work has changed, and the critic, whose task is to evaluate the change, must put down their tools; there is nothing for them to do. But there is another bridge. If the literary expert has also the historian's skill, he will insist that every work of art must be understood and enjoyed in terms of the creator's intent and of the impact it made on the men and women of its day. To appreciate Shakespeare's *Hamlet*, he must know exactly what Shakespeare was trying to do and how an audience of the year 1601 viewed his result. To this end, the literary historian establishes exact texts; discovers the sources and explains the genesis of a work; expounds its diction, metaphors, and ideas; investigates the life of the writer and the culture of his age; and reports on the reputation of the author in his own time and in subsequent periods. This is primarily a technique for the study of letters anterior to our own day, but it is also useful for comprehending modern writers like T. S. Eliot or James Joyce. The modern critic, who does not approve of this at all, approaches his task with a third point of view. The worth of a work of art, says he, exists entirely in its current import. The true value of Shakespeare's *Julius Caesar* is the value that it has for us in 1945. What it meant to Shakespeare or to any Elizabethan is of as small matter as what it meant to a man of the eighteenth or nineteenth century; it means much more when it is translated according to the vocabulary of Freud or Marx. This is simply another way of learning from literature, and the wise historian of letters does not avoid it although he feels that it is better fitted to the study of contemporary writers than to those of the past.

If I was correct in saying that the modern importance of the study of literature is to provide the reader with illumination and a sense of recognition and if these experiences are enhanced by the multifariousness of the planes of their realization, the critic and the historian should not exclude each other but learn from each other. The critic who has in his gift the manifold experiences of the sensitive contemporary has much to offer the historian who is sometimes blinded by his preoccupation with the past; yet he can also learn much from the historian who attempts, but, of course, never fully succeeds in recapturing the experiences of men now dead. I do not ask for a marriage between these two groups; I have seen too many historical scholars trying to work as critics and too many critics attempting the historical function to advocate such a miscegenation. All that I would have is a sort of Platonic friendship, for I think that they may read each other with tolerance and that together they have much to contribute to the education of the lay reader of literature. For one talks of the past fluently, and the other is at ease in the present, and between them one may perceive the ghost of the future.

The modern critic, however, is surer of the commonplaceness of his talent than I am. He writes essays urging the historian to give up whatever he is doing and turn to criticism. As I understand it, however, criticism is the rarest of talents; and when as an historian I look back through the long avenues of time, I discover that good critics are far rarer than good poets. I know of only three English critics whom I would consider first class and I have doubts about one of these. To be a good critic is a gift vouchsafed to very few men and the doing of something important badly is not my notion of decorum. It would be far better, I think, for a man with a second-class mind to devote himself to literary research, which requires a much smaller talent and which offers a variety of graded tasks at which people of lesser ability may labor. I shall not pretend that all literary research is valuable or that it is all grist for the critics to grind. Much of it is trivial and highly unimportant; much of it does little more than attempt to reduce the great man of letters to the stature of an assistant professor of English. And yet there is an apology for this second-rate kind of research in literary history;

it is, after all, a form of intellectual activity and as such it has a human importance. It is against this sort of research that the modern critic storms; yet, I am sure he would not want this type of person to turn to criticism. A second-class performance in the arts is, after all, a form of blasphemy. It is far better—in spite of Robert Browning's objections—to spend one's life working arithmetic problems correctly than to fail constantly at solving quadratic equations.

There are two important types of research in literature. The first type moves towards the penetration of a literary work's meaning and artistry. It seeks to elucidate the work in such a fashion that the multiform experiences of illumination and recognition may be doubled for the reader. The second type of research, using the literary work as a text, departs in the direction of the history of ideas and seeks to establish the intellectual climate of the period that produced the work of art. The findings of both schools are important to the first-class critic if he were willing to pay some attention to them. For most pedagogical purposes the first method is alone valid, though in higher studies the results of the second method are of great significance.

I could illustrate what I mean with many examples from each department of literary research, but I shall avoid the special prejudice involved in dealing with famous and familiar examples to show you what can be done with six very average lines from a not widely read play of Shakespeare's. In the first act of *Richard II*, the frustrated Henry Bolingbroke says,

> O, who can hold a fire in his hand
> By thinking on the frosty Caucasus?
> Or cloy the hungry edge of appetite
> By bare imagination of a feast?
> Or wallow naked in December snow
> By thinking on fantastic summer's heat?

Now all that the average reader—in fact, all that the modern critic, if he will play the game by his own rules—can say is that here we have three interrogative statements modified by a prepositional expression with a redundant use of the word *thinking*. He might add—if he is not Mr. Ransom, who eschews the didactic—that Bolingbroke is saying that thinking of the better does not enable one to endure the worst or that a present extreme is not banished by its imagined antithesis. As a "dryasdust" historian working towards the lines, I am permitted to see in the first pair the veiled legend of Prometheus bound to a rock in the Caucasus for bringing fire to men. This legend governs the key words *fire* and *frosty*, and one can see how the image was conceived. I remember at this point the apotheosis of Prometheus as a philosophical symbol in Shakespeare's age; and though the critic may argue that Shakespeare was probably not a philosophical adept, I can reply that many a modern Freudian novelist has probably never read Freud, that we are born Freudians as our parents were born Darwinians. The word *Caucasus* also carries me into further spheres of speculation, for I remember how dreadful those summits seemed to a traveller of Shakespeare's age and how menacingly they are registered on the maps of his time. In other words, I begin to feel the fervor that kindled the mind of Shakespeare when he wrote these two lines and to perceive the mental responses that they awakened in the more sensitive members of his audience. I am carried out of the present and share a definite experience with men of the past. But the excitement does not stop here. The remembrance of the legendary Prometheus shaped without question the next two lines in which the *hungry edge* of appetite is whetted on the *bare imagination* of a feast. The connecting link is probably another classical legend, that of Tantalus, who was tortured in Hell by unattainable food. If the fable of Tantalus is the basis, then the last two lines are brought in by the memory of Hell—the subject of so much Renaissance art and so many Elizabethan treatises—a Hell in which the damned souls are alternately carried from the roaring heat through the Lethean waters to a quiet waste of snow. This idea, kidnapped by Shakespeare from the geography of the Hereafter, is given a local habitation in Tudor England,

> Or wallow naked in December snow
> By thinking on fantastic summer's heat.

This is one aspect of how the literary historian may work when he focuses his commentary on the lines of the poet, but he may also use the text as a point of departure. These lines might suggest a study of the Promethean myth in Shakespeare's time. In that case, the historian will collect all that the Elizabethans said about Prometheus and try to determine what forms the pattern of the legend took, what were its symbolic implications, and what we can learn from it about the myths of the twentieth century. The "frosty Caucasus" might interest another historian in a study of Renaissance orology, and he would proceed in a similar fashion to gather from literary and non-literary sources all that he could learn. In both of these cases, literature is not the center of the study but is used rather as illustrative and supporting documents. The essential result in the first study is a contribution to the history of philosophy and in the second to the history of science; nevertheless, both studies would also be of great value in the interpretation of literature. The investigations of Professor Lovejoy and his students into the history of primitivism, anti-intellectualism, and similar subjects have enabled us to see things in the works of writers that we had not noticed before, and, consequently, to participate in ancient experiences that are closed to the ignorant. The worth of this type of research is clearly seen when we witness the floundering of the critics and the old-line literary historians (not to mention the struggles of the few surviving specimens of the "moonlight and Blahblah" school of impressionistic interpretation) before some work of literature that is perfectly clear once its atmosphere of ideas is understood.

But the methods of research perfected by the literary historian are not valid for a comprehension of older literature alone; for he who attempts to read modern writers without them loses a depth of meaning and understanding that is an essential part of the aesthetic experience. Two modern poets of importance, Allen Tate and Wallace Stevens, continually revise their poetry, and part of the value that they have for the reader resides in the protean quality of their thinking and emotions. In this they are in sympathy with an age that is amorphic, changeable, uncertain. The critic, however, should according to his self-announced offices deal only with the final state of their verse, but, realizing that in this way he would partially erase their full poetic magnitude, he blandly talks about revisions and development as if he were just a literary historian. But let me give you another instance. One of Eliot's later poems, "Burnt Norton," comes out of the modern concept of time and has, as a consequence, a certain intelligibility for the average man who knows how to read; nevertheless, its summary of the current predicament is more pointed for him who has read Boodin, McTaggart, Bosanquet, Royce, Gentile, and the modern physical philosophers. I do not suppose that Eliot has read all this speculative literature, but by living in this age, he has inadvertently made its unit concepts part of himself. By understanding these theories before we go to his poem for a second time, we add to the experience that we had when we read it with only the general background of an educated modern. Perhaps, in a sense, we "make" the poem ourselves by the knowledge that we have of its milieu, but I shall not quarrel with this result, for to me it is simply another aspect of the multivalence of the poetical experience. I shall conclude with these two examples of the value of the historian's methods for the enjoyment of modern literature although I could place many others on exhibition. One has only to read the average current essay in artistic evaluation to see how these time-honored procedures are employed for the elucidation of modern writers by many of the modern critics who say that they scorn them.

So the research of the literary historian, provided that it is done with sincerity and discrimination, is important in our era to somewhat the same degree that literature itself is important. We have realized that the study of literature is an inseparable part of the life of any man who wishes to transcend the suspiciously one-sided data of the materialists and read in the true book of nature without wearing the astigmatic glasses of science. For this reason, the study of literature is not an escape from life but an escape into life from a twilight land of half existence, where everything is ordered according to the fallacy of time, and man is known more by his differences than by the eternal pattern of his nature. It is the literary historian, I think, who does much to erase these differences by explaining them, and who, consequently, stands not only as an interpreter between the present and the past but also as one who helps to gloss the present for the present. Through his better services, he enables us to recognize ourselves in that body of the world that is said to be dead and in that body of the world that seems to be alien. And from this it comes that the light that never was on land or sea can fill us with a great illumination, and we can perceive not alone the truth of our own infinity but the reality of our eternity.

HISTORY AND SOCIAL RECONSTRUCTION

Avery Craven

PROFESSOR OF AMERICAN HISTORY
THE UNIVERSITY OF CHICAGO

A THOUGHTFUL HISTORIAN once made the remark that Ulysses S. Grant fought nobly for a noble cause without ever once recognizing its nobility. However that might have been, today there is a very positive notion abroad that the good soldier should know exactly what he is fighting for and should believe thoroughly in the superiority of his own national values and assumptions.

The idea, carried further, demands of the average citizen in a democracy a knowledge of national traditions and national accomplishments. We are at war not only with other nations; we are at war with bitterly hostile systems and values. We might win our battles with only vague understanding of what is at stake in the conflict, but few would be bold enough to say that we can win the peace unless we know what it has all been about and just what we, as a nation, stand for and want in the days ahead.

The impact of such thinking on the study of history has been marked. Agents of public information have aroused concern over the lack of knowledge of American history shown by those who have come through our public schools and colleges. Surveys have been made; campaigns have been started to increase the time given to history and to make our teaching more effective towards preconceived ends. The danger from neglect of the discipline has been exchanged for the danger of unwise overemphasis. Not that a wider and more thorough study of history would be an evil, but rather that the study of history should be thought of *only* in terms of its uses for practical ends as determined by existing public opinion.

All scholars to a degree, of course, feel the pressure to render practical service in times of unusual stress. Some can easily turn from what we call "the academic" to the utilitarian without danger to their personal or professional integrity. Scholars in the humanities and the social sciences run the greatest danger. The historian, especially, is subject to pressures and dangers of peculiar strength and appeal.

In wartime, and often in other periods of unusual stress, the historian is under pressure to use his subject for the purposes of what is being called "social action." There seems to be a widespread feeling that history has some peculiar value and force which can be used to forward causes. The past, if brought to their service, will add the respectability of age and the prestige of example. "The Fathers" are always desirable allies. Past events teach wise lessons and offer sound guidance to faltering feet. The historian, as the guardian of the past, is therefore expected to respond to the patriotic or moral urge and come forward with the hosts of yesteryear to help fight the battles of the present.

The idea is a worthy one but fraught with grave danger both to history and to society. The historian is both scholar and citizen. It is difficult for him to remain entirely antiquarian amid the swirl of crowding events. It is only natural that he should want a hand in affairs and that he should enjoy the prestige of being an authority. One recalls the stirring words of Professor J. Franklin Jameson at the beginning of World War I urging "scholars to come out into the market place in order to use their knowledge energetically and boldly," and the almost identical appeal of the Mississippi Valley Historical Association's committee, issued only a few weeks ago, encouraging its members "to enter into the market-place with their books, meet and learn to answer the interpretations of men who either derive the force of their arguments from an appeal to the past or else neglect it." They close with the warning that "if the sound historian fails to supply his contemporaries with readable history that is to the point, they will go elsewhere for it, to unsound historians."

In both of these cases the idea is, of course, to supply "sound history" for constructive purposes. But one must also remember the chauvinism of German historians which passed as "sound history" and the gentle but sure way in which some American scholars, during World War I, drifted into positions almost as biased and ultra-nationalistic as those of the enemies they condemned.

It is not a simple matter or one to be lightly dismissed. The South should know this from the way in which the history of the great sectional struggle which culminated in the American Civil War has been "soundly" written from 1865 to the present, by impartial historians with a northern point of view. So completely has that point of view become orthodox history that the one way for a southern historian to demonstrate his emancipation from the backwardness and ignorance of his native section is to incorporate that point of view regardless of the evidence in hand. Jefferson Davis saw deeper into the future than most others and understood more profoundly the practical import of history when he declared that one of the greatest losses sustained by the South in defeat was the fact that the victor would write the history of the war. For that reason the South has never regained moral standing in national thinking.

It is therefore extremely important that in these days when history is again called upon to take its place alongside of anthropology and sociology in producing "social action," we try to answer two basic questions about the discipline: What is the nature of history? What are its uses?

Carl Becker has defined history as "the memory of things said and done." He has insisted that every man knows "some history" as an essential support to his everyday living. He takes the simple act of paying the winter's coal bill and finds memory of details reinforced by careful research in a vestpocket memorandum; a conflict of data cleared up by comparison of documents; and then satisfactory action taken on the basis of such "critical scholarship."

Of course what Becker has in mind is the simple fact that we are oriented in our present and prepared for our future by the memories of things past. We extend what he calls our "specious present" backward and forward. Out of a varied set of happenings in days gone before, ours and those of our ancestors, we select such data, true and untrue, as enlarge and enrich our immediate purposes and enable us better to anticipate the future. History and life are thus united. In subtle fashion we constantly recall the past and weave it into our present needs and desires, material and emotional, selecting whatever fits the occasion and using it as the basis for our next steps. This, says Becker, is "the natural function of history," whether formal or informal.

So defined and so assigned, there is only one distinction between "everyman's history" and that of the professional. There is, in fact, only one distinction between myth and history. And that difference has nothing to do with either "purposes" or "uses"; it relates only to the quality of the materials which go into the memories involved. Myth is simply history which has been discarded because a sounder fact basis has been found upon which to build the tales of the past. The scholar in history merely has a wider and more certain foundation for the memories he presents to his readers than does the man who goes on hearsay or who accepts uncritically any information available. But even he must face the fact that the things which he recalls for a people are those which they wish recalled, those which are significant because of present values and understanding, and that his own work will, with changing age currents, fall back into the discard where myths are kept.

Few will deny that the modern historian, equipped with his elaborate critical research spirit and method, has done rather well in uncovering source materials and reducing them to their sound fundamentals. He need give little ground to the natural scientist in the quality of his procedure and results. He has summoned a goodly crowd of new witnesses and examined them with a skill quite comparable to that of his legal friends. As a fact-finding animal he need blush only slightly unless his humility be a trifle greater than that of his learned colleagues. But the uses and abuses of history will not permit him to stop with mere fact finding. He must "interpret" facts and events for mankind—select and arrange them into patterns such as men require for present needs and future steps. And there is where the trouble begins.

For when the historian ceases to ascertain, scrutinize, and evaluate data with scholarly precision and begins to select "memories of things said and done," to arrange them, and to explain their related meanings, he is only offering for the purposes of his age and its future his own opinions, however superior and scholarly they may be, and however loudly he may shout the words "historical interpretation" to cover his procedure. All the factors of time and place and station which enter into his own make-up and values leave their impress on the story he tells. He has become a creative artist. His so-called facts are only pigments. His tools may be of the latest scientific make. His procedure may conform to the rules which masters have laid down. Yet, when all is said, pigments and tools and rules by themselves do not make even impressionistic pictures. Or, to change the figure, the scholarly historian may pan the streams of time for golden nuggets. He may purify them by improved refining methods. He *may* present them for view in some exhibition case, called a source book. But he has not, by this, rendered the greater service required. If he fails to go on with his task, some greater historian will mint his precious gold into a circulating medium for society's use. And when this is done each coin will bear the image of its creator on its face; the date it carries will be that of his own era; and the motto inscribed will be one to which his own people pay lip service. Such are the necessities of the case.

In this brief description of history, as research and interpretation, the whole matter of whether history is a science or a humanity is suggested. Complete *objectivity* is the obligation of the scientist; the quality of *art* is largely measured in terms of self-expression. Subjectivity is not a fault in the humanities. It does not cancel scholarship. The question of whether the historian is a true scientist or whether he is of the humanities becomes one, therefore, of determining, as far as possible, in what ways and in what capacity the historian may be completely objective, or, if you wish, may be scientific. And, on the other hand, in what ways may he still preserve his scholarship and yet perform his functions with that delightful subjectivity of the philosopher, the student of literature, or, to be blunt, most of the so-called social scientists?

Few, I believe, will question the possibility of a large degree of scientific objectivity on the part of historians in assembling and describing certain types of information regarding past events. It is quite possible, for instance, to exclude all personal wishes and all shades of personal bias in ascertaining the quantity of corn produced in Illinois in the decade from 1850 to 1860. Price ranges may also be established with equal personal indifference. It might even be possible to discover and describe the farming methods used in that region at that date or even to say, with some degree of accuracy, what certain individuals thought about the prevailing corn and hog economy. But should the historian wish to explain just *why* corn and hogs were raised, why prices were always just what they were, why certain practices were in use or why this or that economy prevailed, he would move out on to less certain ground, and *opinion* would be mixed with fact. If he should attempt to relate the agriculture of Illinois and her neighbors to the coming of the War between the States, or should he, from this region, seek parallels and draw conclusions applicable to all agriculture, he would advance still farther into the personal darkness. If he presented a complete picture answering what, how, and why, and set it in "proper relation" to all other facts before and after, as historians are wont to do, the critical outside observer who was asked to read his book might well do some investigating himself. He might find it useful to know why this particular historian happened to be interested in the agriculture of Illinois for that period; just what he thought of present-day agriculture; and how he wished future developments in this line to run. He might even have to know something of the whole larger social philosophy of this historian—his notion of what kinds of factors shape developments and just how forces are related in events—if he were to pass final judgment on the matter of the historian's objectivity and subjectivity.

All of which is not saying that historians are deluded or dishonest. Or, on the other hand, is it admitting that they always introduce personal elements knowingly or deliberately. Ofttimes they are completely unconscious of personal preferences or of the influence of world currents. Yet simple unconsciousness does not produce objectivity, nor does consciousness completely destroy it. A sound knowledge of the past may give the right to influence the future. And even were the historian consciously, instead of subconsciously, "plotting his lines out of the past into the future," he would not be deceiving. He would, in fact, be revealing truth as any artist reveals it—as everyone in the humanities reveals it—by a philosophy as sound as his own intelligence and with facts which might be as sound as scientific methods can make them. And who, after all, does not know that such men have often spoken with a knowledge and a wisdom greater than that of many who have seen a small unrelated segment of something, not understood, through a powerful microscope, and who have then proceeded to fit their unrelated facts into some elaborate preconceived hypothesis or theory which may be completely discarded by the next generation? If the historian, patterning his conduct after the "legitimate scientists," were only wise enough to hail new findings which destroy the validity of his previous work with loud acclaim and as new evidence of historical wisdom, he might achieve greater renown. But instead he accepts each new turning as evidence of his own ignorance and as new reason for greater humility. And renown is seldom erected on humility.

Let us hope that some day the historian will accept his role in the humanities—no less scholarly for that reason—and understand the basic importance of a sound and comprehensive philosophy to his work of finding some sense and order amid the confusion of past events, some lines which run safely and sanely back into a well-established past and on into a more rational future. May he find his curiosity ever great enough to secure all the truth possible without selfish twisting. And by the same token may he expect the next generation to discard his history, without feeling that his contribution has been weak or in vain.

If he can do this, his product may still be powerful enough to scare the Sons and Daughters of this or that; yes, practical enough in its influence to worry crowned heads and those which seek crowns. He may even go on shaping national policies, let us hope less and less by emotion, and more and more by "hard and cold facts" set to a sound philosophy of life (whatever that is).

What I have said about the nature of history suggests most of what I have to say in answer to the second question: What are the objectives of history in education? What can the historian contribute to the individual student and to the larger society of his day?

Some understanding of objectives in history is undoubtedly essential to good teaching. The person who knows what he is after, the peculiar values in the discipline in which he deals, and the ends possible of attainment, is, of course, more efficient than one who sees only an immediate task to be done by any means at hand. We can hardly deny the desirability of clear-cut and definite objectives in any teaching.

But the matter of objectives in history is a complex and puzzling one. I may as well confess to you at once that I do not know exactly what purposes history serves in the development of an individual or the building of the social order of which he is a part. I have sometimes questioned whether those who know the past best are any wiser for present emergencies than others, or whether one generation has ever profited by the experiences of those who have gone before. I am not certain that a study of the American Revolution, the Barbarian Invasions, Southern Reconstruction, or the Protestant Revolt always adds to the richness of personality or the improvement of the world in which the student lives his life. And, what is more important, I am not certain that the history teacher should of necessity definitely aim that it should do so. Is it desirable that those who teach history have in mind certain ethical ends to be achieved? Should the teacher advocate any particular social program or say what is to be considered "good" and what "bad"? Is it possible for a historian to set up ends to be achieved in the social order without becoming unhistorical—a propagandist striving to indoctrinate his pupils with restricted ideas of values? To have objectives in history that are positive, that are of an ethical character, that aim at the establishment of set views or social practices, is a most dangerous thing. Austria and Prussia sought through their teaching of history to create definite national attitudes, and we can now give as little approval as some might grant to the present Russian effort to fix the economic and social patterns of its children.

And yet we cannot escape. As I have said, we must, within the limits of our time and space, select certain facts which we shall present, and, in any effort at order and sequence, we must arrange those facts and stress some things and slur others. Such a process must be to a very large extent a matter of personal choice and disposition. The history we teach becomes, in spite of ourselves, to a large degree, a matter of our own personality and our own philosophy of life. When we diverge from that pattern, it is liable to be fashioned by the accepted values in the social order about us. We shape the approach as the D.A.R., the American Legion, or the dominating economic groups might wish it, and unconsciously assume that it is just a part of our duty as teachers or a necessity for our own highest comfort. Whether we like it or not, we have objectives of our own choosing or that have been chosen for us by others.

That being the case, the historian may just as well frankly consider his objectives and take such steps in their clarification and formulation as is consistent with the "science" to which he pays tribute. What is unconscious or what is consciously done for him by others he may as well do for himself. And do it in as historical a way as possible.

He may begin, I think, by insisting that we teach history in order that history may be learned. The first great objective is bluntly and purely the imparting and acquiring of historical information. We believe that every educated man is well-informed; that every well-informed man has not only knowledge of the world about him but also an understanding of the origins of the present and a realization of other orders and civilizations that have existed before. It is not necessarily a matter of being able to profit by the experiences of others, but rather the possession of a rich background on which to contemplate the existing order, and a field into which to make mental excursions for rich associations with men long gone and events that have already worked themselves out into conclusions logical or illogical. Good old Thomas Fuller in 1638 put it this way:

Now know, next Religion, there is nothing accomplisheth a man more than Learning. Learning In a Lord, is as a diamond in gold. And if you fear to hurt your tender hands with thornie School-questions, there is no danger in meddling with History, which is a velvet-study, a recreation-work. What a pitie is it to see a proper Gentleman to have such a crick in his neck that he cannot look backward! yet no better is he who cannot see behind him the actions which long since were performed. History maketh a young man to be old, without either wrinkles or gray hairs; privileging him with the experience of age without either the infirmities or inconvenience thereof. Yea, it not only maketh things past, present; but it ableth one to make rational conjecture of things to come. For this world affordeth no new accidents, but in the same sense wherein we call it a new Moon, which is the old one in another shape, and yet no other than what hath been formerly. Old actions return again, furnished over with some new and different circumstances.

The first value of history is as a humanity. It is merely a part of the equipment of a gentleman—that great object of all education. It is a part of the educational job of passing along from one generation to another a people's cultural heritage.

Stating the objective in terms of the theme, we may say that our first object is to get at the truth—to see things as they were in their own time and place. History has been too much "bunked" and "debunked." My first feeling, as I follow the pages of the average textbook in history, is that the men and women found there do not act the least bit like the folks with whom I associate day by day. In election time the people in the textbooks studied the issues, voted from conviction, and the results indicated a clear-cut division for or against a principle. My human beings vote from prejudices (their own and those inherited from their fathers), from interests, reactions conditioned by an immediate environment that has nothing to do with principles. In fact, they are about as far from being cold, rational machines as it is possible to be. By the same token, the great leaders to be found in textbooks are, as a rule, quite too godlike for comfort. The pictures which I got of Washington, Lincoln, Lee, and Davis in my school days were such that, with all my later study, I have never been able to make these men quite real to myself, and I have had to find my greater interest in lesser folk that I could discover for myself and know to be as human as the interesting people who live all about me. And yet, what bothers me most is the honest conviction that when my human beings and their world get into the history books, they and it will be just like those already there.

It is on the assumption that our heroes have been painted as cold, stilted, "cigar-store-Indian" men, demigods, that the modern biographer has started his campaign of debunking. I read a biography of Daniel Webster not long ago, the object of which seemed to be to show that a man might become a national figure in America, renowned in song and story, who was a drunkard, who opposed his nation in wartime (even resisting the draft), who accepted fees from both sides of legal cases, who took retainer fees from the United States Bank while he was a member of the Congress considering its possible injury to democracy, who pressed legislation to make good certain legal claims against the government so that he might profit by collecting them, and who died saying, "I yet live," that he might receive one last drink of brandy which had been promised. The historian might confess that all charged was true. But it was not all the truth. Neither is the usual picture of Webster, which has been retouched into a perfection quite foreign to the great Daniel. The debunking biography at least made him human. The "godlike" statesman slinks out of sight and Daniel reels down the street or sings in his deep rich monotone with Jenny Lind at the concert, rising to bow at the applause. If I must take my choice between such unrealities, I believe I would take the human Webster rather than the others. I can at least understand him and probably do something for him with my students. I could do nothing with the old demigod. But why must I choose between these two extremes?

Our problem as historians is to make men of the past real. To make them as human as they were, but to catch also that upward striving that is the divine in us all. Should you tell students that Webster was somewhat inebriated when he made a great speech? Would saying that carry the same impression of moral make-up to the youth in front of you that the fact carried to the man of his own day? Have you already created the age spirit of Webster's time, so that his drinking assumes the right proportion to other things in his life and makes clear the lack of moral implications in "getting drunk" on certain occasions in Webster's time and place? Have you yourself learned what the old Negro preacher insisted on—"The World Do Move"? If not, keep still about Daniel.

It is your duty to leave men in their own age. But it is your duty to give as much of the humanizing material as is necessary to balance correctly the other side of the picture. Historical characters must be left both human and aspiring. We need gods as little in history as we need villains. We need the truth if history is to be real, but balance is an essential to truth. And if it is to be interesting, the men who move through it must be like the men who live about the world today and those who live inside our students.

A further step in attaining the objective of reality, I have just suggested. You and your students live in a real world. Government is not all in the book. Part of it is just downtown or over there in Washington. The farmer outside our towns is still quite close to the old "average American," and the factory down the street is a vital part of the Industrial Revolution. We must keep our present geared up with the past if the past is to be real. We must assume that what we experience today is essentially like that which preceded it, or else we are under the obligation to show by comparison the changes that have come and how they have come. We must, above all else, keep that continuity between the "now" and the "then" which alone can give reality to both.

By the time we begin teaching history to children they have discovered that there is no Santa Claus. Yet the usual description of government and how it functions, as taught in our schools, is as far from reality as is the good old St. Nick. Government is run by those with enough interest in it to go to the trouble of making it pay them, and your student will find that out some day and laugh at you if you have not made it clear. Impractical, cloistered school teachers, who still believe in myths! Men "run for office" because they wish office, and political parties are groups who would like the job of running the government. Why must we deal in abstractions to the point where "political bosses" become disreputable and all officials become "heroes"? And our picture of past economic and social orders is as bad. We know so little of how and why men behave as they did in that old order that the medium of contact with the present is almost lacking. We, as teachers, are a bit abashed when we discover that, in spite of the foundations on which the modern business world rests, the practices which bring success in the present are so far from those we have pictured as to make us appear to our students, when they have gone into the real world, as impractical idealists. The present, as a reality, must be projected back into the past as certainly as the past is to be related to the present.

But we must ever remember that in the United States the real order is a democracy. It is possible for us to control it. History teaches that *change* is a constant in human affairs. Your students may in a democracy make reality approach an ideal. If we may not idealize the past, we may at least glorify the future. The materials for an honest comparison between conflicting ideals and systems are found in history. Even when interests and pressure groups forbid the social scientist to make a fair examination of present society, history may teach that there have always been two sides to all issues and that the one which dominated at one time did not always endure. Without indoctrination of any kind, history may furnish the materials from which a forward-looking attitude may be created. Men of the past did dream dreams. They set up ideals to be achieved in the future. And these ideals set for a people are as real as their subsequent actions. Who can read the Declaration of Independence or any of the other great expressions of faith written by "The Fathers" without realizing that those men expected the great "experiment in Democracy" to lead to "the pursuit of happiness" rather than to the defense of property? They expected men of the future to be born well and to have in any social and economic order a chance for "well-being." It is an ideal that must ever be kept in mind in the changing setup of material conditions. It lays on the teacher of American history, if not on others, the duty to teach faith in America as a land where change is as much a gospel as stability; where we have not achieved the ideal set until all men can be born well and have a chance to a high degree of comfort through honest toil, and where the few shall not have place and power above their own honest efforts. The acquiring of historical information not only has its relation to the present, but it has a part in the shaping of the future according to past ideals within the premises of past practices.

But history teaches more than change. It teaches permanency as well. There are some things that weather storms and are passed on from the experience of one age to another as a heritage to stability. Experience might be worth something whether we have permitted it to be or not. The benefit of the doubt belongs to that which endures. Constitutions, institutions, and even traditions give to the body politic that form and force which bones give to human bodies. History teaches the wisdom of slow change and careful weighing of values. It emphasizes the fact that "change" and "progress" are not necessarily synonyms!

These last suggestions, it seems to me, have particular meaning for the South as a section. The great values which distinctly belong to the South as an historical unit are in grave danger of being lost because of ignorance and misunderstanding. The slavery struggle so stressed that institution that those things which would have made the South a cultural entity under any labor system were forgotten and discredited along with slavery. The poverty of postwar days and the eagerness to share in the good things of modern American life have still further weakened those values. A sound conception of southern history might help to save them.

In this connection I would stress the fact that southerners, from the days of Thomas Jefferson and John Taylor, have somehow insisted that agriculture is a superior type of economic endeavor—that it constitutes a way of life as well as a means of living. They believed that a farmer might also be a gentleman; the farm a home, its acres more than a commodity to be bought and sold. Southerners early made peace with nature, sunk their roots deep into red and yellow soils, and knew the attachment to place and things and people. Some of them turned living into an art which expressed itself in well-proportioned houses, beautiful gardens, and gracious relationships. A few even stressed "being" above "becoming" and left a tradition of good manners in terms of James Petigru's definition that "Politeness is nothing more than the habitual consideration for the feelings of those we converse with and the making it a rule never to give ourselves the preference."

These are things in which this nation, as a whole, has been desperately poor. Their loss will be a nation's loss. The historian would do well to play his part in their salvation!

So when I, as a historian, hear men suggest that all the South needs is economic diversification, I am a bit disturbed. Happiness is not entirely a matter of things; it is more than prosperity. It has to do with a way of life and a set of values. Traditions cannot be ignored without cost and the South by merely becoming like the industrial North will not automatically end all her troubles or gain all satisfaction. She might gain something of richness by looking backward as well as ahead.

And here at the University of North Carolina, Roulhac Hamilton has builded the finest collection for the all-around study and understanding of a section that exists in the United States. In so doing he may have served not only a profession and a section but also a nation.

A second objective of history has to do simply with the historical method. We must be scientific in as far as our subject allows; we must be artists from that point forward. History should be a discipline in "the scientific attitude." No other study offers more opportunity for the development of the critical faculties. The habit of weighing all evidence, of seeing all sides to all questions, of examining all witnesses as to their competency and their accuracy, is an objective that is paramount. To reveal the complexity of men and events, to make clear that right is seldom all on one side either in the affairs of men or nations, to enable a student to distinguish between emotions and reason and to keep his balance between conflicting interests, is a thing that the historical method should do.

Furthermore, the ability to relate events in their proper sequence, to strip off non-essentials and to get down to fundamentals, and the ability to present the findings of such investigation so that the fair and honest hearer will be convinced, is not just an ideal with the practical history teacher. The whole subject, if properly taught, is made up of materials which require these abilities. Too often the teacher secures all these benefits for himself by retaining the historical processes and passing out to the student the finished product of historical synthesis. At some places in every course in history, time should be found for turning the student loose with the raw stuffs of the past without the slightest interest being manifest as to whether he acquires information or gets beyond the realization of complexity, bias, passion, frail humanity, and the necessity of taking care in the formation of judgments. We history teachers are too much interested in "informing" rather than in "training."

A recent newspaper editorial declared that "there is nothing more painfully obvious than that the persistent and costly errors of democratic government are the direct result of a failure of the critical faculty in the mass of voters, to say nothing of their leaders. . . . A sound system of education would do more than is being done to give the generality of our people more ability than they show to remember and compare facts, to weigh them, and to resist . . . 'mendacious emotions.' Until this habit of mind becomes more general, democratic society must continue to blunder painfully and often. It must continue to be the prey of the demagogue and the false prophet. It must fall far short of the self-mastery and the efficiency which are essential to its rich fulfillment, if not indeed to its bare survival." It ends its plea by saying that "what is learned at school will be modified, corrected, illuminated by experience and mature reflection, but sound mental habit, capacity for observation and straight thinking, the resistance to demoralizing emotion are a permanent resource, more precious than rubies, to the individual and to the society which possesses them."

It is rather difficult to know just what transfer of skills acquired in history is possible to other fields. One objective, however, that must be kept in mind is that the student learns how to gather information for himself. Knowing where and how to find things in history should afford training of a rather general kind and it should implant in the individual a desire to find things out for himself all along the line. To make inquisitive people as well as critical ones is possible where the notion is early planted that all knowledge is not found in a few books and that much of it is subject to considerable discount by the man who knows how to dig for truth. If "history acquiring" ends with school, we may well question the value of our discipline. If no permanent attitudes appear from our teaching, we may as well follow the advice of one of our most brilliant leaders and flee "from the world of reality to a land of abstraction."

But I am convinced that there might be a value for social and individual betterment in history whether past actions reveal its effectiveness or not. The newspapers of our day, the propaganda of interests, the claptrap of the politician—these are things that need to be carefully weighed and evaluated before the individual reaches conclusions as to truth. The advertising craze has set artificial values that must ever be reduced to their proper por-

portions. The good old lady that bought certain supplies because "the advertisements spoke so highly of them," might have been saved some of her bitterness if she could have suspended judgments, examined her witnesses, and weighed the evidence. Yet she was no more foolish than some folks who pick the candidates to receive their votes by the same method. Democracy, itself, needs intelligent conduct.

Still more doubtful is the matter of transfer of abilities into the more subtle realm of ethics. It is probably quite negligible. But one cannot help but hope that the student trained in a field where cause and result are ever apparent, where unsound practices are constantly proving their power to destroy civilizations, may somehow sense the fact that honest effort and being are more to be depended upon than "profits" and "putting things across." It is a hope; it should remain so. The history teacher must not become, in any sense, a preacher. If the facts do not speak for themselves, it is futile to try to twist them for the purpose. If the method does not in itself give the skills here mentioned, to some degree, it is useless to try to impose attitudes upon the student. We are offering a tool, not a full set of digested reactions. We are scientists, not social workers. We are artists who make the past relive, not as a photograph would present it, but as a rich soul would offer it rekindled with the life of his own understanding. But we need not deny our science with our art.

Thus under the two great objectives of information and method, it is possible for the teacher of history to make his contribution to what Professor Beard has called "the many-sided personality" and the more perfect social order. It is our contribution to the task of general education. It is a part that is rather uniquely our own. If we can translate such objectives into the practical class-room effort without that conscious purpose that distorts, we may enlarge the vision of our profession and again become practical folks in our impractical way.

THE PHYSICAL SCIENCES AND INDUSTRY

RESEARCH AND INDUSTRY AS A FACTOR IN SOUTHERN DEVELOPMENT

Milton H. Fies

CONSULTING ENGINEER, BIRMINGHAM, ALABAMA
TRUSTEE AND TREASURER, SOUTHERN
RESEARCH INSTITUTE

WILLIAM ALEXANDER PERCY, distinguished Mississippian, whose death relatively a short time ago was an immeasurable loss to the South, wrote great prose, but greater poetry. He said this:

> When I have made my tablet of the laws
> To guide the flight of my young Enzios,
> "Thou shalt not" shall be missing from its rubric.
>
> . . . .
>
> If men would but forget what not
> To do, and fix their wills and uttermost minds
> On what to do and do it—they'd breed the world
> With loveliness and power beyond all guessing!

If I read correctly the "wills and uttermost minds" of the men of the South, they have definitely fixed their resolution on what to do and they propose to do it. They have determined to cease emphasizing the South's deficiencies and refer to them only that their underlying causes be clearly recognized and overcome, and have resolved that their own hands shall mold their destiny.

For nearly three-quarters of a century we in the South have known what our economic deficiencies have been. We have proved our case beyond impeachment. As a matter of fact, we have spent too much time proving it. If we are not now completely aware of our status and the underlying causes we shall never become aware. What we should do is to gauge our strength and apply it, now that we have gathered sufficient strength to gauge. Henceforth we should "throw off the fatal temptation to worship our dead selves and perpetuate our past mistakes." We have come fully to know that throughout history the failure of creativeness has done more to destroy peoples and civilizations than the Huns and Vandals of all time.

I need no other proof of the importance of research to the future progress of the South than the Sesquicentennial program of this great University. The underlying reason for the choice of subject is compelling and understandable. It is interesting to note that, while the theme of this occasion delves into all phases of research, there is much emphasis placed upon the material— that is, applied research. It may well be that we have come to believe that while man cannot "live by bread alone" he cannot get along very well without bread. This program indicates that the South renounces forever the disposition on the part of some of us to turn this area over to "the absolute power of existing circumstances"—if I may quote the great Frenchman, Renan. It is the aim of our people to do something about the "existing circumstances." They realize that a "predatory economy" cannot last forever, and with their full vigor have determined to remove that which is predaceous in the South's economy. At long last we have reached the stage where dreamers are practical men.

To stress the material aspects of research is to avow that there is a fundamental relationship between culture and economic well-being; between life, liberty and the pursuit of happiness, and bread and meat; to understand that the influence of the home and through it the building of character and stamina in a people can never be strong when the roof of the home leaks and when cracks in the walls invite the elements; when ordinary comforts which induce and protect vitality are not generally afforded our people. Our schools and universities and our churches, yes, and our democracy itself face futility until we can bring this influence of the home more generally into the lives of the people of this Southland.

There is little latitude for home influence where so great a proportion of a people move about as do so many agricultural workers in the area and where the living conditions for their families are degrading.

I make this point because the South is essentially agricultural
—that is to say, agricultural products constitute its greatest
source of income; and rural houses—such as they are—constitute
the homes for the majority of its people. It may well be that
much of our backwardness has its genesis in shacks where pre-
natal influence with its immeasurable effect is appalling; where
the "fondest hopes" of childhood's hour decay. This condition
mocks at the security of the family; it weakens the foundations
for the good life because the family "bottoms them all."

Is there exaggeration in this apprehension? I shall refer to
Alabama to emphasize conditions, the correction of which is
possible through only two means. And it is fair to state that
conditions in Alabama are not unlike those in other southern
states.

In Alabama where 70 per cent of its population is rural, the
proportion of farm tenancy is 59 per cent, and 58 per cent of the
tenants are white.[1] Farm tenancy has numerous economic and
social effects which involve the whole population in one way or
another. It is estimated that in 1940, rural-farm dwellings
occupied by tenants each had an average value of $340. Eight
per cent of the rural-farm population have had no schooling; 27
per cent have had schooling from the first through the fourth
grade; and only 4 per cent finished high school. The average
year's value of farm products sold and traded by crop and self-
sufficing farmers in Alabama in 1940 was $278. This includes
most of the tenants, and 96 per cent of all the farmers in the
state. Their health status is lower than their financial status.

Now it is all too obvious that this sort of thing cannot go on
forever. It is the very basis of the South's ills. There are only two
routes out, and we must of necessity travel both. These means
are: first, improved farm practices to raise the standards of living
for our farm population through soil conservation; new uses for
the land; new and improved varieties of economic plants and
animals; better practices of farm management; better utilization
of energy on the farm; and better organization of our agricultural markets at home and abroad. Increased agricultural effi-

1. Figures quoted in this paragraph are from a Report submitted to Hon.
Chauncey A. Sparks, Governor of Alabama, by The Farm Tenancy Committee, Novmber, 1944.

ciency in production would supply a greater market in direct proportion to the increased farm income and would tend to support locally an increased industrial production.

But improved farm methods and farm living standards cannot completely solve our problems. If only one half of what we hear about the future of cotton proves true, a more critical situation will yet confront us.

The other route is by the expansion and development of industry in the South, thus more nearly to achieve that long-sought and much-talked-about balanced economy.

To solve the problem of low agricultural income in the South we shall be compelled to go outside the field of agriculture itself and into the whole field of the South's economy. If our regional industry fails to provide employment for the people who are no longer needed on the farms because of increased physical productivity in agriculture (which we must achieve) and because of the inelastic character of the demand for agricultural products, then the South indeed faces a bleak future. Either a large fraction of its farm population must shift to non-farm employment or the South must resign itself to being the nation's most depressed area in the future, as it has been in the past. The manner in which the job can be accomplished is indubitably through development of more industries. I can think of no force at the moment which can aid so immeasurably as can research.

We have this one great assurance—the South has the raw materials; and above all we have the differential possibilities, because up to the present time the industrial differential has been negative and not positive as it should be. By "differential" I mean the difference in two forces, or that which gauges the ability to move forward. As the South has advantageous climate, matchless resources, excellent sources of power, waterways, basically good labor, our difficulty is timing. And what we must understand is that the industrial timing of the South is critical for the reason that growth today is not slow or over a great number of years, but is rapid and can be influenced and controlled. No greater pioneering frontier was ever open.

Here is what I mean. If the products of industrial development and production were listed and plotted against each generation since Genesis the line would run very close to zero for the first 5,800 years, and only within the last 200 years would it begin to rise. For the last 100 years it would rise rapidly, and for the last 30 years the line would be almost vertical. The South must move forward now. Action is our *sine qua non*.

The absence of research in the South in the physical sciences has been a very much larger factor in the relative slowness of industrialization than we have acknowledged. There is something more than coincidence that the territory generally referred to as the area north of the Ohio and east of the Mississippi River, accounting, as it does, for 61 per cent of all the wage earners, for 60 per cent of the value added by manufacture in 97 out of the 3,072 counties of the United States, is strong in research personnel and plentiful in patentees. A study made by the Southern Research Institute shows that between the years 1934 and 1944, a total of 388,000 patents were issued to residents of the United States, according to official data from the Patent Office. These data show that 78 per cent, or 300,000 patents, were accredited to states east of the Mississippi and north of the Ohio, and 11,000, or 3 per cent, were accredited to the nine southeastern states. Obviously, there is an intimate connection between cumulative inventive genius and accumulated wealth producing industry. And let me assure you that the pattern would be little different if it included all the patents issued since the establishment of the Federal Patent Office.

In connection with the study of patents, consideration was given to the location of industrial research personnel in 1938, which is the most recent available data. It reflects the growth and location, to that time, of organized industrial research in the United States, and shows that 89 per cent of industrial research workers of the nation were located east of the Mississippi and north of the Ohio rivers, and that 2 per cent were in the nine southeastern states. Can there be any question as to the deep and abiding relationship between organized research and patents issued, or between these two means and the existence of wealth-giving industrial enterprise?

Patents are largely the result of intensive research, and are usually the step between creative thought and its conversion into physical wealth through the manufacturing process.

Each of the states of Illinois, Indiana, Michigan, Ohio, Pennsylvania, New York, New Jersey, Delaware, Connecticut, and Massachusetts had more industrial research workers than were contained in all of the southeastern states put together.

It is true, of course, that the present concentration of research personnel, and to a large degree that of patents issued, pertain to the existing research laboratories in industry now concentrated in the northern states. And here lies a great significance: it is in the great industrial areas, where the large business organizations are, that the enormous amount of research is being done. This begets more new products and improvements for the benefit of these industries. It is a circumstance which would tend to solidify the present industrial pattern and intensify the already overwhelming economic advantage of those areas.

In the light of these actualities as they relate to research, and in connection with the status of the rural South, can there be any issue as to the importance of, and the potentialities for research to the development and expansion of, southern industry? The founding of the Southern Research Institute, centered in Alabama, marks the beginning of an era in the South which, categorically, is the most significant step which has been taken in all its economic history.

In this statement thus far, generalities have marked its presentation. It is my purpose to be specific and, with full realization of my own personal limitations, to present to you those fields which offer wide scope for decisive expansion and development of industry in the South through research.

The richness of this area in raw materials, and more particularly minerals, to which reference has been made, emphasizes more forcefully today the importance of research as it relates to industrial expansion than ever before in the long history of the South's struggle for economic independence. The significance of these raw materials stresses the urgency for timing.

The South, according to the National Emergency Council, has more than 300 different minerals. This Council stated further that with less than 2 per cent of its seams so far tapped, the Southeast contains a fifth of the nation's soft coal; nearly two thirds of the nation's crude oil is produced in the South, and over two thirds of our supply of natural gas comes from southern fields; in 1935 the South furnished one half of the country's marble output; Florida and Tennessee produced 97 per cent of all our phosphate, and Texas and Louisiana supplied over 99 per cent of the sulphur.

When the reserves of minerals in the South are viewed with regard to the status of the nation, then the light breaks through.

A recent study of the mineral position of the country and a survey of the future has been made jointly by the Bureau of Mines and the United States Geological Survey. The results were made available with full knowledge that data thus presented involved many unforeseeable factors but with splendid understanding that the situation in mineral reserves warranted the approach. It is recognized that new deposits will undoubtedly be found as will also extensions to known ore bodies, but it is believed that the risks and costs involved are too great to warrant the assumption that our present estimates will be greatly increased through future discovery.

These findings on the reserves of certain essential minerals are disconcerting, to put it mildly. We have been jarred by rationing of fuel and gasoline; by shortages of minerals that have been felt at the battle front; and we have come to understand fully, as never before, their tremendous importance in modern life. If it were not for our mineral resources we would be limited to an agricultural economy which alone could not support 135,000,000 people with a standard of living unequalled in all the world. It is these minerals which have made it possible for 7 per cent of the world population here in America to perform 40 per cent of the world's work. And, because minerals are exhaustible, it is right to check and find out where we stand.

To put the matter squarely before you, it is stated that we face exhaustion, in a relatively short period of years, of certain important minerals. Our production of minerals has been almost inconceivable. Between 1880 and 1944, the annual output rose in value from one-half billion dollars to eight and one-half billion—a sixteen-fold increase. Since 1900 the production in our country has exceeded that of the entire world prior to that time. But, unless we are able to improve by concentration our vast reserves of low-grade ores, we shall not be able to sustain our economic well-being. Nor shall we be able to discharge effectively the responsibility in international affairs which we have undertaken. And that is where the South comes emphatically into the picture; where research is fundamentally essential; and where expansion and development of industry are inevitable if we promptly follow the right course.

Progress in converting submarginal resources into commercial reserves can be made through research, whereby methods can be improved in extracting and processing minerals and in reducing costs.

The findings of the Bureau of Mines and the United States Geological Survey constitute a review of our "commercial" reserves of 33 minerals. Building materials were not included because the country has an ample supply. And by "commercial" reserves is meant those reserves which are available under present economic conditions and technologic practices. And here too it was realized that supply, demand, and prices as well as progress in mineral technology are not susceptible of precise determinations. It was emphasized, however, that the rate of discovery of metalliferous deposits has been declining at an alarming rate for the past fifty years.

Of these 33 minerals we have an indefinite supply of nitrogen, magnesium, and salt. We have an ample supply of coal, phosphate rock, and others; but there are 22 minerals of the 33 which have a life of 34 years or less, from copper at 34 on down to zinc 19, petroleum 18, lead 12, bauxite 9, asbestos 3, manganese 2, and quartz crystals at less than one year. All of these estimates are based on their average annual production during the period 1935-1939.

It is interesting to note that the engineers of the Bureau of Mines and the United States Geological Survey fix the life of our commercial reserves of iron ore at 111 years—which is none too long. I know one eminent geologist who questions this estimate as being greater than it should be. This authority states that the Lake Superior district producing some 80 per cent of the iron ores of the country is now faced with the necessity of concentrating low-grade ores, and that no satisfactory method has been worked out. In this field the magnetite iron ores of North Carolina occupy a position of growing importance and have great possibilities.

The South throughout its borders is replete with a great

variety of submarginal minerals. No more striking illustration of probable industrial expansion in mineral production can be presented than North Carolina. This state contains over 250 different minerals, many of which may be on the brink of development. Of the 23 minerals whose reserves are estimated at less than 34 years, North Carolina will, through new and improved methods of extraction and utilization, contribute substantially.

For example: copper in the Piedmont and western counties is beginning to assume importance. Asbestos is mined in several parts of the state; and, though the quantity presently produced is small because of its type, North Carolina asbestos can have wide application as a result of its chemical and high temperature resistance. In this same class of mineral is North Carolina's vermiculite—a mineral wool—which will prove of importance as the use of insulation is extended. Chromium is found in three of the state's western counties. Low-grade deposits of manganese are known to exist in frequent outcroppings in several sections of the state. Tungsten, the reserves of which are estimated at only four years, has been found in Vance County and has been mined by at least two companies.

It may well be that in the silica deposits of this state we shall find quartz crystals, the national reserves of which are zero, in sufficient quantity to strengthen our national weakness in this respect. And who would gainsay that the vast deposits of spodumene near King's Mountain, said to be one of only two such deposits in the country, may furnish alumina through improved concentration, and thus augment the life of our bauxite, the reserves of which are estimated at only nine years, and at the same time make a large contribution to the production of lithium.

The possibilities of increasing North Carolina's mineral production over the sizable total of 21 million dollars in 1940 to a sum far in excess of this amount are recognizable, and this can be brought about through research and the consequent expansion and development of industry.

Many of these submarginal minerals are found in Alabama and other southeastern states, and I doubt not, if the submarginal minerals in all of our southeastern states were viewed from the standpoint of research, and a satisfactory method of mining and concentration worked out, that the Southeast alone could greatly enhance the position of our nation with respect to exhaustible ores.

Since we unquestionably face a shortage of important minerals, it is suggested that the mineral deposits of certain heretofore Japanese-controlled islands in the Pacific be investigated with the aim of increasing the reserves of those minerals whose exhaustion is imminent.

It is, no doubt, superfluous to stress so obvious an item as the possibilities of developing our forest resources through research, or to restate the axiom as to the opportunities of industrial expansion in this field. The South is one of the great forest areas of the United States. Alabama's area is 55 per cent forest. But to drive home the significance of timing even further, it may not be amiss to review briefly a few fundamentals. German industrial economy has had to rely heavily on wood. German scientists have developed, from odds and ends of wood, explosives, motor fuels, textiles, foods, and synthetic-rubber components. In the United States only about 30 per cent of any stand of timber finds its way into finished lumber—the remainder is waste, some of which can be used even in this land of higher labor and transportation costs as compared with Germany.

American mechanization of wood production is the answer, plus research. Carbon compounds in wood take the form of cellulose and lignin. Every ton of dry sawdust or chips yields approximately 1,000 pounds of wood sugar and 500 pounds of lignin residue, a brown powder with dramatic chemical promise. Alcohol distilled from wood sugar mash averages 50 gallons to 1,000 pounds, and it is ethyl alcohol, not methyl or wood alcohol. There is an hydrolysis alcohol plant costing two and one-fourth million dollars in Oregon; there is none, so far as I know, in any other area of the United States.

The potential cheapness of wood-ethyl will give it a place in postwar industry after its habit of absorbing moisture in storage is overcome.

The possibilities of lignin are great. Chemists tell us that, once they determine how the hydrocarbon molecules of lignin link together, they can obtain from it fairly simple coal-tar products, aspirin, sulfa drugs, perfumes, resins, and bulk chemicals.

Treated with certain chemicals, lignin makes vanillin flavor, phenol, cresol, wood alcohol, higher alcohols, and heavy oils; and from these come plastics and various drugs. And if to these we add cork, tannin fabrics, naval stores, laminated flooring and lumber, synthetic plywoods, wood iron, etc., research in the South becomes increasingly significant.

I have omitted any reference to the vast field of research in agricultural products for the reason that another speaker will present it. May I say, however, that our utilization of agricultural wastes will some day immeasurably enhance the South's economy.

Frequent reference has been made in recent years to the necessity for the establishing of industry in the South. If we accept as the basic hypothesis the prevalence of raw materials throughout this region, the occasion for their conversion to finished products is a requisite, considered in the light of population and the strength of southern markets. It is a fair assumption that never before in the South's history has the area's purchasing power been relatively so high.

In a recent report of the Alabama State Planning Board under the caption "Industrial Opportunity in Alabama," 446 types of industries were examined from data obtained from the most recent (1939) United States Census of Manufacture. In this report the industries were ranked as to the national value of products and the ratio of "value by manufacture" to "value of products." The value of products in the Southeast, the value of products in Alabama, and the average annual wage were set out. The study is not unlike the painstaking, excellent compilation made by Miss Harriet L. Herring, of the University of North Carolina, in her book *Southern Industry and Regional Development*, which is more detailed and exhaustive.

Of the 446 types of industries reviewed by the State Planning Board, 176 were classed as not particularly favorable opportunities for industry in Alabama. There remained 270. The national annual total of the 270 items in the Alabama report classified as suitable for manufacturing in the Southeast was 39 billion dollars, and of this only one and a quarter billion dollars was produced in the Southeast, or about three and three-tenths per cent. I reviewed these 270 industries and made a list of manufactured products, each of which has a total national value of not less than 35 million dollars annually, and confined it to those products having less than 10 per cent of the national production originating in the Southeast. I further restricted the cataloging to those industries whose raw materials were in the main either produced or could be available in the Southeast. I defined the Southeast as did Dr. Howard Odum, by limiting it to the boundaries of his "Southern Regions"—eleven states (Virginia, Kentucky, North Carolina, South Carolina, Georgia, Florida, Alabama, Mississippi, Tennessee, Arkansas, and Louisiana.) I chose 10 per cent because I thought it fair to predicate the study on the assumption that an area comprising over 21 per cent of the population of the nation should produce 10 per cent of various manufactures, each totaling a minimum of 35 million dollars per year. This list of manufactured products, ninety-five in number, is illuminating and is submitted in its entirety,* but I shall refer briefly to a few extraordinary items.

Of the annual national production of agricultural machinery totaling $168,000,000, 3 per cent was manufactured in the Southeast—all the raw materials are found in Alabama. The total for the nation of canned and dried fruits, soups, and vegetables was $587,000,000. The Southeast furnished less than 6 per cent, and the raw materials are, or can be, made obtainable in each of the eleven states. Hardware in the entire country totaled $154,000,000, and less than one-half of one per cent was manufactured in the Southeast, with all of the necessary raw materials in two of the states. Household furnishings, except drapes, for the nation amounted to $114,000,000— raw materials in all of the states, and slightly over two per cent produced therein. Plastics—the wonder material for the future —with raw materials throughout the area, totals $78,000,000 for the United States; none produced in the Southeast. Women's and misses' blouses made from cotton and rayon—raw material in large quantities in the area—totaled $42,000,000 for the

*See below, pp. 147-54.

nation; none produced in the Southeast. And in the same category the national market for women's dresses totaled $506,000,-000 with only eleven one-hundredth of one per cent produced in this section. Wrought iron pipe totaled $76,000,000; not one joint manufactured in this area. And so on without end.

The terrific loss to the South because there has not been provided reasonable means to finish its own raw materials is made plain by an analysis of the chemical engineering industries. This analysis showed that the average cost of raw materials employed is about 60 per cent of the products yielded.

These general statistics are presented because they lead unmistakably to another phase of research—market research—which has been neglected too long as far as systematic study is concerned.

Market research has many angles, but so far as I know, we have never made a study of many relating factors. Generally speaking, consumption (or use) data are difficult to obtain on short notice. Such data are of vital interest to industrialists, as they obviously indicate the presence or absence of a ready-made market when they are compared with production data. Research by items of consumption for some base year might be conceivably kept fairly up-to-date by multiplying by a general consumption index. Periodic checks could be made for regular corrections of the base.

This is one type of market research. Other aspects include the buying habits of the people of a region, the advertising media to be used for best over-all results, and the market trend for any particular product. Of these the questions of market levels and market trends are the most important. They will indicate where we are and where we are going. Such research will speed industrialization by pointing the way to both existing and potential enterprises.

As an example of this way-pointing, let us assume that a southern manufacturer of road machinery contemplates the production of farm tools. In the contemplated field he would be dealing with, to him, a new type of buyer, an unknown market level, and an unknown market trend. If data were readily available, he might find a strong but dwindling market for farm tools and a fair and rapidly growing market for garden tools. He could quickly make his decision, whereas if the necessary data were not available, either an unprofitable venture or the delayed entrance into a profitable one might result.

The men and organizations whose industrial development activities are known to me are convinced that the South is the Number One area of the nation from the standpoint of future manufacturing. If this is true, then this type of research will give them another tool, or it will "add a step to the sword" with which they are trying to cut the economic bonds of the South.

If you accept the premise that we have the raw materials, the markets, and the skilled labor, and the means of financing industrialization, then it is incumbent upon us to face one grave deficiency—that is, as far as the immediate future is concerned. The number and the quality of the men who engage in scientific study in our universities throughout the country, and more particularly throughout the South, are the startling signposts on the road to "scientific bankruptcy" to which Dr. Arthur Compton referred recently. We have made a serious mistake in drafting the relatively few advanced students to serve on the fighting fronts, while other nations that have had similar experiences in previous wars maintain their stock piles of research specialists. As soon as the war with Germany ends, unless we are to be hopelessly handicapped scientifically, it is imperative that scientists serving in the armed forces be relieved of their duties in order to develop processes for peace. Students who were in scientific courses in our great universities or who will enter scientific schools should likewise be given opportunities to resume their studies immediately. This is more emphatically true in the South than in other sections of the country because of the fact that we were short of this type of men to start with, and because the "drag of talent" out of the South in past years has intensified this situation.

If the South is to develop through research with ensuing expansion of industry, business in the area must understand its responsibility for education, and particularly education in the sciences in our southern institutions. Dr. Howard Odum referred to the South's incompetence in this respect when he stressed that "there is no institution [in the South] equipped for advanced instruction and training for land study and use, or for other highest technical equipment necessary for the development of an agrarian culture. Nor is there anywhere in the South a technical engineering school of the first rank."

That the South is penalized for its own omissions is attested by this predicament: Of the 1,828 southern-born persons in the 1933 *Who's Who in America* who took their graduate training out of the South, 1,092 were at that time located outside the South. This means that approximately 60 per cent of the South's sons and daughters of *Who's Who* distinction who leave the South for graduate training never come back.

Data here presented seem to warrant the conclusion that the South is a heavy contributor of its best leadership to other parts of the nation, to the South's own disadvantage. Modern industry in the South in its own defense, if it is to develop and expand, must with vision recognize this deficiency by joining hands with our southern educators to overcome it. This cannot be accomplished by a penurious attitude; rather does the situation demand magnanimity and co-operation.

Moreover, with all the darkness in the world today—we must stress science as one of the great humanities. What we want of our future executives is a liberal arts training in history and economics, in philosophy, and in good English, and likewise an intelligent interest in science and technology.

I have endeavored to emphasize in this discussion the prolific quantities of raw materials in the South, with the disproportionate means of finishing these raw materials. I have reviewed the unquestioned existence of the South's markets within its area. I have proved the absence of research personnel and research educational facilities, and have illustrated what has been accomplished through research in other sections.

If the accumulated savings of our people are invested wisely in the development of the area, in fifty years the absentee owner will have become an extinct specimen. If our financial leaders will reasonably risk what has been termed by them as "risk capital," which has reached unheard of totals in this part of the country, we shall simultaneously develop our own financial market. If these financial leaders of the South sell the South short their woes will have no end. If northern manufacturers fail to interpret the growing conviction among the South's citizens that they should trade at home for a fair share of their wants, their balance sheets will reveal their lack of discernment.

This need for improving the status of the South by the establishment of industry and the balancing of its economy may be deemed a far cry from "I'll take my stand." But if southern culture and tradition assay to a fraction of the estimate, and if southern people are really as individual as described, industrialization will be absorbed by the South without a loss of sectional distinction. And that distinction will be maintained because it has its roots in southern history, which is an enduring reality of the region—a history which points out a direction, designates a purpose, and enhances the significant experiences of its people. The discoveries of science as we turn to them shall never take precedence over this experience, nor can pragmatic liberalism drive this area from its regional characteristics.

ANNUAL PRODUCTION IN CERTAIN INDUSTRIES IN THE NATION AND THE SOUTHEAST†

PRODUCT	ANNUAL NATIONAL PRODUCTION		RAW MATERIALS	
	Amount (over 35 million)	Per cent in S. E. (under 10 per cent)	Items Involved	S. E. Sources
Agricultural Machinery	$ 168,000,000	2.85	Hardwood, Iron & Steel	Ala.
Aluminum Ware (Kitchen, etc.)	37,000,000	*	Aluminum Sheets & Ingots	Ala. & No. Car.
Artificial Leather & Oilcloth	43,000,000	—	Cotton Cloth, Clay Fillers, Petrol Products	Area
Batteries	118,000,000	0.95	Zinc, Lead, Graphite, Acid	Ala. & Tenn.
Biscuits, Crackers, Pretzels	201,000,000	2.57	Flour, Shortening, Milk, etc.	Area
Bolts, Nuts, Washers, & Rivets	84,000,000	*	Iron, Brass & Aluminum Bars & Rods	Ala. & No. Car.
Bread & Bakery Products	1,211,000,000	9.00	Flour, Shortening, Milk, etc.	Area
Brushes	48,000,000	*	Synthetic & Imported Bristles—wood	Area
Canned & Dried Fruits, Soups, & Vegetables	587,000,000	5.30	Fruits & Vegetables, Salts, etc.	Area
Carpets & Rugs—Wool	140,000,000	*	Imported wool & Jute Yarns	Area
Cement	193,000,000	7.06	Limestone, Shale, Silica & Fuel	Ala. & Tenn.

*No data.

†Excerpts from Table I in *Industrial Opportunity in Alabama*, Alabama State Planning Board, November, 1944.

ANNUAL PRODUCTION IN CERTAIN INDUSTRIES IN THE
NATION AND THE SOUTHEAST (*Con.*)

Product	Annual National Production		Raw Materials	
	Amount (over 35 million)	Per cent in S. E. (under 10 per cent)	Items Involved	S. E. Sources
Cheese	108,000,000	4.22	Milk	Area
Children's Dresses	$ 51,000,000	0.17	Cloth (Cotton, Rayon, etc.)	Area
Chocolate & Cocoa Products	99,000,000	—	Imported Cocoa, Sugar & Milk	Area
Cleaning & Polishing Preparations	90,000,000	0.22	Clay Fillers, Abrasives, Pigments—Oils	Area
Coal Tar Products (crude)	43,000,000	7.03	Coke Oven By-products	Ala. & Tenn.
Coated & Glazed Paper	84,000,000	*	Pulp—Clay Fillers, Alum., etc.	Area
Coats, Suits, etc. (not fur)	314,000,000	0.06	Wool, Worsted, Cotton & Rayon Suitings	Va. & New England
Cold-Rolled Sheets & Strips	70,000,000	—	Steel Billets, Rods, & Bars	Ala. & Tenn.
Colors & Pigments	84,000,000	*	Coal Tar Dyes— Ochres, Carbon Black	Ala., Tenn., & La.
Condensed & Evaporated Milk	210,000,000	6.73	Milk & Sugar	Area
Converted Paper Products	161,000,000	*	Paper, Board, etc.	Area
Cotton Narrow Fabrics	49,000,000	2.86	Cotton Yarns	Area
Creamery Butter	492,000,000	3.48	Milk & Cream	Area

ANNUAL PRODUCTION IN CERTAIN INDUSTRIES IN THE NATION AND THE SOUTHEAST (*Con.*)

PRODUCT	ANNUAL NATIONAL PRODUCTION		RAW MATERIALS	
	Amount (over 35 million)	Per cent in S. E. (under 10 per cent)	Items Involved	S. E. Sources
Cutlery & Edge Tools	60,000,000	*	Steel, Cast Iron & Wood	Ala. & Tenn.
Doors & Windows (Metal)	$ 48,000,000	*	Steel	Ala., Ga., & Tenn.
Drugs & Medicine	365,000,000	4.96	Various Imports & Domestic	Area
Electrical Appliances	146,000,000	*	Copper, Steel, HeatingElements	Ala. & Tenn.
Electric Lamps	85,000,000	*	Glass, Heating Elements, Copper & Brass	Area
Enamel—Iron Sanitary Ware	126,000,000	*	Silica, Pig Iron, etc., & Fuel	Area
Envelopes	50,000,000	*	Paper—Fine & Manila	Area
Flat Glass	102,000,000	*	Silica Soda Ash & Fuel	Area
Flavoring Extracts	139,000,000	2.64	Imports & Domestic, Coal Extracts	Area
Footwear (except Rubber)	735,000,000	3.72	Leather & Cotton	Area
Forgings (Iron & Steel)	105,000,000	*	Steel & Iron	Ala. & Tenn.
Glass Containers	158,000,000	*	Silica, Soda Ash & Fuel	Area
Grey Iron Castings	208,000,000	4.65	Pig Iron, Coke & Sand	Ala. & Tenn.

ANNUAL PRODUCTION IN CERTAIN INDUSTRIES IN THE NATION AND THE SOUTHEAST (*Con.*)

PRODUCT	ANNUAL NATIONAL PRODUCTION		RAW MATERIALS	
	Amount (over 35 million)	Per cent in S. E. (under 10 per cent)	Items Involved	S. E. Sources
Hardware	154,000,000	0.47	Iron, Steel, Brass, & Alloys	Ala. & Tenn.
House Dresses, Aprons, etc.	114,000,000	2.48	Cotton & Rayon Cloth	Area
House Furnishings (except Drapes)	114,000,000	2.15	Cotton & Linen, Rayon Cloth	Area
Insecticides	93,000,000	4.88	Domestic & Imported Chemicals, Fillers, etc.	Area
Knitted Cloth	69,000,000	8.30	Cotton & Rayon Yarns	Area
Knitted Outerwear	104,000,000	*	Cotton, Rayon, & Wool Yarns	Area
Laundry Equipment—Domestic	61,000,000	—	Iron, Steel, Aluminum & Brass	Ala. & Tenn.
Leather Tanning	346,000,000	3.88	Southwest & Imported Hides & Tan Acid	Area
Lighting Fixtures	126,000,000	*	Brass, Aluminum, Iron & Steel	Ala. & Tenn.
Machine Shop Products	360,000,000	4.57	Brass, Aluminum, Iron & Steel	Ala. & Tenn.
Malleable Iron Castings	53,000,000	*	Iron	Ala. & Tenn.

ANNUAL PRODUCTION IN CERTAIN INDUSTRIES IN THE
NATION AND THE SOUTHEAST (*Con.*)

Product	Annual National Production		Raw Materials	
	Amount (over 35 million)	Per cent in S. E. (under 10 per cent)	Items Involved	S. E. Sources
Malt Liquors	526,000,000	4.46	Sugar, Malt, etc.	Area
Meat Packing	2,648,000,000	4.59	Livestock	Area
Mech. Power Trans.	170,000,000	*	Iron, Steel	Ala. & Tenn.
Men's & Boys' Suits	598,000,000	4.71	Wool, Worsted, & Rayon Suitings	Va. & New England
Machine Tools	126,000,000	0.06	Brass, Aluminum, Iron & Steel	Ala. & Tenn.
Men's Neckwear	46,000,000	0.52	Rayon & Cotton & Wool Cloth	Area
Mirrors	50,000,000	8.90	Glass	—
Needles, Pins, etc.	38,000,000	—	Steel, Zinc, Aluminum & Brass	Area
Office Furniture	55,000,000	2.82	Steel & Aluminum Sheets	Ala. & Tenn.
Oven Coke & By-Products	342,000,000	5.89	Coal	Ala. & Tenn.
Paints, Varnishes, etc.	435,000,000	4.62	Pigments, Turpentine, Oils, Clay	Area
Paper & Paper Board	933,000,000	8.16	Timber, Salt Cake, Lime & Sal.	Area
Paperboard Containers	383,000,000	6.33	Paperboard	Area

ANNUAL PRODUCTION IN CERTAIN INDUSTRIES IN THE NATION AND THE SOUTHEAST (*Con.*)

PRODUCT	ANNUAL NATIONAL PRODUCTION		RAW MATERIALS	
	Amount (over 35 million)	Per cent in S. E. (under 10 per cent)	Items Involved	S. E. Sources
Perfumes, Cosmetics, etc.	147,000,000	2.02	Alcohol, Clays, Olive Oil, etc.	Area
Pickled Fruits, etc. Sauces	73,000,000	7.43	Fruits & Vegetables, Vinegar, Sugar	Area
Plastic Materials	78,000,000	—	Sul. Acid, Urea, Phenols, Alcohol	Area
Poultry Packing	138,000,000	1.54	Poultry	Area
Preserves, Jellies, etc.	38,000,000	5.46	Sugar—Fruits	Area
Printing Ink	49,000,000	1.26	Lampblack— Linseed Oil, etc.	Import
Radios, Tubes, etc.	276,000,000	*	Hardwoods— Glass—Aluminum and Steel	Area
Refrigerators, Mechanical—Domestic	279,000,000	0.12	Steel, Aluminum, Insulation	Ala. & Tenn.
Robes, Lounging	40,000,000	0.28	Cotton, Rayon, & Wool Suitings	Area
Roofing—Roll & Built	108,000,000	3.85	Asphalt, Jute, Pigment—Slate & Gravel	Area
Screw Mach. Products	83,000,000	—	Iron, Steel & Brass Rods	Ala. & Tenn.
Signs & Advertising Displays	88,000,000	5.03	Glass Tube, Sheet Steel	Area

ANNUAL PRODUCTION IN CERTAIN INDUSTRIES IN THE
NATION AND THE SOUTHEAST (*Con.*)

PRODUCT	ANNUAL NATIONAL PRODUCTION		RAW MATERIALS	
	Amount (over 35 million)	Per cent in S. E. (under 10 per cent)	Items Involved	S. E. Sources
Soap	303,000,000	0.01	Animal & Vegetable Fats, Clay Fillers, Caus. Soda	Area
Sporting & Athletic Goods	65,000,000	1.08	Wood, Steel Aluminum, Leather Textiles	Area
Stampings (not Auto)	178,000,000	*	Sheet Steel (Tin) Aluminum	Ala. & Tenn.
Steel Barrels & Drums	49,000,000	5.44	Sheet Steel	Ala.
Steel Castings	135,000,000	*	Steel (Ingot & Scrap)	Ala. & Tenn.
Stoves and Ranges (Cast)	223,000,000	9.67	Pig Iron, Sand, & Coke	Ala. & Tenn.
Tableware—Glass	97,000,000	*	Silica, Soda Ash & Fuel	Area
Textile Machinery	93,000,000	4.76	Iron, Steel, Wood, Brass	Ala. & Tenn.
Tin Cans & Tinware	373,000,000	*	Tin Plate	Ala.
Tires & Tubes (Auto)	581,000,000	*	Sulphur, Carbon Black, Rubber, & Fabric	Texas, La. & Area
Vitreous Enamel Products	44,000,000	7.54	Enameling Steel, Sand & Soda Ash	Midwest & Area
Wire (from Punch Rods)	177,000,000	—	Steel Rods	Ala. & Tenn.

ANNUAL PRODUCTION IN CERTAIN INDUSTRIES IN THE NATION AND THE SOUTHEAST (*Con.*)

PRODUCT	ANNUAL NATIONAL PRODUCTION		RAW MATERIALS	
	Amount (over 35 million)	Per cent in S. E. (under 10 per cent)	Items Involved	S. E. Sources
Wirework	159,000,000	0.65	Wire	Ala.
Wiring Devices	94,000,000	*	Iron & Steel	Ala. & Tenn.
Women's & Misses' Blouses	42,000,000	—	Rayon & Cotton Suitings	Area
Women's & Misses' Clothing	40,000,000	0.27	Wool, Rayon & Cotton Suitings	Area
Women's & Misses' Dresses	506,000,000	0.11	Rayon & Cotton Suitings	Area
Women's & Misses' Cloth Underwear	91,000,000	*	Rayon, Silk & Cotton Cloth	Area
Women's & Misses' Knit Underwear	37,000,000	0.39	Rayon, Silk, & Cotton Yarns	Area
Women's Pocketbooks	56,000,000	*	Cotton, Rayon, & Wool Cloth & Leather	Area
Woolen & Worsted Mfg.	698,000,000	6.02	Woolen & Worsted Yarns	Va. & New Eng.
Wrought Pipes	76,000,000	—	Steel Sheets (Heavy)	Ala.

NEEDS AND OPPORTUNITIES FOR RESEARCH IN INDUSTRY

Reuben B. Robertson

EXECUTIVE VICE-PRESIDENT, CHAMPION
PAPER AND FIBRE COMPANY

IN HISTORY'S BALANCE-SHEET war, of necessity, must show a deficit. Debits will always exceed credits as long as value is given to human life. The aggressor nations in their sordid way endeavored to convince themselves that an excess of material gains over material losses could be shown that would justify their aggressions, but the loss of human values was ignored. Someone has said that the Nazis believed in wholly wrong things, but believed them with frenzied zeal, while Americans believed wholly right things, but in a casual sort of way. For a time it looked as though that frenzied zeal would carry the wrong into ascendency. When once fully aroused, however, America proved that she could be even more zealous in the carrying out of her sound principles than the Nazis were in carrying out their insane and inhuman ideas.

While always insisting that there can be no over-all credit balance in favor of war, we must admit that there are some by-products of war that may be properly placed on the credit side of the ledger. War does lessen internal strife, it does compel national unity—it encourages the spirit of sacrifice over the spirit of self interest; it does stimulate invention and the conversion of invented ideas into operating realities. Such influences are carried forward into the days of peace with beneficial effects.

Innovation, invention, and discovery in normal times must be subjected to the tests of a realistic world. "Can we afford to apply the funds needed for the development of an appealing idea?" "Will it, after completion, yield adequate financial return?" The negative answers frequently and necessarily given

155

to such questions have administered the "knock-out" to many a contender for honors in the field of invention.

The "musts" of a struggle for national existence are so compelling that these practical questions of peace time must be relegated to the background. When we need ships to supply our armies on foreign soil, it is speed and quantity production that count—saving in dollars is secondary. When our armed forces demand planes that can out-travel and out-shoot the best the enemy can offer, the only questions asked are: "Can it be done?" And "How soon?" When faced with such problems the scientist and the inventor go ahead, freed of the ingrained inhibitions of peace time. Their style is no longer cramped by cost restrictions. War has in this way accelerated by decades technical progress in the fields affected by it. Following the usual and necessarily cautious course of private enterprise we should not have been ready for safe air transport across Pacific wastes for many years to come. The expensive lessons of the Burma Road taught much about high-altitude transport that will have postwar application.

Air speeds of four hundred miles per hour and the still higher speeds of the jet-propelled plane would still have been matters for deliberate and careful engineering study, rather than realities which will readily find adaptation to postwar needs. Electronics, plastics, synthetic rubber, all show the evidence of this wartime acceleration. Many other examples of hastened development resulting from wartime needs can be quoted, such as the "miracle" medicines atabrine, penicillin, DDT, sulpha drugs, plasma, etc.

Shortly before our Civil War, a patent examiner was reported to have recommended that the U. S. Patent Office be discontinued because all worth-while improvements that could be invented had already been invented! And that was before the day of the internal-combustion engine, the telephone, the steam turbine, and the rubber tire, with their tremendous and far-reaching effects on our daily lives. How completely he underestimated the fertility and resourcefulness of the human mind! Even then the Patent Office records showed the seeds of ideas which led, step by step, to the really miraculous development of today. Even the jet-propelled plane was clearly anticipated in recorded inventions prior to that day, illustrated with some sketches that show a remarkable resemblance to the jet-propelled planes in actual operation today. It has been said, "There is no greater force in human experience than an idea whose time has come." The time for the jet-propelled plane had not come, for it had to await the development of a suitable fuel and the understanding of that fuel which came with the internal-combustion engine. It needed, too, the pioneering work of Professor Langley and the Wright brothers in the field of heavier-than-air machines.

We should not forget, however, that failure in the field of technical development has come to the individual, not only from being ahead of his time, but also from being behind his time. Sometimes the over-cautious defer too long their break with the obsolete. Both vision and courage are needed.

Inventions, sometimes incidental, sometimes epoch-making, are constantly opening up ever wider vistas of possible accomplishment. Scientific research must accordingly not only search but actually "re-search." For, in the stock pile of ideas rejected in earlier days as having little value, are many thoughts that under new conditions and with a broader background of development take on greatly enhanced importance. Lawyers say "time is of the essence in commercial transactions"; and timeliness is certainly "of the essence" in the field of invention. It is not a comforting thought to imagine what might have happened in World War II had German scientists been able to perfect their robot bombs a year or two before they were actually put into service.

Theodore Roosevelt well said that "90 per cent of the value of being right lies in being right in time." "Unconditional Surrender," now a reality, means that many of the "musts" of a wartime economy will cease to provide stimulus for production, for development, for invention. The time has come for us to begin to change our thoughts and our plans from things that destroy civilization to things that better the status of mankind. Our national income, because of the transient stimulus of war, has been at an all-time high: unemployment has been practically nonexistent and social gains have been great. We have learned what a nation, united in objective and working as one great team, can accomplish in the production field. We are unwilling to relinquish, for the postwar days, these results of our entrance into the global struggle. To do so would endanger the system of private enterprise, which is the very cornerstone of national security and national progress.

We converted our industrial machine from peace-time production to wartime needs with remarkable skill and resourcefulness, but we must remember that this conversion was not complicated by the necessity for finding markets, or by considerations of financial justification. Uncle Sam provided the market and Uncle Sam took care of finances. Reconversion will call for even greater skill and resourcefulness, for it means not only production, but also the responsibility for seeking out markets and the justification for capital expenditures. We must again become realistic and ask the questions, "Can the enterprise pay back the capital which it borrows?" "Can it pay a proper return on the investment?"

In the selection of markets we have been wisely warned that "too many plans are based on the hope of getting into the other fellow's business; that does not create new jobs—only new products and new plants do this." We must use the truly creative force of scientific research. The modern methods of market research and analysis form a most important adjunct to scientific study. We must find the economic equivalent of war as a stimulant for maximum production and its concomitant maximum employment. A high level of employment must be realized if we are to escape the very real dangers of readjustment to peace.

Research is bound to play a most important part in providing answers to the many difficult problems which confront us. Individual research, organized or teamed private research, consulting research provided through private organizations, and consulting research provided through public organizations, all are important—all should be used.

In a recent opinion, Judge Thurman Arnold, commenting on research methods in relation to patents, took as an example the classic instance of seeking a needle in a haystack and said, "The old method was to turn everybody loose in the haystack in a grand scramble; once in a long while the needle was found; the research method is to divide the stack into a number of parts and assign one man to each part. The needle was generally found."

Judge Arnold's illustration is good, but we cannot say as much for his conclusions. We think that patents should be issued objectively, each invention resting entirely on its own merits. The granting of patents should not be in any way conditioned on the antecedents or the affiliations of the inventor nor on the conditions under which the invention was created. The Judge's radical departure from former well-established rulings would, if accepted as part of the law of the land, open wide the opportunity for arbitrary and whimsical decisions that would discourage rather than stimulate invention. The precedent would be dangerous in the extreme.

Organized, systematic research justifies itself; it pays dividends in the long run, even when we offset frequent failures against infrequent successes. Mankind has been the gainer as compared with sole reliance on the "flash of genius" type of invention. The two methods are related to each other pretty much as are the crimes of murder and of manslaughter. One is the result of momentary impulse, the other the result of deliberate planning. As the lawyers say, the latter is done with "malice aforethought." Both bring results.

Obviously, the organized "mass" attack on a problem is not available for the resourceful individual who may have an excellent idea but lacks financial reserves and the technical contacts necessary to explore its merits. Unaided individual effort has, no doubt, accounted for by far the greatest number of inventions that have been recorded. Individual effort must be retained and encouraged; it should not remain unaided. Consultation with disinterested scientific agencies should be made available to the individual at modest cost, either through our universities or through some government-sponsored agency.

Organized research makes its own peculiar contribution to national progress. After all, this type of research is a gamble in which the risks of loss are heavy. In the oil industry, for example, there was a day when new oil deposits were readily found through shallow and relatively inexpensive wells. The man of small capital, willing to take the risk of loss on the chance of large gain, felt justified in drilling his own "wildcat" well. Later, as the readily-reached oil resources were exhausted, deeper and deeper wells became necessary and the drilling of wells became the "sport of kings." Capital requirements are now large and the owner must be prepared to accept with equanimity the loss of everything spent, when his effort is rewarded with a "dry" hole. There are many "dry holes" in the field of research. This kind of chance-taking should be undertaken only by those who can afford to lose.

It is estimated that today there are something like 70,000 scientists engaged in organized research with annual expenditures of approximately $300,000,000. Industrial management sponsoring these expenditures is generally content if as much as 5 per cent of the projects undertaken turn out successfully. It seldom happens that an individual can afford to provide funds for the ninety-five "duds" that pave the way for the five successful projects.

After an invention has apparently been perfected, there is still the problem of conversion to everyday use. Practical development of an idea is fully as important as the conception of the idea itself. Donald David, of Harvard, speaking of the scientist, said, "He does a magnificent job in providing the analysis and the diagnosis; in short, he lays the egg. Too often he cackles and leaves the nest and the practical man must hatch it."

The satisfaction that comes from successful accomplishment is always an important reward for research effort, but it should not be the only reward. The incentive of possible financial return appeals to the individual investigator and to the sponsor of organized research alike. Size and affiliations do not change this fundamental motive in human affairs. We must provide the incentive of limited monopoly, granted by the issuance of a patent, or must accept the alternative of suppression of information and prolonged secrecy regarding the details of inventions which should be brought to light. Our legislators of earlier days chose the wiser alternative when they established our patent system. Abraham Lincoln said the "patent system added the fuel of interest to the fire of genius."

Over the years abuses creep into any plan, no matter how sound in basic concept, and those abuses call for correction. We should not, however, "throw out the baby with the bath" and destroy sound fundamentals in our effort to correct abuses that do not go to the heart of things.

Industrial-research groups, even when fully staffed, frequently find it advantageous to farm out specific projects to consulting research organizations—such organizations as the Mellon Institute, the Institute of Paper Chemistry, and the Battelle Laboratories provide facilities that are most valuable to big and little investigator alike. Research along regional lines, along state lines, and for industrial groups are all helpful adjuncts to our over-all program. On the national level such groups as the Forest Products Laboratories, the Bureau of Standards, and other similar groups make their worth-while contributions to the sum total of our national knowledge.

The pulp and paper industry, in which I am especially interested, has long been accustomed to the methods of modern scientific research. To the use of these methods can be credited the production of strong white fine papers from the pines of the South, as well as the successful production of news print from southern pine. During the war period, paper in its various forms has rated high in the essentiality scale. Our Washington agencies could hardly have carried out the slogan which they are accused of fostering, "Pass the buck, throw the bull, and make seven copies of everything," if they had not had efficient support from the paper makers.

The industry has made most valuable contributions to the war, especially in the field of the packaging of food and of a wide range of military supplies. Much has been learned about the wear-resisting and weather-proofing qualities of paper that will be of great value in the days ahead. Research has made possible the substitution, without real loss of quality, of obtainable raw materials for the unobtainable ones cut off by war's exigencies.

Research for postwar operation in this industry begins in the forest and carries through to the ultimate consumer. In the forest we are concerned with the most effective utilization of timber growth. We hope to see timber harvesting so planned that annual growth equals or exceeds annual drain, so that forests will be "farmed" for perpetual annual growth rather than "mined" for temporary gain.

Logging methods are being scrutinized for savings in manpower and in dollar costs because of the necessary close relationship and the delicate balance that exist between the amount of forest products that can be salvaged and the cost of that salvage. All of us hope for high standards of living for our workers in the future. High wages mean high unit costs and restricted markets, unless high levels of productive capacity per man are maintained. Low unit costs obtained in this way permit more complete utilization of forest products and the conservation of a natural resource that is of vital importance to the nation and especially to the South.

I have visited European forests where the utilization was complete, from pine needles to the roots, but it was complete only because low wages and low standards of living prevailed. It is said that Herbert Spencer, piqued because of his defeat in a game of billiards, remarked, "To play billiards well is a sign of a well-rounded education, to play billiards too well is a sign of a misspent youth." Good utilization of forest products is a sign of a well-rounded economy. Too complete utilization may spell economic poverty.

In the manufacture of pulp, only about 40 per cent of the weight of the wood can be used for the production of pulp fibre. The remaining portion of the wood weight, chiefly lignin, today is either burned for fuel or wasted to the sewer. Scientists are busily engaged in developing uses for this lignin in plastics and in some of the newer wood products which give promise of extensive future use. Fatty acids and resin acids, both by-products of the production of pine pulp by the Kraft process, have many possible new uses. Hydrogen sulphide, released to the atmosphere in this pulping process, has given the mills a reputation for being rather "flagrantly fragrant," and, while we must confess that we do resemble, to some degree, the rose behind the garden wall, in that our presence is known even though we can't be seen, still, we are aware of our shortcomings and are making progress towards correction through electrical precipitation and other methods of improvement.

The Southern Appalachians have been one of the nation's greatest sources of tanning materials through the utilization of the chestnut forests. The chestnut blight has killed nearly all of the trees of this variety, leaving for industrial use only the deadened stems, and, while these stems will provide tanning material for probably a decade, the problem of finding a substitute material of forest origin is a definite and pressing one. The study of tannin-bearing trees of the South, conducted by the University of North Carolina under the guidance of Dr. Russell, constitutes a real contribution towards the solution of this problem.

Likewise the study of forest resources of North Carolina recently completed by Dr. Egon Glessinger under the auspices of the North Carolina Department of Conservation and Development is thought-provoking and informative and will undoubtedly be evidenced ultimately by many instances of profitable and job-making development.

Research and the scientific approach have in the case of the Ecusta Paper Company at Brevard (under the far-sighted guidance of Harry Straus) brought progress and prosperity to a community that otherwise had little chance of substantial growth. There farm and factory co-ordinate their efforts for the manufacture of cigarette papers and other high-grade papers using flax as a raw material. These papers in the prewar period came from overseas.

All of the South is vitally interested in cotton: in the methods of its production, of harvesting, of conversion into finished products. The mechanical cotton-picker, recently supplemented by the use of leaf-removing chemicals, is recognized as having great possibilities as a means of keeping cotton production on a competitive basis in the markets of the world. The harvesting of "whole" cotton by machines, similar to those used for harvesting grains, is a matter that is receiving careful study, the plan being to broadcast the seed as in the case of grains and to extract oils and fibre by mass-processing methods. Nice questions of economic balance are obviously involved.

Cotton will also feel the impact of increased production of staple fibre. Such problems will challenge the skill of our best scientific minds.

Research is needed in specific fields of technology, but, for the results of research to find their greatest usefulness, the general "atmosphere" in which industry functions must be sympathetic. Congressional and administrative policies should be geared to plans which encourage rather than discourage the conversion of invention into actual projects of production. It is a barren invention which does not find consummation in actual use.

I have been somewhat familiar with the activities of the Committee for Economic Development, one of whose primary objectives is to create an atmosphere favorable to the spending of risk money. I have had the stimulating privilege of listening in at some of their joint meetings of research scientists and business men where broad questions of national economic policy were discussed in objective and constructive fashion. The scope of the Committee's research studies is indicated by the titles of some of the projects: "Production, Jobs and Taxes"; "Liquidation of War Production"; "Financing Industry during Transition from War to Peace"; "The Special Problems of Small Business."

The Committee's approach to these problems has won almost unanimous approval—one prominent statesman going so far as to say that C. E. D. provides the outstanding and most encouraging point of departure between conditions at the conclusion of World War I and the conditions of today. Then a policy of "drift" prevailed, while today we have a policy of careful analysis, of study and of action based on study and analysis.

In the past there has been a tendency, on the part of the business man, to hold himself aloof from the scientist on the ground that the scientist lived too far up in the intellectual stratosphere and was impractical, while the scientist with equal aloofness was inclined to consider the business man too much "dollar-minded," too narrow in his views, to be worth talking to. The Committee for Economic Development has brought these two groups into close and mutually considerate contact with each other with a broadening of the view point of each. The resultant conclusions show the thoroughness of the scientist as well as the practical judgment of the man of business. The method has been so successful that it could well serve as a pattern for the study of many other national problems.

Payment of the bills for the frightful wastes of war necessarily involves heavy tax burdens and these must continue for many years to come. Efficiency and economy in government have, therefore, become more important than ever. No needless tax burden should be allowed to hamper the free expansion of business. It is quite appropriate, therefore, that research should include the conduct of our public affairs.

Under the skillful guidance of Mr. Coates, The Institute of Government here at Chapel Hill is making a unique and outstanding contribution to efficiency in government. It richly deserves the "sincere flattery" involved in repeated imitation in every state in the Union. These things help to create the "atmosphere" needed for scientific progress.

If scientific research is to have its much desired continuity, personnel replacements must be provided for the normal human casualties that occur in its staff of technically trained men. In peace time replacements have been furnished in steady flow through graduation from our colleges. But, as is well known, this flow of replacements has been interrupted by the diversion of students to war activities. We shall enter the post-war period with a depleted "back-log" of young technicians capable of carrying on in the field of scientific research.

Someone has outlined the specifications for a research worker as follows: "He must have the simplicity to wonder—the ability to question—the power to generalize and the capacity to apply." These qualities are not always easy to find in a single individual, and replacements with men fully satisfying these specifications will be difficult.

We have been inclined to believe that the real expert in research, like the poet, had to be born that way. As Carroll Wilson points out, that view is giving way to the more optimistic one that we can synthesize the inventive tendency. He would "catch the innovator young, then help him to acquire ingenious habits and inspire him to employ them effectively in his living and in his work." His "seven catalysts for inspiration and training" are in themselves ingenious and interesting and will justify careful consideration on the part of those who plan education for scientific accomplishment.

Harry Emerson Fosdick reminds us that there are extraordinary possibilities in ordinary people. Mr. Wilson's catalysts may point the way of conversion from the ordinary in folks to the extra-ordinary.

The South has great natural wealth in its forests, its coal fields, its gas and oil reserves, its mineral deposits, its water-powers, and especially in the spiritual and intellectual power of its people. It has both resources and resourcefulness. These elements linked together in closer co-operation and co-ordination through the methods of scientific study spell opportunity for all.

THE BIOLOGICAL SCIENCES

RESEARCH IN THE FISHERIES FOR THE BETTERMENT OF THE SOUTH

Harden F. Taylor

FORMER PRESIDENT, ATLANTIC COAST
FISHERIES COMPANY

IT IS IN KEEPING with the traditions of leadership of this great University that for the celebration of its one hundred and fiftieth anniversary it has chosen the theme of research in subjects of fundamental importance to the welfare of the region which it mainly serves. The natural resources of the region stand first in any program of research, for it is mainly upon them that welfare must have its foundation, the term welfare including not only economic prosperity but, in the fisheries, the possibility of contributions of importance to public nutrition.

The coast line of the southern states, indentations not included, from the Virginia Capes to the Mexican border is about 2,500 miles long; including defined indentations, it is about 4,500 miles long. While the greater part of the Atlantic Ocean is about two miles deep, the land does not pitch off suddenly at the shore into the abyss of the ocean. There is an under-water ledge, beginning at the low-tide line and gently sloping off-shore to the 100-fathom line, which lies about 50 miles to sea along our southern states, and roughly parallel with the shore line to the southern tip of Florida; it is wider on the southern west coast of Florida and generally in the Gulf of Mexico. This ledge under shallow water around the fringe of land is the Continental Shelf; its area from Virginia to Texas is roughly 175,000 square miles, which exceeds the total area of North Carolina, South Carolina, Georgia, and half of Florida. The marine resources accessible to the southern states are mainly on this ledge and on similar shallow water areas in the near-by Bahamas and West Indies.

The fisheries of this under-water area have been exploited since the founding of the colonies, and have contributed to the nutrition and the economic welfare of the South. Considering the large area of sea bottom, and the fact that every square mile of it is a natural food factory, the total yield of the fishery has not been and is not now of impressive magnitude, and, as will appear, the South is not making the most effective use of what is produced. In a typical recent prewar year the total production of the fisheries from this 175,000 square miles of bottom, off the eight coastal states of the South, was 622 million pounds, of which 303 million, or nearly half, was menhaden, used almost entirely for the manufacture of oil, fish meal, and fertilizer. The value of all fish products including menhaden and sponges was 13 million dollars. Four groups, menhaden, mullet, shrimp, and oysters, total 500 million pounds, or 80 per cent of the quantity, and 7.6 million dollars, or 58 per cent of the value. Exclusive of sponges and menhaden, the fish available for human food was 317 million pounds worth 12 million dollars, or a million dollars a month divided very unequally among eight states. A large but unknown part of the 317 million pounds of food fish was shipped to northern markets as a cash crop, but even if it had all been consumed in the eight coastal states, whose population is 25 million, the per capita consumption would be twelve pounds whole fish, or one pound per month, but actually not more than one half pound per month, since on the average less than 50 per cent of whole fish is suitable for human food. It is probable that a half of the production of the South is shipped elsewhere, so that, say, three pounds per capita per annum is the amount consumed as human food in the South. For the nation as a whole it is about eight or nine pounds.

It is from the elementary facts that any research program must begin. These are the elementary facts, so far as they are obtainable. They indicate either that our southern marine area is of low productivity or that full advantage is not being taken of our natural resources. It appears on the face of the facts that these 175,000 square miles of sea could yield a great deal more of fishery products than they now do. After the war we shall have great numbers of young men who will need employment and economic security and who will make good fishermen; we have an unexcelled network of the roads over which other young men could drive trucks to transport them, and the dietary of the South could certainly benefit from the produce of the sea.

For the more ambitious part of any fisheries research program it is necessary to examine broadly the characteristics of the fisheries as a natural resource industry, especially in the South, its foundation, its peculiarities, and its problems, for, while some of these characteristics point to great values and call for action, others set definite limits to what can or should be done by public action to realize them.

Of all the natural resource industries, the fisheries are the only one that does not deplete our national wealth. On the contrary, everything of value brought from the sea to the land is a net addition to our total wealth. For ages the rains have been falling on the land, washing out the soluble nutrients and carrying them down the rivers to enrich the sea. By this process the sea has become an inexhaustible reservoir of nearly all the soluble nutrients of the world—not only of the familiar fertilizers, fixed nitrogen, phosphorus and potash, but of the indispensable array of trace elements such as iodine, fluorine, boron, manganese, copper, zinc, and indeed whatever additional elements may yet be found necessary to life; for they are all there, and in such quantities that if the whole of mankind took all of its chemical supply from the ocean, or dumped into it all of the chemicals it possesses, not the slightest detectable change would be made in the composition of the sea. The plants and animals at sea are collectors and concentrators of these elements, and when we bring them ashore we return to the land a tiny fraction of what has been taken from the land. The ocean is not only quantitatively the biggest, but qualitatively the most perfect source of nutriment in the world.

Yet the ocean is not full of fish. Vast reaches are nearly barren. Plants grow rapidly in the sunshine at the surface until they have used up the least abundant fertilizers, and then stop growing, because at most places there is little or no vertical circulation of water which can replenish the fertilizers from the nearly stagnant reserve in the deep ocean. Life is therefore abundant wherever the shape of the bottom and the movements of water caused by wind, tide, differences of temperature, and rotation of the earth bring the rich bottom water up to the surface sunshine—on the shallow spots, submarine ridges, and fringes of the continents, such as that off the southern states. There the chain of life begins, as it does on land, with plants which are the food of tiny animals, and these of larger animals, and so on up to fishes which we can use. Such spots of abundant life are the North Sea, Norwegian Sea, the waters around Newfoundland, off our Northeast Coast, on the fringe of the American Pacific Coast, Alaska and south to Japan, and numerous other places including the continental fringe of the eastern side of North and South America.

The great fishing ports of the world are situated near these shallow areas and ledges—in England, Germany, Norway, Nova Scotia, in Boston, Seattle, and San Pedro, U.S.A., and in Japan. At such ports the landings of fish are large enough to support the operation of mass handling and manufacturing machinery, oil extraction plants, fish meal plants, freezing and cold storage warehouses, attendant and supply industries, and transportation for wholesale quantities with correspondingly low cost. In this respect the southern fisheries appear to be at a disadvantage since, for one reason or another the fisheries are scattered over a coast line 2,500 miles long, many of the fishes are migratory or seasonal, and no place under present conditions can count on a sufficiently large and continuous supply to support mass production at low cost with regular employment of labor.

In another way the geographical distribution of fishes on the earth may affect the South. In polar and sub-arctic waters, the number of species of fishes is smaller but the population of a given species tends to be greater than in tropical or sub-tropical waters. The cod, herring, salmon, haddock, halibut, mackerel, and several of the other large-volume varieties are all northern, cold water fishes. In the tropics is found a great profusion of kinds of fishes, many beautiful and interesting, but not numerous and of little value. The waters of the southeastern United States seem to be a middle ground between the fertile arctic and the relatively barren tropics.

Another fundamental characteristic of the fisheries is that the supply of fish is limited but inexhaustible. The ultimate supply of the products of life is a definite quantity per square mile of sea and is limited by the concentration of the least abundant essential nutrient in the water and by the amount of sunlight, just as the productivity of land is limited to so much vegetation and can nourish such and such a tonnage of animals per acre. In this sense the supply of fish is limited. The productivity of a given area of sea can be estimated, but such an estimate has never been made of the southern continental shelf. In the English Channel the annual productivity is about 4,000 tons of vegetation or 710 tons of glucose per square mile of sea. The actual take of 622 million pounds of useful fish off the southern states is about 1¾ tons per square mile. We do not know what is the basic production of vegetation in our southern waters, nor how much vegetation is required to produce a ton of fish. It would be a proper part of any research program to make such estimates. On any reasonable assumption, the catch looks low indeed.

The supply of any sea fish is inexhaustible. We hear that the whale or some other fish is approaching extinction by over-fishing. Yet it is obviously impossible to exterminate a strictly marine fish for profit, because the profit disappears before the fish does. It is of course true that the capture of fish of a given species thins out the population. As the population is diminished, the amount that can be caught per unit of effort falls off, the cost of catching per man-day increases in inverse proportion to the amount remaining in the waters, and the return of profit diminishes, until a point is arrived at where the fisherman's effort is just rewarded by the wages he could obtain in other employment, or a just barely acceptable return is realized on capital. In this process, of course, the less efficient fisherman or proprietor is forced out before the more efficient, and, at any given rate of capture, if it remains constant, an equilibrium is established between the birth and death rates of the fish. Thus there is an automatic self regulation of any commercial fishery. The amount of fish obtained by intensive exploitation of any particular fishery, when it is in this state of economic balance, may be regarded as the basic economic yield of that fish per square mile of sea surface. It remains to be proved that man can do anything to increase this basic useful yield over a period of years. This statement is no doubt over-simplified, but in any event over-fishing does no permanent harm, because the supply, being self-replenishing from an inexhaustible source of nutrients, will always come back if the pressure of over-fishing is lifted. Much of our legislation and regulation of fisheries is unscientific and based on false assumptions, imaginary conditions, and hoped for effects, and the cost of enforcement is almost never included, as it must be, in arriving at an over-all economic value of a fishery.

Such are the fundamental biological characteristics of the fisheries. Before we pass over to a discussion of the fisheries as an industry, another biological matter must be considered, namely, the nutritive worth of sea foods, particularly in the South.

It will be in order first to examine the state of nutrition in the states bordering this submarine shelf, before attempting an appraisal of what may be on the shelf and how great is the need for it.

Judged by the knowledge of nutrition of thirty years ago, the dietary of the South and of the whole country was generally adequate; we considered ourselves a nation of very well fed people. By the standards of the knowledge of nutrition today, the dietary of the South, and of a large part of the whole country, for that matter, is seriously deficient. Thirty years ago we were taught that a sufficiency of proteins, fats, carbohydrates, and minerals was adequate provided it contained an assortment of about twelve or thirteen chemical elements. Research of the past twenty years has added much to our knowledge of dietary requirements, and greatly extended the list of essentials. It is no longer sufficient that each person consume seventy five or a hundred grams of protein per diem; the protein must contain adequate amounts of at least ten amino acids which the body cannot make for itself but must obtain already made in its supply of food; that is to say, the quality or composition, as well as the quantity, of proteins is of vital importance.

Then there is the long and growing list of organic substances which are essential to life and normal health, but are sufficient in triflingly small quantities, and obtainable only from external sources, preferably the food. These substances include the vitamins. The more these substances are studied, the more complex their relationships appear to be, for not only are there upwards of a dozen of them, but for several of them there are also anti-vitamins, or substances which have the opposite or nullifying effect. It may turn out that the presence and relative amounts of these antis will be as important as the vitamins themselves.

Finally, the list of essential chemical elements has grown from twelve or thirteen to around twenty, among them the "trace" mineral elements, quite essential to good health but sufficient in very small quantities; among these are iodine, necessary for thyroid gland function, fluorine for teeth, and several others, such as copper, manganese, cobalt and zinc, and boron, molybdenum and titanium required by plants. The prevalence of these trace elements in the soil on land is decidedly spotty and in places inadequate, if not entirely absent. If these elements are not present in the soil, they cannot be present in the crops that grow on the soil nor in the flesh of animals that feed on the crops. Widespread deficiencies of iodine and fluorine are known, as well as of cobalt, manganese and zinc, and boron. Though not exactly a "trace" element, calcium is one of the most generally inadequate essentials in our dietary. Calcium and phosphorus are an interrelated pair; both are essential to life but a relative excess of either tends to remove the other from the body tissues. Our diet generally has a deficiency of calcium with respect to phosphorus with a resulting negative calcium balance in the body.

The absence or insufficiency of any of the essentials makes the whole diet inadequate; conversely, a relatively small amount of food containing the essentials, otherwise lacking, can supplement the main bulk of the diet and carry a value and importance all out of proportion to its quantity. In the light of the facts here briefly summarized and from numerous other evidences, clinical as well as statistical, the diet of the southern states is generally inadequate, especially in the quality or supplementary elements, though it must be said that the subject will bear much more study in detail than it has had. We need not here go into the causes of this condition except perhaps to point out that southern agriculture has never specialized in food production so much as in cash crops, such as cotton and tobacco.

In all these circumstances it is clear that what is wanted is, for economic reasons, perhaps an increase in the total quantity of food of native southern production kept and consumed in the

South, and less imported from elsewhere, but in any event, and especially for dietetic reasons, a supplement of quality foods which, when added to the customary diet, will provide the food elements which are necessary but generally inadequate.

How well do sea foods meet these requirements? It must be admitted that the scientific information in hand, obtained experimentally and analytically, on the nutritive values of sea foods for man, is far from what we ought to have. Nevertheless, there is some information, all favorable. A great deal of chemical work has been done on sea water. It is known to contain at least forty-eight chemical elements, including all of those both abundant and rare, that are of value to life. No one has ever been able, by dissolving salts in fresh water, to make artificial sea water that will support marine life satisfactorily. Natural sea water has properties or trace ingredients in proper proportions to provide all the requirements of life, and we do not yet know what all of them are. Marine organisms collect and concentrate some of them in their bodies far beyond their concentration in sea water, and exclude others or have them in reduced concentration in accordance with the requirements of life. We have adequate data to prove the sufficiency of iodine in sea foods generally. It is highly likely that the flesh of fishes contains all the ten necessary amino acids, though in any research program this statement should be proved analytically on a variety of fishes and shellfishes before we count on it absolutely. Likewise, we know that some of the vitamins are in satisfactory quantity in some fishes. There is no doubt as to the fat solubles A and D, both of which have their main commercial sources in fish liver oils. We also know that they are of general prevalence in quite significant quantities in the body fats of many, if not all, fatty fishes. We have little data concerning the water soluble vitamins in sea foods. We know they vary considerably from species to species, and that some of them are present in some fishes in significant amounts, especially in the roes, which are often discarded as food. In all this field, a great deal of routine analytical and experimental feeding should certainly be done.

Perhaps the best direct over-all evidence of the value of fish as a quality-supplement to other and incomplete foods comes from feeding tests on chickens. The diet necessary for the growing of chickens has been scientifically elaborated perhaps as thoroughly as any other requirement in applied dietetics. The bulk, i. e., 90 to 95 per cent, of the chick's diet is cereal, which provides most of the energy for growth and activity. Cereal, however, must be supplemented with essential proteins, minerals, vitamins, and trace elements to secure a high rate of survival, rapid growth, and productivity of eggs as well as a high yield of chicken body weight per unit of total food consumed. From 5 to 10 per cent of supplement to the cereal, if it contains all of these essentials in suitable proportion, is sufficient to make completely effective 95 to 90 per cent of cereal. In well confirmed feeding tests on chicks with the four leading commercial protein supplements—skimmed milk powder, fish meal, meat scrap, and soya-bean flour, fish meal stood at the top of the list, even excelling milk powder, the next best supplement. These results were expressed in terms of weight of chicken per unit of total food containing the different supplements. The results are, in all probability, accounted for by the essential amino acids and the trace mineral elements in marine fish. Menhaden fish meal, besides the known common elements, carbon, hydrogen, oxygen, nitrogen, sulphur, potassium, sodium, calcium, iron, magnesium, phosphorus, iodine, and chlorine, has been shown by spectrographic analysis to contain also aluminum, barium, chromium, copper, fluorine, lead, lithium, manganese, nickel, niobium, silicon, silver, strontium, titanium, vanadium and zinc—in all, twenty-nine of the chemical elements!

These results show the superiority of fish in supplying the essential but small volume ingredients. If we may apply to human nutrition the results from experiments on chicks, they also show how far a small amount of fish can go in making adequate an otherwise inadequate diet. It seems highly probable that, even if the volume of fish in tons procurable in the South is not impressively great, its importance would be so, if it were disseminated well in the general diet of the southern people. As I shall undertake to show later on, it is highly probable that of all food materials known to man those which would rank at the very top in terms of high quality at low cost—all-around value, would be certain fishes, such as herring, sardines, menhaden, and probably also mullet.

The first element in rating the business worth of an industry is competitive cost. Here, too, fish are unsurpassed; indeed, no other animal, domesticated or wild, comes near sea fish in yield per unit of effort, which is what cost comes to in the end. Two examples can be taken where accurate statistics of cost of catching are available for comparison with the cost of producing the most efficient domesticated farm animal, the pig. The United States Department of Agriculture estimates that in raising corn and feeding and marketing pigs on a highly productive farm in Iowa, one man-year of effort will yield 50,000 pounds of pig. In the otter trawl fishery of Boston, one man-year yields 200,000 pounds, or four times as much, of cod, haddock, etc., as one man-year will produce of pig. Considering the trace elements, the cod liver oil and its vitamins A and D, the codfish will probably excel pork in all-around food value, as a supplement to other incomplete foods, even if it does not do so in calories. The pig is by far the most efficient of the farm animals in accounting for its food, so that it is not necessary to consider cattle, sheep, and poultry. In the case of the California sardine, one man-year produces 500,000 pounds, or ten times as much of food, of undoubtedly higher all-around dietetic quality, · as the same effort will produce of pigs! This is the justification for the statement made above that *for all-around dietetic quality and value, per unit of effort or cost to produce, no food product known to man excels or even equals the fatter varieties of ocean fish!*

This difference in efficiency rests on fundamentals, is not industrially accidental, and can never be reversed. It is well known that the production of nitrogenous or protein food by raising crops on land and feeding the produce to animals is one of the most inefficient operations of agriculture, and wasteful of land, soil fertility, and labor. If it were not for the need of quality supplements derivable from animal tissues, the world could feed itself much more efficiently if it went all-out vegetarian. About three-fourths of all the food consumed by warm-blooded animals (including man) goes merely to supply the heat to keep their bodies warm, and a large additional fraction goes to furnish the energy necessary for supporting their own weight and for other body activities. Therefore, the weight of animals is only a small fraction of the total weight of the food they have consumed, and only a tiny fraction of the total remains in their bodies as eggs, as milk, or as flesh suitable for human food at the end of the process. In the fisheries most of this waste is circumvented. Fishes are cold-blooded animals, and none of their food is used to keep their bodies warm; they even do not have to support their own weight and for these reasons are far more efficient converters of their food into flesh than any land animals; in the fisheries no land is used, no fertilizer, and no labor for cultivation, and, as said above, the product is a net addition to our total national wealth. What more could be asked of any food-producing industry?

Indeed, while our subject here is the southern United States, it is well to bear in mind that the world as a whole is none too well off for food, even with its present population. At least half of the world is under-fed, especially in the quality foods, to a far worse extent than the worst anywhere in the United States. Efficient agriculture not only needs fertile soil but at least twenty inches of rainfall annually on reasonably flat land. The rainfall map of the world shows that the area of the earth where these conditions prevail is confined to certain very limited regions of the land. Yet in only one or two spots is full advantage being taken of the sea. I have estimated, for example, that we could take an additional 1,500 million pounds of codfish from the North Atlantic, and as much more herring—or an additional three billion pounds of high quality food, which is nearly as much as the total of edible fish now taken in the entire United States.

Why is it, then, with all these advantages, biologic, economic, and nutritional, that the fisheries have never achieved the dignity and importance of the other natural resource industries? There can be no doubt that full development of the fisheries industry would be a great asset to the South, and one would think that the ordinary forces of competition, enterprise, and discovery would long ago have developed the potentialities. Why have they not done so?

No doubt many tangled factors, biologic, geographic, economic, social, legislative, and those involving public policy have conspired to hold back development of the fisheries industry. It would be the function of a comprehensive program of research to untangle and evaluate these many factors and chart the course of action to be taken.

A most important part of such a program would be in the field of economics and public policy. Expressed broadly, the fisheries have not been very lucrative or attractive to ambitious young men as a career. Aside from a few branches of the fisheries, such as those of the salmon, sardine and otter trawling, where some degree of advantage does exist, the industry as a whole has afforded little more than a labor wage to those who are in it, after allowance is made for business losses from insolvencies and bad debts. As an example, here in North Carolina, the alewives or river herrings are among our lowest-cost, nutritionally most valuable and most prolific fishes; yet the catch in the state in 1938 was almost exactly what it was in 1902, eleven million pounds in both years, and the price was the same, too—one cent per pound. Yet, within that period of thirty-six years, the purchasing power of the money which the fisherman received for his labor declined by at least half. This condition prevails in most sections of the fisheries.

All of the big and prosperous industrial enterprises have a variety of forms of protection from unlimited competition—patents, well known trade marks, favorable locations, possession of sources of raw materials, requirement of large capital investment which excludes the small competitor, organized research, the efficiency that goes with mass production, and many others. It is well known that the basic commodity industries possess these advantages to a lesser extent and are more competitive and less profitable. This factor has been recognized by public policy in agriculture, which, since its product is essential to public welfare, receives the most elaborate assistance from federal and state governments at public expense. The farmer at least has a monopoly on the land which he cultivates, and the government provides him with scientific knowledge in the fields of soil fertility, the breeding of superior stocks of plants and animals, the extermination of pests, farm machinery and engineering, and the preservation and marketing of produce. It also provides exemptions of various kinds and economic and statistical studies, to say nothing of direct personal aid by county agents, support of prices, and financial compensation.

The fisheries, except in a few special cases, have no protection or advantages, natural or acquired. The fish industry is perhaps the most perfect example that could be found of pure, naked competitive commodity economics, without benefit of any government aid, federal or state, that amounts to anything. It does have legislative restrictions or regulation of its operations, which are often unwise and ill advised, and which may hamper its efficiency by prohibiting the most efficient methods of fishing. However, the fish industry pays its share of taxes to support the agricultural program.

An equally difficult field is that of economics. Although fish are, as said above, among the cheapest foods at the source, they are not necessarily cheapest at their destination because of the economic and technical factors of distribution, and the antiquated custom of restricting the choice of fish to Fridays. In the South, although there is now available a fine network of roads, the industry still follows the line of least resistance by shipping a large part of its product to northern markets. Because of their perishability fish do not lend themselves readily to distribution in small towns and in the country in either fresh or frozen condition. The southern states generally are populated in the country and in a great number of villages, small and moderate-size towns, with few large cities, so that the region is generally unfavorable to an economic system of distribution. These conditions have been much improved, however, by the creation of a network of excellent roads.

Perhaps the greatest difficulty of all is in the willingness or unwillingness of people to eat fish. The health appeal is a feeble one and is responded to by only a few "food cranks." As a general rule people do not consume what is good for them, but what they want; and what they want is usually what they have been brought up on, for in nothing are people more set in their ways than in their foods. Nowhere in America, except in New England, have people generally included much fish in their diet, and it will not be easy to change their customs.

The theme of American industrial efficiency is mass production of standardized products and of all possible by-products. In the fisheries these advantages are present in only a few special cases. In the southern states a relatively small production is spread over 2,500 miles of coast line, and, so far as is known, the principal varieties are seasonal and migratory, and therefore too undependable and not in sufficient quantity of standard varieties at any point to support mass production, use of automatic machinery, steady employment of labor, and working up of by-products at low cost.

Most fishes are less than 50 per cent edible as human food. The unsuitable portions make excellent fish meal for poultry. If all the human-edible portions of the 317 million pounds of southern fish, exclusive of menhaden, were prepared and shipped separately to market, not only would shipping weights be cut in half, with greatly improved convenience to consumers, but the inedible residues, if available in sufficient concentration, would produce 32 thousand tons of fish meal, which could supplement or reinforce 320 thousand tons of poultry feed. Yet, as things are, there is little, if any, fish meal manufacture in the South, and the raw material for it goes into the consumer's kitchen garbage pail, after freight has been paid on it.

Surely all these factors of government policy and economics merit a place, perhaps first place, in any scheme of research in the South.

In the field of marine biology, the larger duty of research is to appraise the productivity of, and the values in, these waters, collectively and broadly, as well as in detail, on the principal species, as a guide to public policy and regulation. To begin, the dietetic values of sea foods should be determined by chemical analysis and experimental feeding far more extensively than they have ever been before. Determinations should be made on the chief varieties of sea foods for amino acids, vitamins, calcium, and mineral trace elements; and comparative feeding tests should be made to establish what the nutritive worth of sea foods really is.

A chemical and biological appraisal should be made of the fundamental productivity of the 175,000 square miles of sea surface hereabouts—what there is, and whether we are already drawing too heavily on the supply or whether the resource is still largely untapped. If production can be increased, then where, in what species, when, how much? And what shall we do with the product? Methods are available for estimating basic production of vegetation, and, therefore, of all life at sea. Such studies would indicate whether emphasis in public policy should be in encouragement of exploitation or in restriction and regulation.

Such studies might also show that the growth of vegetation in sea water outruns the conversion of that vegetation into animal life, and that vegetarian fishes might be advantageously transplanted from other parts of the world, such as the California or Mediterranean sardine, to increase the total amount of grazing and therefore of fish substance in the sea.

It is important to remember that fishes cannot pass between the Atlantic and the Pacific without traversing polar or subpolar water, and few fishes can do either, since most species live within very narrow ranges of temperature, and few of them could successfully traverse the Atlantic from east to west. Much valuable and successful transplanting was done by the United States Fish Commission in the 1870's and 1880's, but this has now been largely forgotten. The shad and striped bass fisheries of the Pacific Coast originated in this way. Many areas of the world have valuable species which cannot come here under their own steam, for example, the soupfin shark of the Pacific Coast, whose liver is the richest known source of vitamin A, which in turn is obtainable commercially only from fish livers. The visible supply of this vitamin is far below the probable postwar demand for food fortification, and it is the only one of the common vitamins not synthesized, and not likely to be. The soupfin shark inhabits waters up to 70 deg. F. on the Pacific coast and its abundance has declined seriously there, where it has already yielded millions of dollars of value. If it is deemed safe to do so, this fish might be introduced to the Atlantic as the basis of a new and profitable industry. The stone bass of South Africa is another excellent source of this vitamin. Indeed, this whole field of the possibilities of transplantation is hardly explored at all. There are many places in the world which have aquatic conditions similar to these here in the South—around South Africa, Argentina, and the whole southeast coast of Asia and the Indies.

Airplane transportation now makes possible what would have been impossible in the past, namely, transport of fish eggs or delicate young fish from distant places. It now becomes possible to bring here the snoek from South Africa, the pearl oyster from the Indian Ocean, the Japanese crab, and any of a great number of other valuable species. However, all questions in this field go back to the fundamental volume of plant production in these waters, and for that reason a measurement of chemical fertility and the basic yield of vegetation is essential to any really far reaching program of research.

Regulation of the fisheries should be based solely on knowledge of the factors which control animal populations, and should have as its purpose the highest possible permanent level of yield. Any proposed restrictive measure should of course be demonstrated or have in its favor a high degree of scientific probability that it will actually accomplish its purpose. In 1863-65, T. H. Huxley, then a member of a Royal Commission investigating the condition of the fisheries of Great Britain, laid down the principle *"No restriction without scientific justification,"* which was enacted by Parliament in 1868 and has ruled in Britain ever since. Such regulation as we now have, differing greatly as it does from state to state, and even from county to county, is usually the result of attempts by legislators to compromise the pulling and hauling between sport and commercial fishermen, and between groups of the latter, so as to keep everybody reasonably happy. Regulation often takes the form of prohibiting use of the most economical methods of catching, such as trawlers and pound nets, on the ground that they are too destructive. The object of any fishery is to kill. If regulation is needed, the amount, rather than the method, of catching is the thing to be controlled. The most efficient method is always to be encouraged. Scientific studies of the factors that govern fish populations deserve a prominent place in any research program, and should be the basis of legislative control.

A good system of collection of statistics is the basis of a survey both of potentials and of regulatory measures. Without good statistics, neither can be done well or wisely. There is not in existence and never has been an adequate statistical service for the fisheries. The U. S. Fish & Wildlife Service takes a canvass of southern fisheries about once in five years. This is obviously sufficient to give only a general idea of production. Adequate service should be continuous and uniform over a natural biological area, such as the southern states from Chesapeake Bay to Texas. It would be advantageous to have a uniform system in all of the southern states.

Biological research can also point out what fishes are excessively destructive of other fishes, as blue fish and striped bass are known to be, and encourage the catching of them; the starfishes are well known to be highly destructive of oysters, and make good fish meal when dried and ground. Biologists can seek new grounds and the hibernating places of known economic species, make surveys of other economic animals and plants such as sea weeds, and prospect for sources of wanted materials such as 7-dehydrocholesterol in the molluscs now used to make vitamin D.

In most of the sea fisheries man is singularly helpless to do much of a constructive nature to improve biological conditions because of the magnitude of the sea and inaccessibility of its contents. But with the inshore molluscs, such as oysters, which are attached and accessible, man can do much. In fact, oyster culture is extensively and profitably practiced, the product is elegant and nutritious, and an excellent source of calcium and the mineral trace elements. Oyster culture is at its best along shores which are indented with bays, sounds, and lagoons, such as those of North Carolina, Florida, and Louisiana. Here there is no practical limit, except that of finding the market, to the possible expansion of a lucrative industry.

A fascinating extension of this general idea is in the possibilities of culture of other plankton-consuming marine animal species in enclosed bodies of salt or brackish water. The oyster lives on plankton or microscopic vegetation. The limiting fertilizers of plankton are believed to be nitrogen, phosphorus, silicon, and, in water of higher temperature, possibly carbon dioxide. If, now, we seal off a salt water lake of, say, a square mile, and supply artificially these three elements, we should get a very profuse growth of plankton, in which animals that subsist on plankton should grow very rapidly. This method of aquatic farming would be very different from that of cultivating trout, now commercially practised, for in trout culture the whole food must be produced and supplied to the fish. Here we supply only the least abundant elemental traces of the natural fertilizers, just as we do on farms, and let nature produce the food where it is wanted.

Results of experiments on fertilizing sea water, recently reported from Scotland, indicate the practical possibilities. Two lochs or inclosed bays of salt water were chosen for the experiment. One of these, having an area of about eighteen acres and an average depth of two meters, with 70,000 cubic meters of water, was fertilized in the first year with 600 pounds of sodium nitrate and 400 pounds of superphosphate, or 45 kg. of N and 17 kg. of P, but no silicate. The other lake near by received no fertilizer. In the fertilized lake, additional fertilizers were put in during the second year, quantitative measurements of the plankton or microscopic plant life were made before, during, and after fertilization, and the amounts of the fertilizers in the water were determined chemically. Immediately after the fertilizers were added there was a dramatic rise in vegetation of three to four times the original amount, and the fertilizers disappeared from the water within four or five days, showing extremely rapid and complete utilization.

Since microscopic vegetation is the nourishment, directly or indirectly, of all animal life, the growth of animals in the lake immediately leaped forward. Marked baby flounders put into the lake grew in thirteen months an amount equal to two or three years in the North Sea, itself a very rich feeding ground. The average density of the bottom fauna increased 240 per cent and the "useful" bottom fauna, suitable for food for flounders, increased 215 per cent; the lake became, for the time, one of the richest areas of marine life on record.

These experiments, obviously preliminary and subject to much improvement, point unmistakably to great possibilities. Nutrients are converted, under suitable conditions, almost immediately into living substance and the whole chain of life is started. What the upper limit of such conversion would be with increased and continuous addition of fertilizers, instead of small amounts occasionally, we do not know, but it must be very great. With proper control by skillful biologists to establish the best possible and economically most valuable chain of consumed and consumers, such enclosed bodies of water could become veritable food factories.

The coasts of North Carolina, Florida, and Louisiana are particularly inviting prospects for success in such undertakings. Perhaps no better place could be found in the world than the sounds, bays, and lagoons enclosed by the off-shore sand bar of North Carolina, less than two hundred miles from where we now stand. It is easy to visualize an enclosed or semi-enclosed salt water lake, with a soup of plankton, and a well chosen assortment of plankton converters leading by one further step directly to human food. Oysters, clams, and scallops are plankton consumers, and with perhaps a trace of copper added to the water should grow with extraordinary speed. Shad could be landlocked and grown for market. Baby menhaden or alewives, which are also plankton consumers, ought to make perfect sardines which could be grown right at the canneries. Bottom feeders, such as crabs, should take care of the sedimented plankton.

I have made a few rough calculations of the quantitative relationships. Most fishes contain about 20 per cent protein, exclusive of fat, or $3\frac{1}{2}$ per cent nitrogen, and about $\frac{1}{15}$ as much phosphorus. This works out to about five tons of fish to a ton of sodium nitrate, which at $27 per ton would be $\frac{1}{2}$ cent per pound for the fish produced. It is doubtful that the land farmer can make as efficient use of fertilizer as this. In the first place, because of the expense of bagging the fertilizer and the lost motion and expense of retail distribution, he has to pay nearly twice the bulk f.o.b. works price, whereas the marine farmer could have his fertilizer delivered in bulk in car lots. Then, if in our lake some of the fertilizer is frittered away to useless animals, much of the farmer's fertilizer is drained away by rainfall and seepage, or goes to useless stems, leaves, and roots of plants. It would be a proper experimental research to determine and account for the fertilizers used.

Preliminary to such actual experiments it would be necessary to make a general reconnaissance of coastal waters, their salinities and fluctuations in salinity, income of fresh water from streams and rain, and loss by evaporation and escape to the sea. Chemical analysis should be made of the known minimal essentials and of acidity or alkalinity. The dissolved free and combined CO_2 content of the water must be included in these studies, for this is the only source of carbon; it is less soluble in warm than in cold water and therefore might be a limiting factor in southern waters. The actual biological experiments on small bodies of water should be designed to furnish the data from which calculations could be made on costs, efficiency, and general worthwhileness of artificial fertilization as an economic undertaking.

A sportsman's paradise could be created in such manner by including game fishes in the fauna, but it should be borne in mind that sport fishing and economic food production are not the same thing and should not be combined in the same body of water. Game fishes are predators, consume a great quantity of other fishes, and therefore are not the most economic sources of food; yet they should not be scorned, for, after all, sport and recreation need no defense, and economically a sportsman may spend up to $100 for each fish he catches, making good business for hotels and boat operators and promoting general prosperity in resort places.

Undertakings to fertilize large bodies of water would probably be unsuitable for private enterprise, for obvious reasons. If careful scientific study should find them sound and practicable, it might be in order for the state to provide the fertilizers at public expense, a small modicum of aid to the fishermen as a parallel to the bountiful public aid to agriculture. A few thousand tons of fertilizer would produce a few million pounds of highest quality sea foods.

In the field of technology, a great deal of work needs to be done for the development of the fishery resource industries of the South, but, if nothing more were done within the next five years than to divert the 300 million pounds of menhaden from industrial manufacture of oil and meal to consumption as human food in the South, the whole effort of a research institute would be well repaid. It is doubtful that, at the commercial value in 1938 of 0.29 cents a pound, with its exceptional fat content, high grade proteins, vitamins, calcium, and all the trace elements, a greater bargain than the menhaden could be found in the entire world of food of the kind needed in the South, even after the cost of preserving and distributing is added. To be compared with menhaden's cost of less than $\frac{1}{3}$ cent per pound is 7.6 cents per pound for hogs in the same year. Surely some satisfactory method can be found for preserving menhaden and getting it distributed in the South. I see no reason why baby menhaden would not make excellent sardines, the better grades of which are imported at high prices from Norway, France, and Portugal. This is only one example of the possibilities of technological research in southern fisheries. Much valuable and even necessary work can be done in applying the techniques of freezing, canning, salting, etc., to the distribution of fish in the South, and the manufacture of by-products.

Measured by any appropriate standard—such as the addition fisheries can make to the South's natural resources, or their potential contribution to a well-balanced nutrition—one of the South's needs—or the low cost of additional delectable foods to bring esthetic variety to the daily diet, or increased opportunities for gainful employment—measured by any and all of these standards, the fishing resources of the South rank high in their promise that a well and imaginatively planned program of research, diligently executed, will bring rich results. A neglected field offers the greatest opportunities. No field in the South has been more neglected than that of her fisheries.

RESEARCH AND THE SOUTHERN FARMER

George J. Wilds

PRESIDENT, COKER'S PEDIGREED SEED COMPANY
HARTSVILLE, SOUTH CAROLINA

I T HAS FREQUENTLY been stated that America is great because of her natural resources. This is partly true but it is not the whole story. With natural resources even greater than those of the United States, there are some nations which have not advanced far beyond the primitive stage. There is something lacking.

A. L. Ward, writing for the National Cotton Seed Crushers Association, expressed it well when he said that America's greatness lies in her human resources and her skill in using them.

But this also is not the whole story. I believe that America is great because of the ability, the inventiveness, the initiative, the faith, and the courage of her people, and because, under the American system of free enterprise, her people have had the opportunity and encouragement to use these qualities in the development of her mighty natural resources.

The method by which we in America employ our various abilities is generally referred to as "industry." It may be farming, mining, manufacturing, or one of the service trades, but, whatever the field of effort, "industry" is simply the way we make our living. It is the way we employ our natural and human resources, the way we transform the raw materials of nature into useful products, and the way we provide ourselves with the necessities and comforts of life.

Industry, in turn, is born of the two great fundamental approaches—research and education; research to improve the old and seek the new; education to disseminate the findings of research into those channels where they will make their maximum contribution to society. There is no better example of research being applied to education than that which is being employed right here by this great institution whose Sesquicentennial we are here to celebrate.

We use the word "research" so often, and we are all so familiar with its general meaning, that I wonder sometimes if we are completely aware of its full and rightful implication. Dr. Julian F. Smith of the Institute of Textile Technology, Charlottesville, Virginia, has given an interesting interpretation. Says Smith, "Research is to ask nature questions and get her answers."

Man, if he is willing to play the game of life with nature as a partner and not as an opponent, is not confined to guesswork. He can ask questions and get answers. But great skill is required of the questioner and it is sometimes an arduous task to interpret the answer. When nature seems to answer a question wrongly, it is because man either asked the question in the wrong way or misread the response. Also, nature isn't particularly concerned about man's time or patience, for to interpret properly one of nature's answers may call for a dozen new questions, each bringing in some new ones of its own.

In seeking nature's answers, painstaking and systematic experimentation has preceded every worth-while development, whether it be in agriculture or in manufacturing. In fact, progress has been proportionate to the extent and quality of research, and in no country has research been so broadly employed, and its benefits so widely used, as in our own. When we consider for a moment the great industries of America, which are so symbolic of her industrial might, we can measure their success and their greatness in almost direct proportion to their programs of research. The DuPont Corporation, which enjoys a substantial portion of its volume of business from products that did not exist ten years ago; the Ford Motor Company, which introduced mass-production methods into the automobile industry; the Thomas Edison enterprises, which created a whole new field of products, previously unknown, but which have brought untold health and happiness to millions of people; General Electric, Standard Oil, McCormick-Deering, and many others—all bear witness to the power of research, and give America a standard of living not approached by any other country.

The story of agricultural research in this country is as inter-

esting and romantic as any phase of our development. One of
the earliest records of research in this country applies to agriculture. In the year 1669, according to Carrier, "The Lords
Proprietors sent an expedition to settle on the Ashley River
which is memorable because of the provisions made for the
fostering and encouragement of agriculture. Joseph West was
placed in command of the expedition. . . .

"West was instructed to stop at the Barbadoes and procure a
supply of: cottonseed, Indigo seed, Ginger roots . . . some canes
[sugar canes], Olive setts, half a dozen young sows and boare.

"Special care was ordered to be taken of all these and the first
efforts at culture should be experimental to 'find out the soil to
which each species of plants was best adapted and the season of
the year most favorable for planting,' also to provide seeds and
cuttings for the use of the plantation. Cattle were to be imported
from Virginia."

Carrier further states that "the experimental work was to be
done with a 'man or two,' the rest of the people to be 'employed
about planting Indian Corne, Beanes, Pease, Turnips, Carrots,
and (Sweet) Potatoes for provisions.' 'Information as to the
proper season for planting corn, beans and pease, was to be obtained from the natives.' " This in 1669.

Thoughtful, scientific leaders in subsequent years appeared on
the scene. Men whose contribution to the progress of our agricultural development is more appreciated with the passing of
the years; men who thought through the problems, and then put
science to work in their solution.

Jonathan Lucas, of Charleston, prior and subsequent to 1800,
harnessed the tide, both ebb and flow, to operate his rice mill,
and used this phenomenon to dam up fresh water and irrigate
his fields of rice.

David R. Williams, of Society Hill, South Carolina (period of
greatest activity—1808-1830), a writer, publisher, member of
Congress, governor of the state, and a general in the war of 1812,
pioneered in cotton manufacturing and in the manufacturing of
cottonseed products. He reported his experience in using cottonseed meal as a feed and predicted the use of cottonseed oil for
human consumption. He conducted experiments to determine
the effect of spacing on cotton and, from the results obtained,

recommended for maximum yield three-foot rows, a hand width in the drill. For length and strength of fiber he recommended greater distances.

Thomas G. Clemson, founder of the college that bears his name, helped to organize the "Agricultural Bureau," now the United States Department of Agriculture. (His period of greatest activity was 1865-1888.)

David R. Coker, Hartsville, South Carolina (1870-1938) a scientist, philanthropist, and plant-breeder of world renown, developed full-length short and long staple, upland cottons, with wilt and disease resistance and higher yields per acre. His work in grains was also outstanding.

I mention these men from South Carolina only because I happen to be familiar with their work. Others were equally distinguished in their contributions to agriculture.

There is no agricultural product of importance, the development of which is not closely allied with research and experimentation. Cotton, so synonomous with the South, provides one of the most interesting studies in the book of American agriculture. Cotton was introduced into the English colonies in Virginia and the Carolinas soon after they were founded, but its expansion was slow because of the difficulty of separating lint and seed and because of the greater profit in tobacco. It remained for research, the invention of the cotton gin by Eli Whitney in 1793, to give cotton growing and manufacture the impetus that it needed to become America's greatest export crop.

But cotton research did not stop with the invention of the cotton gin by Whitney—it only began. We hear of cotton's backwardness, from a research standpoint, so often that we are inclined to overlook some of the progress that has been made.

Forward-thinking leaders many years ago recognized the fact that the foundation of a cotton improvement program must come in the development of improved strains and varieties. Government and private breeders set out to make cotton growing more profitable by developing varieties that would improve per-acre yields and that would give better staple lengths. They were successful to a large degree. Then along came the boll weevil and the cotton industry in America appeared doomed. Some of the great agricultural writers predicted that within ten years from the advent of the weevil cotton growing in this country would bè extinct, and that Southern farmers must look to other sources of revenue. The plant breeders set about to develop earlier maturing varieties—varieties that would set a crop ahead of the mass emergence of the boll weevil. You know the story; although we still lose many millions each year to the boll weevil, the development of the early maturing varieties, plus the successful research on methods of controlling the weevil with insecticides, gave new birth to the cotton growing industry.

But the breeders' problem was not ended. Cotton diseases became a serious handicap to production in many areas, and it was necessary for the breeders to set about on a program of breeding disease-resistant varieties. This work has been successful to the extent that some of our best per-acre yields are now made in areas where some of the diseases are most prevalent. Cotton diseases, however, still take an annual toll of over two million bales.

But again new problems entered the picture. Within recent years, and especially since the war started, the attention of the cotton industry has been focused sharply on competition from synthetic fibers—fibers that are uniform in strength and length and that are being produced on a mass-production basis at a cheaper and cheaper rate. It became generally recognized that breeders not only should seek to develop varieties that would give higher yields, higher lint percentage, earlier maturity, and disease resistance, but that efforts must be turned toward developing cottons with stronger fibers, finer fibers, and greater fiber uniformity. The United States Department of Agriculture made testing facilities available that enabled the breeders, textile mills, and others to get scientific tests on small samples to determine these fiber properties. Within the four or five years that these testing facilities have been available, much progress has been made, and many cotton leaders believe that we are entering a new era of cotton marketing and processing, based on the breeding, production, and processing of cotton to exacting specifications.

I, for one, am not willing by any means to admit that cotton is licked. Thoughtfully planned and carefully executed programs of scientific research and experimentation, beginning with the breeder and carrying through all phases to the manufacturer, plus revitalized educational and selling programs, will keep cotton competitive.

Leaving the breeder, we enter into the broad research fields of cultural practices, including planting and spacing methods, insect and disease control, fertilization, cultivation, land utilization, and many other features. The United States Department of Agriculture, co-operating with the various state experiment stations, has performed magnificently in these fields. Even at this time these groups are in the process of surveying, revaluating, revitalizing and more adequately co-ordinating their programs of cotton-production research, determined to meet cotton's challenge squarely and intelligently.

The American Farm Economic Association at this time is engaged in launching a broad, fundamental research program that should prove of inestimable value to our cotton economy. Co-operating with the various state educational institutions and the United States Department of Agriculture, they are undertaking the most comprehensive study of southern land utilization ever attempted. It is just as important to know what lands should not be in cotton as to know what lands should be in cotton. It is equally important to work out land-utilization programs for farms taken out of cotton production. These are some of the objectives of the study now being planned.

Just as progress is being made in breeding and cultural practices, so it is being made in the field of harvesting, handling, and processing.

The South has been cursed with an abundance of cheap labor. The result is that our methods of producing, harvesting, and handling cotton have, in many respects, become antiquated. We sat by and watched the wheat growers, the corn growers, the cane growers, the fruit and vegetable growers, and most of the other farmers of the nation become highly mechanized in their operations, but we plodded along with our cheap hand labor. It took a war to bring us to our senses.

Within the past two years we have heard more about mechanized cotton production, harvesting, and handling than in all the years previous. For the past two years one of the largest Mississippi Delta plantations has gone completely mechanized. They plant and cultivate with four-row power equipment. They control weeds with a flame-throwing machine. They chop with a mechanical chopper. They control insects and defoliate with an airplane. They harvest with seven mechanical harvesters. Costs of production have been reduced several cents per pound.

The manufacturers of cotton are not idle by any means. The war has stimulated their research by leaps and bounds. Several big and well financed organizations are in the picture, seeking to improve manufacturing techniques and to develop new uses.

One of the most interesting new uses is cotton insulating material, developed by the Department of Agriculture. It has possibilities of consuming as much as one half million bales annually. Many people believe that chemical treatments of cotton will open up a whole new field of cotton consumption. Already we are seeing substantial volumes going into laminates for plastics. As synthetic fibers are developed and expanded, we find more and more cotton going into blends with these synthetics, because most of them do not have some of the more desirable qualities of cotton.

Since the beginning of the war many of the leading textile mills have set up large research organizations under their own roofs. The mills are becoming research-minded. During the past few months two conferences of breeders and spinners have been held, looking toward continued progress in the development of cottons to meet exacting spinning requirements.

When historians speak of cotton they stress its use as a textile material, but again it remained for research to discover that the tiny cotton seed, originally considered a valueless nuisance, contains a treasure undreamed of during the thousands of years that cotton was produced for its lint alone.

The National Cottonseed Products Association has given us some interesting information concerning cottonseed. Although centuries ago the people of India and China devised crude methods for obtaining oil from cottonseed to be used in their lamps and for medicinal purposes, it is only during the past fifty years that research has pointed the way to the great wealth which the seed actually contains.

The uses for cottonseed oil range from shortening and margarine to miner's oil and soap; the uses of its kernel, from livestock and poultry feed to linoleum, synthetic leather, and phonograph records; its hulls, from roughage feed to chemicals for use in the manufacture of synthetic rubber; its linters, from upholstery and absorbent cotton to rayon, high-grade smokeless gun powder, and moving picture film. Certainly, in the story of the once discarded cottonseed do we find an outstanding example of science and research at work in behalf of agriculture.

Let us look for a moment at another great American crop—corn—and see what research has done for it. It was in 1933 that the first hybrid corn was planted on a commercial scale. Iowa planted only o.7 per cent of her acreage to the new hybrids and her average yield was 40 bushels per acre. Ten years later, in 1943, she planted 99.3 per cent of her acreage to hybrids and her yield was 61 bushels per acre. Illinois, during the same period, increasing her acreage of hybrids from about one half of one per cent to 96.1 per cent, increased her yield from 27 bushels to 50 bushels. Not all of that increase in yield is attributable to hybrid corn, of course, but certainly it has been a highly instrumental factor.

It is interesting to note what we in this section were doing with our corn during that some period, while Illinois and Iowa were stepping up their per-acre production over 50 per cent. During the ten-year period from 1933 to 1943 North Carolina's yield increased from 18½ to 22 bushels per acre, and South Carolina's from 14½ to 16 bushels per acre. Neither state was planting more than 2 per cent of its acreage in hybrids.

It is encouraging, though, that government and private agencies in these two states, as well as a number of the other southern states, have vigorous programs of research under way to develop hybrid corns especially adapted for southern culture. These, plus radically new fertilizer practices, give promise of doubling our per-acre yield. In North Carolina the experimenters are using hybrid seed and determining by research the proper rate of seed and fertilization to obtain maximum yield on the various soil types.

It hasn't been many years ago that our tobacco fields were a discouraging sight to look upon. The stalks ranged from runts to giants. Some were infested with disease while others went through unharmed. Some ripened early while others ripened late, and some were coarse-leafed and some were fine. Farmers were losing millions of dollars annually in both production and grade. Then research came to the rescue. Through the work of experiment stations and private breeders, we have seen tobacco varieties standardized. Now we look upon fields that are uniform in appearance, in maturity, and, to a far greater extent, in grade. Pure seed stocks are available to tobacco farmers, and yields have increased tremendously. Work is now progressing rapidly on the development of disease-resistant varieties, which are adding more to quality and returns. If it were not for the breeding and introduction of the Granville wilt resistant (Oxford 26), fifty thousand acres of the best North Carolina tobacco soils would be unsafe for planting. This one tobacco will easily contribute over four million dollars annually to the income of the North Carolina farmers.

Let us look for a moment at the small grains—oats, wheat, barley, and rye. Again through the efforts of our experiment stations and our private breeders, research is putting more millions into the pocketbooks of southern farmers. Where once we saw our grain fields ravaged with disease and insect losses, we now see varieties that are resistant to these plagues, that are far outproducing varieties we knew in the past, and that are giving us the uniformity so necessary for quality. Southern farmers are learning that they can grow small grains profitably. Since 1930 the wheat acreage in the southeastern states has increased 180 per cent, and in 1943 the second largest cotton state, Mississippi, produced more wheat per acre than any major wheat-growing state.

In small grains, as in other fields of agricultural research, we have not finished the research job by any means; in 1943 alone disease losses in oats and wheat were over 26 million dollars. When we pause to pat ourselves on the back because we have bred a variety that is resistant to a disease, our patting is very often interrupted by the appearance of a new disease, or a new race of an old one, which comes up to remind us that nature isn't of a mind to play with one who is prone to stop and pat himself on the back. But we are making progress; we are learning a lot; and southern agriculture is the beneficiary.

In 1921 the sugar industry of Louisiana produced 331,000 tons of sugar. Then disaster came in the form of Mosaic disease, red rot, and root rot. By 1926 the Louisiana sugar industry was bankrupt, its production down to 48,000 tons.

A co-operative research program was organized among the office of Sugar Plants Investigations of the Department of Agriculture, the Louisiana Agricultural Experiment Station, and the American Sugar Cane League. In a short time disease-resistant varieties of cane were bred, and the sugar industry started its comeback. In 1938 Louisiana produced 491,000 tons; more than ten times its 1926 production. Here, certainly, is an excellent example of research saving an industry.

The story of research in the fruit and vegetable industry is a never-ending one; it is a story that parallels the growth and development of trucking as a major southern industry.

By way of example, take the matter of fertilization. For many years in the past we have thought about fertilization mostly with regard to what we term "major" elements—nitrogen, phosphate, and potash. We have known that there were "minor" elements, such as manganese, boron, zinc, iron, and copper, but they had not come in for too much consideration. "We are now finding out that these so-called 'minor' elements are minor only when considered from the standpoint of the quantities needed—not in importance," states Dr. L. G. Willis, of your own state, a pioneer in these investigations.

The Florida Experiment Station, under the direction of Dr. Harold Mowry, has accomplished outstanding results in this field. He states: "Deficiency symptoms and application rates and methods have been determined for one or more of the six elements—copper, zinc, manganese, magnesium, boron and iron— on citrus, tung, corn, pecans, peaches, avocados, mangoes, celery, beans, tomatoes, potatoes, pasture plants and numerous ornamentals, with the list increasing. Few crops would be grown on the organic soils of the Everglades without copper, and the tung tree is a failure in many areas without zinc. Heavy annual celery losses due to 'crack-stem' were entirely overcome with boron, while carpet grass sod with a single application of a combination of copper, zinc and manganese was established in a few months where ordinarily two years would be required. Citrus nutrition practices have undergone a pronounced transformation and now include zinc, copper, manganese and magnesium and occasionally boron and iron.

"Appreciation of the values of the minor or secondary elements and of research on their use may be gauged by the magnitude of application. During the 12-month period ending June 30, 1944, Florida consumed for agricultural purposes some 19 million pounds of copper sulfate, nearly 23 million pounds of manganese sulfate, some $3^{1}/_{3}$ million pounds of zinc sulfate, and large quantities of magnesium." Last season, Florida produced over 260,000 carloads of quality fruits and vegetables. While by no means wholly responsible, the minor elements played no minor role in that accomplishment.

Dr. H. P. Cooper, of Clemson College, in his research as to the need of lime, has found 80 per cent of the South Carolina soils to be too acid for profitable agriculture. In the correction of this condition he has found that the use of lime brings about an aggravation of minor element deficiencies. These deficiencies must be recognized and corrected.

Just as research is on the move in behalf of our crops, so it is on the move in behalf of an expanded livestock industry in the South. Since 1930 milk production in the South has increased 130 per cent, and beef cattle production 40 per cent. Through research and education we are improving our pastures, our feeding practices, our quality, and our general know-how. Through experimentation we are learning how to fit a livestock program into our regular farming program.

In 1935 a group of scientists, chemists, agricultural leaders, and industrialists met in Chicago to form the National Farm Chemurgic Council. Chemurgy (a coined word from the Egyptian "Chemi," the origin of Chemistry, and the Greek word "Ergon," meaning work), is not a new type of research. However, in giving it a new name, Chemurgy was distinguished as a type of research. It means putting science to work in industry in behalf of agriculture. It means maximum utilization of maximum production.

One of the first undertakings of the National Farm Chemurgic Council was to co-operate with Dr. Charles A. Herty of Savannah, Georgia, in the development of southern slash pine as a source of paper stock and newsprint. This work is well known to all of us. Taking the once almost valueless southern slash pine, Dr. Herty perfected a process that made paper making a major southern industry, and gave the nation paper stock and newsprint at a time when supplies were getting dangerously low.

A most interesting project in chemurgy is at work right here at this institution, under the direction of Dr. Frank K. Cameron, Professor of Chemistry. I refer to the work that is being done on the utilization of the whole cotton plant. It envisages, as I understand it, the production of a cheap source of cellulose, at the same time conserving the oil from the seed. While it is not expected that the production of whole cotton will take the place of cotton as we now know it, there is a real possibility of gaining new markets that our present product cannot touch.

An early development in the chemurgic list of achievements was the discovery and development of industrial uses for soy beans. Little known in this country twenty-five years ago, the soy bean reached a 1943 production of more than 140 million bushels, and its uses in industry are truly amazing.

At Laurel, Mississippi, there stands a tribute to science and agriculture working hand-in-hand—a plant manufacturing starch from potatoes. Erected in 1934 by the Bureau of Agricultural and Industrial Chemistry, the plant has served as an experimental project to perfect the system of extraction of starch from sweet potatoes, and in so doing has established a market for this high quality starch far beyond their ability to produce. It has been found that sweet potato starch possesses qualities of tapioca starch in specialized applications for which corn starch is less well or not at all suited. It has established a market for itself for baking, for pudding mixtures, confectionery, etc. It is being used for remoistening gums in the manufacture of envelopes, stamps, and labels. At the same time it is giving superior performance, and bringing a premium, for laundering starch.

When nature answered the question of how starch could be made from sweet potatoes, then it became necessary to ask nature another question, "How can we increase the starch content of sweet potatoes?" The results of this experimentation have been striking. Dr. Julian C. Miller, of Louisiana State University, reports the development of a variety with 10 per cent higher starch content than the standard variety, Porto Rico.

Following the lead of the great Negro scientist, Dr. George Washington Carver, we find many of our southern institutions making a great deal of progress with various applications of the sweet potato. Dr. Miller sent a small sample of dehydrated sweet potatoes to the Army in 1942. The Army was interested and wanted a two-thousand-pound sample for a feeding test. The results were so good that by last year the Army used 20 million pounds of this product, and a new industry was born.

As a result of the findings at the Laurel Starch Plant, and the work of Dr. Miller and others on sweet potato breeding and culture, the United States Sugar Corporation at Clewiston, Florida, is now constructing, at a cost of seven million dollars, a starch plant that will have a daily out-turn of 150 tons of starch.

So goes the story of research and southern agriculture. It is an endless story of patience, hardships, disappointments, and failures. But it is also a story of successes.

Many of the reasons for the failures are obvious. The South is rich in natural resources. We have two thirds of the nation's soils with a rainfall of 40 inches or more. Millions of acres of this land are not in cultivation. We possess 193 million acres of forest lands. We have sold many of these virgin forests for a song, or have seen them swept away by forest fires. Twenty-seven per cent of the electric power is produced in the eleven southern states; yet millions of people still use the most primitive methods of lighting and heating their homes. Large quantities of phosphate, lime, sulphur, gypsum, lead, zinc, asbestos, asphalt, and many other products are in or under our soil, waiting for research to mine and develop them. More than two thirds of the nation's oil and natural gas are in the South, oftentimes sold for a pittance to enrich other sections.

The South is also rich in its human resources. We have the people, but look at their plight—one half of the farm people of the nation live in the South on one third of the nation's cultivated land—and receive one fourth of the nation's agricultural income.

The average income of the South's people, as a whole, per capita, is $25.50 a month. Millions of our homes are classed as substandard and unfit for human habitation in a civilized country. We have had the most eroded soils, the poorest housing, the greatest illiteracy, and the lowest health record in the country. Truly we have been the Number One problem of our nation.

But we believe that today we see the distant dawning of a New Day for our Southland. Our eyes are open. We have commenced to learn. We have called upon education and research to help us with our job.

Now, more than ever before, we must think and plan carefully. Through co-ordination and co-operation we must pool all of our resources and our abilities, thereby giving assurance that southern agriculture and the nation as a whole will reap full benefit from our research efforts.

RESEARCH, THE FOUNDATION OF THE FUTURE

THE MORAL RESPONSIBILITY OF
RESEARCH

David E. Lilienthal

CHAIRMAN, TENNESSEE VALLEY AUTHORITY

T HE OPPORTUNITY this occasion affords me to salute the
University of North Carolina on its 150th anniversary is
an honor that I highly prize. This university is characterized by a rare combination of qualities. It has the stability of
age—being the oldest existing state university in the country—
with the vigor and the forward-look of youth.

It is, therefore, quite appropriate that you have chosen to
signalize your 150th birthday by a conference on research and
regional welfare. For research, too, combines these qualities of
age and of youth. Research is built upon all that has gone before; but it searches the sky ahead. May I say at the very outset
how greatly impressed I was by the little booklet entitled "The
Need for Research," issued prior to this conference by your
Sesquicentennial Committee. This brochure deserves the widest
possible reading not only throughout the South, but everywhere
throughout the country. And such a wide reading and understanding of what is so clearly and beautifully written therein
will certainly further the purposes of this conference more than
anything I could possibly say tonight. With what has been said
in this leaflet, and in earlier papers on your conference program,
I find little basis for difference.

It would be quite pointless for me to repeat what has previously been said and written in the course of the proceedings of
this conference about the need for research or its importance in
the development of the South and of the country. Assuming that
what I shall say will be projected against a background of what
other speakers and the author of "The Need for Research" have
said, I am devoting myself in brief remarks to one point, a general—that is, a generalized—point but a fundamental one, de-

scribed in the title I have chosen for tonight's discourse, "The Moral Responsibility of Research."

Of the central importance of research in modern life there is today little dispute. Thoughtful men see this clearly. Millions of people the world over sense it almost instinctively. They have seen the wonders of radio and plastics and penicillin. The war, furthermore, has dramatized for untold millions what amazing things research can accomplish.

Scientific research has become the right arm of modern technology, that Great Lever by which men's brains and imaginations move the very world and wrest out of the resources of nature greater and ever greater security against hunger, cold, disease, and want. There is no need for me to underline these propositions to such an audience as this.

We can build a firmer foundation under our feet in the South, in the United States, and throughout the remotest regions of the world with the modern fruits of research, and through the methods of creative intelligence that research exemplifies. This is one of the great and shining facts that sustain faith and confidence in the future and in the prospects of world peace in the minds of many, many people—sustain it at the very time when destruction, not creation, has swept the world with a fury never before known.

I believe our confidence in what research and technology can do in furthering civilization and in maintaining confidence in the idea of progress can be justified. I believe, furthermore, that men can direct research and technology so that they can move mankind toward the fulfillment of the greatest promise for human life and the human spirit in all history.

But this result is by no means inevitable. By no manner of means is it inevitable that scientific research and technology will work for good, whether here in the South or anywhere else. It is equally possible that they may yield a harvest of bitter fruit. The burden of my remarks tonight is again to remind ourselves that the problem is not only one of securing more and more funds for more and more scientific workers in private or public research. In terms of human happiness and freedom, the case is not that simple.

More funds for research is not enough. More fine laboratories, more extensive projects in social research are not enough. More use of technology, whether in our South or in South America or China, is not enough. Those who encourage a contrary belief are playing a dangerous game or are quite blind to the realities. For, unless research and technology are consciously related to a central purpose of human welfare, unless research is defined and directed by those who believe in and who have faith in people and in democratic ends and means, it may well be that the more money we spend on research the further we miss the mark. It is like trying to reach your destination in an automobile that is going in the wrong direction; the faster you drive the farther away from your goal you will be.

In the midst of all the technical discussion of particular research projects, in our justified optimism over the improved outlook for funds for research in the South, we must not, at our peril, overlook the simple but fundamental importance of the purpose of research. We must fully recognize that there is a responsibility on those who foster research for the human consequences it produces. Nor must we underestimate how fundamental are these considerations because their application to a particular circumstance will not always be easy—may often be difficult.

The direction of research is secure only in the hands of those, in private business and public agencies, who have faith in people. Research must be carried on by methods and for ends that are in furtherance of that faith in people.

Some research is initiated or carried forward by those who have no faith or concern with broad human welfare. People, to them, are only a "market." They are nothing more than a market to whom to sell new gadgets; a labor stockpile with which to make the gadgets; a political market to be cajoled and organized and voted. Some research is directed by those with little confidence in the people of a democracy, in their good sense, their capacity to choose wisely when they have the facts.

Research under such direction will further the human spirit only by accident, by sheer coincidence.

Contrast that with research directed by those who believe in people, and to whom the interests of people come first.

Such research is born out of a faith in humankind, which is

only another way of saying a faith in life itself. Such research asks first what do people want—not what do the researchers want, nor merely what those who control the research want to sell to people, but what people want.

It asks, do the people have the facts about what they can have, what their natural resources and the state of science permit them to have; what their alternatives are? For what they want must be determined by the people in the light of the facts as to what they can have; and wide public access to the facts therefore becomes crucial.

The purpose of research, then, largely determines whether it is likely to further human well-being or threaten it. What I am saying is simply that the purpose must be a moral, an ethical one. We know what amazing things research can do to increase the destructive powers of armies and navies—the enemy's and our own. We still must ask: What can research do to nourish and strengthen the human spirit? What can research do to strengthen men's freedom? Can a democracy consciously use research to further human welfare?

In our justified enthusiasm about research and technology, those are questions we can neither ignore nor dodge. They are the ultimate questions. They must be faced. No rattling off of statistics of increased productiveness, of new factories, of new gadgets and inventions based upon research provides an answer to those questions.

On these propositions there is the greatest difference of opinion. Some pay lip service to the general idea I have here outlined, but their actions disclose that they fear and oppose any such concept of the purpose of research and technology. Some do not even bother to dissemble; they flatly oppose such ideas; they deny that research or its products and use bear any such moral responsibility. There are men who control large sectors of industrial and physical research who have used research further to entrench vast economic monopoly. Others of like mind have used and are planning to continue to use research and technology to drain the raw wealth of the South and other interior regions of America in order to further, unreasonably, their existing stake in other American regions. There are those, furthermore, who use research and, after the war, propose a gigantic expansion of such use in the exploitation of countless millions of people and their resources in distant undeveloped parts of the world, for their own limited and special advantage. Those are clearly not ethical purposes for research.

People are rather vividly aware, today, of what technology can do for them; of what fruits it can bring to the millions who live in insecurity, who still must work unreasonably hard, who still have far less than enough to eat, who still are inadequately clad and poorly housed. They know that research and technology could go far to change that. The fantastic scientific accomplishments in the war have added greatly to popular education on that subject. They sense, these many millions of people, the great issue of our time: For what purpose shall research and technology be used?

TVA affords one illustration. The widespread interest in the TVA in the Valley and in the United States is largely based on a growing understanding and respect for research as the foundation for an improved standard of living and wider choices for people. For TVA is built upon research. And to the several score of Chinese who have studied the TVA at first hand, to the scientists from India, to the administrators from Australia and New Zealand, to the journalists from Iran and the agricultural scientists from Brazil—to most of the nearly four hundred representatives of fifty-seven foreign countries who visited the Tennessee Valley in recent months—the TVA seems to stand as a graphic symbol of what research and technology can do in putting in the hands of the people modern tools to meet modern problems and aspirations of men and women not only of the Tennessee Valley but of many lands the world over.

At Muscle Shoals, for example, the TVA has one of the largest, if not the most extensive, public research laboratories in the country. The stream of visitors and the people of the Valley —businessmen and farmers—there see what a vast difference exists in the results of research, depending upon the character and nature of the purpose of research itself. The TVA's research in soil fertilizers, for example, is directed toward the end and purpose that the land of the region should be handed on, strengthened, and fortified, to generations yet to come; that the present owner or user of land has a responsibility to future human beings who will live on that land and derive their livelihood and their opportunities for individual development from it; that research in soil fertilizers has a further purpose of providing not only wider diversification in the use of land but a diversification of human choices which research can make wider and more varied. Research in soil fertilizers, therefore, having such ethical purposes behind it, yields different results from what it would if no such ethical purposes drew the research forward and guided it. The same proposition holds true in private industry. There are some companies in the field of lumber and lumber products that use research to perpetuate the forests for future generations rather than to exhaust those forests in a short span of years and thereby deprive human beings of opportunities for their development and the development of their communities. The purpose behind such research in private industry is likewise an ethical one and accepts a moral responsibility for the consequences and the uses to which technology, applied to natural resources, shall be used.

Great is the promise of research and great indeed are the expectations of the peoples of the world. But we must remember that research can be ever so intelligent and yet fail dismally to advance the cause of man's freedom and happiness. A good many of you are familiar with the play by Karel Capek, the Czech playwright, called "R. U. R." The play deals with the invention of the robot, a mechanical man. In the first act Domin, the general manager of the factory making these robots, explains how the inventor, Rossum, got the idea. "Anyone who has looked into human anatomy," Domin explains (I am now quoting from the text of the play) "will have seen at once that man is too complicated, and that a good engineer could make him more simply. So young Rossum [the inventor of the Robot] began to overhaul anatomy and tried to see what could be left out or simplified."

The play continues: "He said to himself, 'A man is something that feels happy, plays the piano, likes going for a walk, and in fact wants to do a whole lot of things that are really unnecessary. But a working machine must not play the piano, must not feel happy, must not do a whole lot of other things.' "

"Young Rossum," the manager goes on to explain, "invented a worker with a minimum amount of requirements. He rejected everything that did not contribute directly to the progress of work—everything that makes man more expansive. In fact, he rejected man and made the Robot. Mechanically the Robots are more perfect than we are. They have an enormously developed intelligence, but they have no soul."

Research must have a "soul." Intelligence is not enough without a spiritual and humane purpose. Research that is only "enormously developed intelligence," research that leaves out the primary driving force in human affairs—the spirit of men— can lead only to one catastrophe after another—one war after another, each more horrible and mechanically perfect than its predecessor, can lead only to the exploitation and devastation of natural resources, and finally to the most terrible catastrophe of all, a non-moral rather than a moral world.

The most heartening fact about modern life is that as a people we can shape our destiny. We are not robots; neither are we at the mercy of forces beyond our conscious control. Science and the skills of management, the constantly wider understanding of how to get things done—these add up to the conclusion that we can deliberately and consciously direct and shape the course of events.

The universities can play a great part in this process of shaping our destiny through the deliberate use of research for human welfare, perhaps as important as that of any other of our institutions, not excluding government.

The enormous influence of the University of North Carolina, and the even greater influence it may exert in the next half-century illustrate what I have in mind. Here you are led by a President who has earned national standing. President Graham not only believes that human welfare and justice come first, but he has at times dared face powerful opposition in support of his convictions. At Chapel Hill you have a faculty of the highest repute. The people of this state apparently expect this University to be not merely a vocational school, but a leader in the discovery and translation of the truths of science and the feasible methods of achieving human progress. You have plant facilities for research. You have men and women of fine training and good purpose to put these facilities to use in the interests of all the people. We may hope that the people of this state will be farsighted enough continually to support and to increase these research facilities and this staff as the best single investment of their funds that they can make for the furthering of North Carolina and of the country.

As you carry forward on this campus in the years to come an expanded program of research in the physical and social sciences, you have an opportunity second to none to emphasize the supreme importance of purpose in the initiation and carrying out of research, the supreme importance of an ethical and moral purpose. With that as your foundation, wisely and realistically carried forward on a hundred fronts, you will affect the minds of tens of thousands of young men and women. Through these graduates this University will be sitting in upon the making of literally millions of decisions, decisions made by men and women at their work, on their farms, in their factories and offices and homes. You will in this way help to establish one of the most important principles of modern life—that we are not inert objects on a wave of the future; that we need not, as did Germans and Japanese, blindly accept the evil consequences of a technology that has no soul; that we are a democracy, and in a democracy the people search out the truth, and upon the truth build the foundation of a free and a humane society.

WARTIME SCIENCE BUILDS FOR PEACE

Georges F. Doriot, Brigadier General, U. S. A.

DIRECTOR MILITARY PLANNING, OFFICE OF THE
QUARTERMASTER GENERAL, U. S. ARMY. FOR
THE UNDER SECRETARY OF WAR
ROBERT P. PATTERSON

"SCIENTIFIC THOUGHT is not an accompaniment or condition of human progress but human progress itself." These words of the eminent nineteenth-century British scientist, William Kingdon Clifford, retain their force despite the uncertainties of our time. We move in all things under the sign of discovery and invention; our maturing control of the forces of nature is an unwavering beam in troubled, darkened years.

It is said by some that war means a serious interruption of the activities of science. Others blame science for the terrible aspect of modern warfare. The first, when pressed to the limit, is too sweeping; the second is the product of confused thought. Plainly, war has its impact upon the development of pure science and especially upon the emphasis of applied science. It affects the education and training of men and women with scientific aptitudes, as it affects everyone. These results are part of the cost of war; they are among the many reasons why the overwhelming majority of civilized people find war repugnant and tragic. But it is clear to us, I believe, that these costs are linked to the preservation of our country and can be borne by a strong, free, determined people. Only sacrifice and resolute effort enable us to redeem the hope of men, that high hope for which so many offer their lives.

As to the view that science is responsible for the savagery of war, it is to mistake the servant for the master. Wars are made by men, not by machines or formulas. The infinite resources and flexibility of science make it adaptable to either war or peace. One may reflect sadly that ethics and politics and the science of society have not kept pace with the advance of science and technology. The complaint is widely heard. It is a challenge to society, not a rebuke to science. We Americans must recognize what science has done to arm and equip our fighters, to save lives and heal the wounded, to improve the welfare of men and women at home and on the fighting fronts, to shorten the war and speed the peace.

There is something more for which we are indebted to science and to its workers. Much that has been achieved in these war years will be of great value in preserving and endowing the peace. To meet the demands of war requires a gigantic output of effort and the mobilization of all human knowledge. While a portion of that effort and knowledge is focused on the design of new weapons, another portion plays its part in fields covering almost the whole of human needs. Indeed, so interconnected is the structure of science that much of what is learned in the making of destructive tools will serve the constructive works of the future. Throughout the war we have been building for peace in meeting needs perhaps more varied than those of any community in normal times. It is to that aspect of wartime research, to the enduring and enriching victories of science, that I wish to devote my remarks this evening. My examples will be scattered and limited, but I hope they will help bring into a single frame the outlines of an impressive picture.

ADVANCES IN MEDICAL SCIENCE

Of paramount importance are the advances in medical science. The immense progress in the use of sulfa drugs, penicillin, and blood plasma is generally known. So is the development of atabrine as a substitute for quinine in the fight against malaria. I may say, as to atabrine, we have reason to believe in some of its therapeutic effects it is superior to quinine. Wide notice has been given to the effectiveness of DDT in controlling mosquitoes which carry malaria and Dengue fever; the fly and other insects which carry dysentery; and the common louse which spreads typhus, the scourge of former wars. But other wartime medical discoveries and developments are less widely known; to these I turn briefly.

In operations of the brain, spinal cord, and nerves there have been surgical advances of lasting benefit. Army surgeons have made striking use of the metal *tantalum* in cases of severe injury to the skull. Fine tantalum wire turns out to be the best product yet devised to repair severed nerves. Methods developed in Army hospitals in the care and rehabilitation of patients with paralysis resulting from injury to the spine should revolutionize the therapy for this tragic ailment. Other innovations offer promise that many victims of paralysis, formerly considered hopelessly bedridden, may be fully restored, or improved enough to permit them to leave their beds and become useful self-sufficient citizens.

Progress has been recorded in the design of artificial limbs, many of which are so good that users can hold their own in a variety of occupations with men who have no physical handicap.

While the effectiveness of penicillin and sulfa drugs has been dramatically presented, the statistical story of their success is less known. A few data are worth mentioning. These drugs have reduced the death rate from pneumonia from 24 per cent in the last war to 6 per cent in this war. In the treatment of venereal disease penicillin is performing splendidly. Syphilis can now be cured in a matter of days instead of months. The use of atabrine and other malaria-control measures have lowered the death rate from malaria to one soldier in every 10,000 per year. Research in preventive medicine in other fields matches this pace. I underscore the fact that due to inoculations and other preventive procedures, there has been no typhus, no yellow fever, no tetanus, and very little dysentery among our soldiers and sailors, and their general health has been raised to a higher level than ever before in war or peace.

Outstanding progress has been made in the use of blood plasma which has been broken down into its various constituents, each revealing, as research probes more deeply, new specialized uses. The protein taken from blood plasma has been developed to counteract measles. Studies are under way on the power of plasma constituents in combatting scarlet fever, diphtheria, whooping cough, and other diseases. Transfusions of red corpuscles from the blood are now used against anemia, and preparations of the corpuscles are painted on open wounds to help clear up infection. These are but a few of the gains in a single branch enriched by war research.

In meeting psychiatric problems the Army Medical Corps encounters a grave and ever-widening disorder, which was mounting in civilian life before the war. At least half of the civilian hospital beds in the country are occupied by mental patients. Aware of the importance of prompt diagnosis and immediate therapy for men suffering from battle shock and combat exhaustion, Army doctors have met the problem with understanding, with realism, and with sympathy. Our frontiers of knowledge in psychiatric treatment, although broadened from year to year, are as yet more confined than we should like. Nevertheless, the great majority of fighting men afflicted with psychic disorders of combat origin are able, after treatment, to return to active duty within a few days. Even if no significant methods for dealing with mental ailments have been developed, there is a major gain in the psychiatric experience of a large number of medical men. Before the war there was only a sprinkling of psychiatrists in the country. Not many of our regular physicians had the time or opportunity to concern themselves with mental diseases. Today, of the forty-five thousand physicians in the Army, the large majority have been brought into close contact with psychiatric problems. Since it is such experience that provides the foundation for fruitful scientific speculation, the future offers hope for material improvement in the treatment of mental disorders.

There is a further wartime gain in medical knowledge which should not be overlooked. It has a place even in this thumbnail sketch, because it is the source of an enormous store of information vital to the detection and prevention of disease. Physical examinations have been made of some seventeen million of our young people in Army and Navy Induction Centers. Because we know more about the sight, hearing, posture, physical development, teeth, skin, and general health of our younger generation than ever before, we shall be in a better position to guard and improve the health of the nation in the future. For years to come this information will be studied and analyzed; it will afford unique and dependable knowledge, knowledge which is power in the best sense.

FOOD AND NUTRITION

Closely allied with developments in medicine are those which have extended and deepened the science of nutrition. We have learned, on a grand scale, what men like to eat, what men need to eat, and what can be provided to keep them fit.

From the beginning the Army had the job of providing adequate rations for men scattered over the world, facing every conceivable extreme of temperature and climate. It was not only our business to furnish adequate rations, but to package them so that they could withstand long, hard journeys over land, on sea, and through the air. Packaging meant more than pink ribbons and cellophane: packages were going to war and new principles were needed to design them. Rations required protection against falls of thousands of feet from transport planes; against hours or days of immersion in fresh and salt water, mud and volcanic ash; against insects and mould and ice and jungle heat; against the natural deteriorative processes of time and the manifold hazards of ordinary handling. And when packages have served these functions, the ration itself must be not merely edible but palatable. Soldiers, no matter how hungry, will not eat unless the food is good. And it is good. Neither effort nor expense has been spared to make it so. And to improve it further, the researches of the Quartermaster Corps, industry, and university will go on until the war is ended.

A few days ago I talked to one of the officers who have had an important share in the research and development work of the Quartermaster Corps. A comment he made may be of interest. "The way we know our results are good," he said, "in nutrition and clothing, is that we receive few complaints. Soldiers won't say this or that is good, but if it's bad you can expect to hear from them. That's why we have confidence in our rations."

Early in the war it was found necessary to develop large-scale methods of dehydrating fruits, meats, cereals, and vegetables. Had it not been for this method we would have been unable to supply our soldiers with many of these important foods. Now we have learned that such a large variety of products lend themselves successfully to dehydration that their use in this form, even after the war, will continue. Success in this method of provisioning our men was attended by other advantages. For there was developed the taste for certain important and nutritious foods so as to vastly increase the demand for them after the war, thus contributing both to the health and economic prosperity of the nation. One example of an increased use stimulated by the Army is that of the sweet potato. The dehydration of this valuable food has popularized and substantially increased its national consumption. The Army requirements alone for dehydrated sweet potatoes this year are nineteen million pounds. Pre-mixed cereals, compressed into discs and blocks for Army rations, are another joint development of the Army working with industry. While cereals in this form are not likely to become the fashion for America's breakfast table after the war, nor even to be packed by the considerate wife for the fisherman's holiday, they offer fair possibilities for emergency feeding in areas devastated by war, flood, fire or other disaster. Besides being highly nutritious, they may be shipped and stored without refrigeration and special handling.

An advance has been recorded in the preparation of powdered whole milk and ice cream mix. It should prove of lasting importance. Production and consumption of milk and milk products have been relatively low in the South, because of difficulties in providing adequate refrigeration. Developmental work initiated by the Army now makes it possible to dehydrate milk and ice cream so that they may be safely stored over long periods *without* refrigeration. Nutritional values have been maintained and improved by this method; our soldiers tell us that even palatability has increased. After the war, when the Army demands for dried milk and ice cream subside, expanded facilities for production can be utilized to supplement and correct the present inadequate distribution of the fresh products. They can, moreover, be manufactured and distributed within a price range attractive to all income groups, and so made available to that portion of the population which needs milk most and gets it least.

In canning and preserving all types of foods, better methods have been devised. These should be a boon to agriculture and industry countrywide. There is a further betterment which should be mentioned even in this brief account. It concerns eating *habits*. We have over twelve million men in our Armed Forces. They come from every class and from every section of the country. In civilian life their eating habits varied according to locality and custom, apart from economic factors. By excellent feeding programs the Army has familiarized many, during critical periods in their lives, with a more wholesome variety of foods than that to which they have been accustomed. We have inculcated a wide awareness of good food and improved habits of diet which will be transmitted from our fighting men to their families. This cannot fail to raise materially the living standards and health of the entire nation. Our people will demand more, they will produce more, they will buy more. Thus there will be a new inducement to the most powerful and self-sustaining of all economic cycles.

IMPROVEMENTS IN CLOTHING AND TEXTILES

Problems similar in magnitude to those faced by the Army in food arose in clothing. It was necessary to offer protection and insure the health of men subjected to temperatures ranging from 130 degrees to 50 below. It was necessary to provide equipment that would withstand relative humidity of 99 per cent and the dry scorching heat of the desert. Clothing and equipment were required which would be suitable for mountain warfare and for jungle use. Items had to be designed so as to survive conditions which the products of American civilian industry were never before required to withstand. The clothing and equipment to meet these specifications had to be made, and they were made. Here are a few examples of what was accomplished.

It was found, when the war started, that many properties such as water repellency could not be evaluated accurately; hence research languished. By establishing dependable test procedures, industrial laboratories of the country took renewed interest in Army problems with the knowledge that their development would be given honest recognition. You have all had the unpleasant experience of exercising on a warm rainy day wearing a heavy waterproof coat. Imagine the soldier so dressed marching for hours, carrying a gun and full equipment. To make matters worse, physiologists have ascertained that under these conditions the individual, besides being almost as wet from perspiration as if no raincoat had been worn, raises his body temperature to the danger point. To solve this problem research was directed to the development of light-weight garments which allowed the body full ventilation while shedding water even after prolonged exposure to rain. Excellent products have been made, light, comfortable, water-repellent fabrics satisfying the need of ventilation. These will be available for civilian use after the war. So adaptable are the new processes that we may expect all outer garments, in the future, to be proof alike against the unexpected spring shower or torrential rains.

Research has succeeded in coupling the property of wind resistance with that of water repellency by adapting certain British methods to American cottons and yarns. Industry working with the Army has produced comfortable and serviceable combat clothing offering a high degree of protection against rain, snow, and wind. New fabricating processes applied to longer staple cotton yielded a fabric which swells when in contact with water, thus tightening the weave to the point of impermeability. Reports from the field on the shelter tents made of these flat ducks indicate that they are water-tight and serve better than any other fabric to keep men dry. Such fabrics will play an extremely important part in civilian life. The flat ducks may be used as coverings for agricultural purposes, for awnings or other water-protective items. It is easy to visualize the extensive use to which such fabrics will be put in replacing the heavier clumsy fabrics used in work clothing.

Before the war, mould and fungi damage to textiles was not of serious concern. Replacements were cheap, and the economic losses were accepted as unavoidable. But with enormous quantities of materials involved and shipping space critical, an altogether different attitude toward the problem was in order. There was much to be learned about the behavior of fungi. A species which is so useful and friendly in bread and penicillin is the ferocious enemy of textiles when they are exposed to moist tropical climates. Starting with almost no background of knowledge in this area, the Army Technical Services, together with the research laboratories of civilian agencies, have discovered preparations which, when applied to almost any organic material, will largely prevent the ravages of mould and fungi. The future benefits of these methods are too numerous to mention. All types of materials, which in warm and humid climate would succumb to deteriorative processes, can be effectively protected. An increase in the life of expensive industrial fabrics can be expected.

Another common and costly annoyance, the shrinkage of woolen fabrics, will largely disappear as a result of a new process for which the Quartermaster Corps of the Army, assisted by the National Research Council, is responsible. This single tiny advance eliminates the homely phenomenon of the vanishing sock which withers three sizes per laundering. The benefits accruing to businessmen, housewives and long-suffering society are obvious.

Among other recent improvements and discoveries are plastic film coverings, plastic insoles to assure the comfort of footwear, families of goggles and sun glasses to meet both general and special needs, and synthetic fabrics of every variety.

The utilization of nylon fibers has been extensively widened. Such war items as parachute cloth, ponchos, screening developed for insect protection, are a few of the examples of new uses for synthetic fabrics, fabrics of light weight and great strength which will fill endless needs in peace, provide new products, and stimulate the founding of new industries.

We may mark another essential point. Scientific research and development in war have promoted the concept of sound specifications as standards for all types of products. Improved manufacturing methods and standards of quality relative to items as diverse as razor blades, baseball bats, fabrics, and rations have resulted. It is an honest concept and should be carried over into the postwar period, for it offers advantages to producer and consumer alike. The consumer will be able to distinguish and demand the product whose quality and value are commensurate with its price; the producer of superior articles will be well armed against the competition of inferior ones.

RADAR AND RADIO

I should like now to turn briefly to other fields of equal importance. When the German Air Force launched its attacks against Britain in the summer of 1940, a single device played a major role in beating back the enemy. It was a device which afforded the defense sufficient warning so that the handful of RAF pilots could get their Spitfires into the air. That device, known as radar, is one of the ingenious, complicated mechanisms made possible by advances in the science of electronics. With its roots in nineteenth-century discoveries in electricity and magnetism, the flourishing science of electrons has furnished man, quite literally, with a sixth sense. National security does not forbid us from speculating on the postwar opportunities and possibilities of electronic devices. Here is a reality which almost outstrips the imagination. Devices embodying electronic principles will permit our ships to move safely on their course through fog and snow, avoid shore lines and hidden obstacles such as icebergs, prevent collisions with other ships. They will make it possible for planes to fly blind safely and to land safely when the ceiling is zero. Accidents in transportation and industry should be sharply reduced. The range of application of electronics to industrial processes cannot yet be conceived. Electron tubes now enable us to measure precision parts, like bearings, to tolerances of millionths of an inch. They count and sort merchandise; they detect dust and gases invisible to the eye; they match colors perfectly. An industrial application of particular interest to manufacturers in the South comes from a property of electronic tubes relative to focusing heat. This, I am told, will be of considerable value to the furniture industry, for in gluing plywood together there has long been the problem of heating the glue without injuring the wood. With electronic tubes the heat can be applied to the glue without affecting the wood, thus eliminating the danger of heat damage. Electronics, in short, will do new jobs, hitherto regarded as impossible, in laboratories, hospitals, industry, commerce, and in daily life; the science will also improve thousands of existing methods and processes.

A twin to electronics is the field of radio, in which long strides have been made during the war. A striking instance is the enlargement of the range of operational frequencies so that new transmission bands are now available. It will make possible the postwar use of the small portable set—the handy-talkie. Not, I suggest, an unalloyed blessing if the last corners of man's privacy can thereby be invaded. I trust there will always be the escape of shutting the thing off.

But the positive aspects are impressive. The opening of new ranges of frequencies will permit radio communications from planes and trains. It bears importantly on television, a field of untapped potentialities, by affording new intervals of usable wave lengths. In television itself we have moved a respectable distance. Very clear images can now be transmitted and projected on screens 18 by 24 feet and they can be projected in full color.

ADVANCES IN AIRCRAFT

In the world of the future we have much to expect from all the knowledge that has been gained and all that has been done during the war in aerodynamics and aircraft production. Aircraft, of conventional type, have seen improvement in their power plant, in design, in size, in speed, and in range. Principles fully worked out, devices already in production, will make flying safer, more comfortable, and more economical. Ideas still forming in the minds of engineers or in the tentative blueprint stage will profoundly influence air travel and air transport.

With all we owe to the more conventional types of aircraft, we must concede that advances in the field of *jet-propulsion* more fully captivate the imagination and foreshadow the trend of aircraft development in the future. A year ago only a few planes could travel more than 400 miles an hour in level flight. Today England and the United States have planes in the 500-mile-an-hour class, craft using the principle of jet-propulsion. There is no doubt that transports after the war, commercial aircraft of all types, will make use of this revolutionary principle. Research, as you know, has shown that we can build power plants which will permit air travel at still greater speeds. We have still to overcome certain aerodynamic problems—increases in drag, for example, which appear when supersonic velocities are attained.

As a layman I am confident that our experts will master these problems.

In developing gas turbine power plants, one of the toughest problems, I am told, was to produce an engine which could withstand very high temperatures. The Germans solved it by a complicated cooling system. We solved the problem by developing an alloy which would withstand the heat. The result is that our planes, not having to depend on this complex cooling system or carry its extreme weight, are bound to prove more efficient.

Jet-propulsion not only means enormous increases in speed; we may also expect substantial economies in air transportation. Jet engines are simpler and less expensive to build and service than reciprocating engines. They feed on kerosene or other low-grade fuels. And in air travel, contrary to other forms of locomotion, it has generally turned out that increases in speed are accompanied by increases in efficiency and a lower cost per passenger mile.

AUTOMOTIVE MATTERS

Let me leave this more glamorous mode of travel and turn to the earth-bound forms of transportation, which, regardless of progress in mastering the airways, will remain with us to the remote future. Every type of vehicular transportation has received an impetus during the war. Never have soldiers of any army been better equipped than ours in all-purpose and special-purpose vehicles. And aside from their combat features all the vehicles give promise of adaptability to useful duties in peace.

There are little vehicles of every kind, shape, and make, which can carry almost anything over almost anything that will bear their weight. Like ants that scurry about, toting grotesque loads five times their size and ten times their weight, the jeeps and peeps and other lilliputians of the automobile world do their work with uncomplaining efficiency. The same vehicles can easily be modified to civilian use, particularly for work on the farm. They can be used for plowing, harrowing, seeding, drilling, cultivating low crops, and harvesting. They can provide power for a buzz saw, hay bailer, threshing machine, milking machine, and stump remover. And they are also buggies-of-all-work.

The war has produced amphibious creatures which can change their duties from carrying men and weapons through the surf onto beaches to meet specialized needs in postwar transportation. Cargo vehicles developed by industry will travel over the lightest snow, ascend inclines up to 45 degrees, traverse the muddiest terrain, and ford rivers, all while carrying and towing good payloads. The use of these carriers in bayou or swamp country, in transporting men and supplies to remote sites of mine and oil operations, suggests itself at once.

Nor can we forget the amazing strength and versatility of that mechanical Paul Bunyan, the bulldozer, which has been developed and extended in usefulness, during wartime, to an outstanding degree. The bulldozer will help us to lay roads, to move mountains of earth, to build airfields. It will perform numberless tasks in repairing the ravages of war and in agricultural, engineering, and industrial pursuits.

THE SCIENCE OF WEATHER

We have good news about that science which deals with our most constant and unreliable companion—the weather. Accurate and dependable information about weather is, of course, essential to the operations of modern armies. The vast operations on the beaches of France, so fateful in their consequences, depended for their success on predictions as to the course of weather over the channel. The weather just about held up, as our meteorologists had told us, but it was touch and go for a few days. During the German counteroffensive in the Ardennes, launched in December of last year, you will recall that there bad weather played into the hands of our enemies by affording a cloak for their build-up and troop movements. During the war encouraging progress has been made in meteorology. An impressive departure is the use of high-frequency radio to detect and track storms. With the aid of weather stations set up by the Air Forces and newly developed equipment of high sensitivity, the tracking of storms through their electrical discharges has become far more precise. Our ability to predict the course of the hurricane which struck the East Coast last fall and to issue adequate storm warnings saved the country $250,000,000. It saved $100,000,000 worth of shipping and $40,000,000 worth of cargo; and many farmers, forewarned, were able to reduce materially the destructive effects of the storm.

Electronics finds one of its applications in weather forecasting. By means of electronic reflectors installed in weather balloons and electronic equipment on the ground, the direction and speed of movement of weather disturbances can be accurately followed. Reliable predictions will be of value equally to commercial airlines, farmers, and the many industries which in their operations are affected by weather. I say nothing of the anxious baseball fan.

From these scattered examples, chosen almost at random, I hope it is possible to gather some impression of the invaluable work which science has performed in the war years. I have omitted mention of many new avenues and products, as great as or perhaps greater in importance than those selected. The subjects come readily to mind: rubber, fuel, metals, plastics, bridge, road and airfield construction, new skills, new methods; all vital to our survival in war, all destined to promote the welfare of the nation and the entire world.

To the workers of science, to its leaders, to the research laboratories of industry, university, and government, the people of America must give thanks for shielding them from disaster, for lessening human suffering, for designing the weapons of justice, and for building wisely even in war to meet the needs of peace. Science, the most thoughtful of man's activities, rests on firm foundations. On the best of the past it builds the best of the future. Science is what man is. It can be a force for good or a force for evil. It is great when it embodies and expresses the life of reason. As to the promise of science and its highest opportunity there are no better words than these from the last unvoiced address of Franklin Delano Roosevelt:

"Thomas Jefferson, himself a distinguished scientist, once spoke of the 'brotherly spirit of science, which unites into one family all its votaries of whatever grade, and however widely dispersed through the different quarters of the globe.'

"Today, science has brought all the different quarters of the globe so close together that it is impossible to isolate them one from another.

"Today we are faced with the pre-eminent fact that, if civilization is to survive, we must cultivate the science of human relationships—the ability of all peoples, of all kinds, to live together and work together, in the same world, at peace."